Elia Kazan

Elia Kazan

The Cinema of an American Outsider

Brian Neve

Published in 2009 by I.B.Tauris & Co Ltd
6 Salem Road, London W2 4BU
175 Fifth Avenue, New York NY 10010
www.ibtauris.com

In the United States of America and Canada distributed by
Palgrave Macmillan, a division of St. Martin's Press, 175 Fifth Avenue,
New York NY 10010

ISBN: 978 1 84511 560 9

A full CIP record for this book is available from the British Library
A full CIP record is available from the Library of Congress

Library of Congress Catalog Card Number: available

Designed and typeset by 4word Ltd, Bristol, UK
Printed and bound in India by Thomson Press India Ltd

Contents

Illustrations

Acknowledgements

My first thanks go to Leith Johnson and Joan Miller, Co-Curator and Archivist respectively at the Wesleyan Cinema Archives. Leith and Joan were unfailingly efficient and helpful during my two visits to the Elia Kazan collection at Wesleyan Cinema Archives, and I'm very grateful to them. Also I should acknowledge immediately the assistance of a funding body, the Arts and Humanities Research Council, which awarded me a Research Leave Award so that I could spend the whole of the 2004/05 academic year on the Kazan project and away from my University duties. I'm grateful to the AHRC for their patience with this project, and my thanks also go to Roger Eatwell and others in the Department of European Studies and Modern Languages at the University of Bath for helping to facilitate this leave of absence.

Like others I am very much in the debt of a number of librarians and archivists. Two people who were of great assistance to my Los Angeles research were Haden Guest, then of the Warner Bros. collection at USC, and Ned Comstock at the Archives of the Performing Arts, USC. Haden worked hard to ensure that I got through the material in the time, while Ned was as usual a mine of information on possible sources. My other major debt in Los Angeles is to Barbara Hall at the Margaret Herrick Library, Center for Motion Picture Study, Academy of Motion Picture Arts and Sciences. I am particularly grateful to Barbara for drawing my attention to Kazan letters and references in the numerous special collections at AMPAS. In New York my thanks are due to Charles Silver of the Film Study Center of the Museum of Modern Art. Charles has written excellent appreciations of Kazan's work for MOMA retrospectives and I also felt an empathy with his more personal remarks on the director and the blacklist, recorded in the folders on the director in the MOMA Film Department.

I am also very happy to thank others who helped me in my research. First in this list I need to mention my friend, the film researcher Joan Cohen, whose help and hospitality in Hollywood over the years has assisted me in numerous ways, and has been highly appreciated. Amongst academics who have helped me I must first express grateful thanks to Peter Lev of Towson University and Joanna E. Rapf of the University of Oklahoma. Peter made invaluable comments on two early chapters and drew my attention to several additional sources; I benefited in particular from his expertise on Twentieth Century-Fox. Joanna made very helpful comments on the *On the Waterfront* chapter, and also helped to facilitate my interview with Budd Schulberg. I am also very grateful to Lenny Quart, who has written perceptively on Elia Kazan, for his advice and friendship over the years and for some specific criticisms of a draft of my Introduction. I thank Peter Krämer of the University of Kent, who again made useful comments on two draft chapters and encouraged my notion of writing this book when we ran into each other some years ago at the Margaret Herrick Library, and also Will Straw, who sent me some material on *Boomerang!* Val Holley also read the chapter on *East of Eden* and made a number of valuable suggestions. I am most grateful to him. I also thank David Culbert for permission to reproduce, in revised form, my article on Kazan's first 1952 testimony, which appeared in the journal that he edits, the *Historical Journal of Film, Radio and Television*, 25, 2 June 2005.

While working at Wesleyan I was fortunate enough to meet Robert Hethmon, a Professor Emeritus at the School of Theater, Film and Television, UCLA. Bob has been generous in making suggestions and allowing me to use a number of his unpublished interviews with Kazan and others. I doubt that he will agree totally with my treatment of Kazan's House Committee on Un-American Activities (HUAC) appearance, but I am very grateful indeed for his friendly assistance.

There are others who have helped me in numerous ways. First of all my love and thanks are due to Helen Humphries for her friendship and encouragement, and also for her valuable thoughts on several sections of the book. It is appropriate also to thank Leith Adams for his generosity and assistance some years ago, when I first studied Warner Bros. material. I'm grateful also to Stuart Hands and Natasha Fraser-Cavassoni for responding to queries, Stephen Paley, Professor Herbert I. London, Lenka Peterson O'Connor and Michael Butler for recounting their experiences, and Dede Allen, Budd Schulberg and Ingrid Boulting for agreeing to be interviewed at some length. Laure Gray is a wonderfully professional translator in Bath who helped me greatly at sessions at which she translated parts of the significant body of work on Kazan written in French. Her work also reminded me to improve my languages if granted another life. Thanks also to Bernard R. Crystal of the Rare Book and Manuscript Library, Columbia University; Ronald M. Bulatoff, Archival Specialist at the Hoover Institution Archives, Stanford University; Charles E. Schamel of the

Center for Legislative Archives, National Archives and Records Administration, Washington DC; Joy Eldridge of Special Collections, University of Sussex Library; and numerous librarians at the BFI Library in London. I also thank Elia Kazan. He responded to several letters and saw me at what was a difficult time. While I think I've written a critical account, I hope it is plain that the films have meant a good deal to me.

Two further acknowledgements: first to Nina Harding of the BFI and Joan Miller at Wesleyan Cinema Archives for help on the stills. If I have fallen short in acknowledging copyright holders I apologise, and will repair damage in this regard in any subsequent edition. I also want to thank Philippa Brewster at I.B.Tauris for her calmness and support, patience with my delays and astute comments on the whole manuscript. My thanks also to John Roost for his work on the proofs. I should add a final note that no-one mentioned in these Acknowledgements is in any way responsible for the faults and limitations of the present work. The buck stops with me.

Finally I want to express my love and thanks to three people, of whom sadly only one, my father George Neve, is with us as I write. Dad has helped in numerous ways and in particular through his great strength and constancy. My mother was and is a great inspiration, and I love her and miss her greatly. I also add the name of my cousin and friend John Williams, who I felt close to all my life up until his sudden and tragic death two years ago. A first class director of film documentaries himself, he loved film and loved talking about film. We used to discuss Kazan and other filmmakers ad infinitum, and I've enormously missed his advice and company as I've brought this long project home. With all humility I dedicate this book to Mum and Dad, and John.

Introduction

When I first wrote to Elia Kazan in 1980, seeking an interview, he responded promptly, telling me that he was pleased that 'you and others' were 'beginning to take films seriously as part of American history and thought'. Yet he would not talk at length, given that he had just started on his autobiography and was devoting himself each day to making progress on it. What he did say, when I visited him in his small office on Seventh Avenue in New York, between 54th and 55th Streets, was not remarkable. The 71-year-old mentioned that not too many of his films had made money, while he responded to a question on his infamous Congressional testimony by saying that by then he hated the Communists, the party functionaries in their headquarters on 12th Street. He referred me to Khrushchev's memoirs and repeated the line that there were no easy decisions, that there were costs either way.[1] I did feel in Kazan's presence a flesh and blood engagement with key strands of American twentieth-century life, from the turn of the century immigrant experience to the art and politics of the Depression years to the Brando and Dean films and the key cultural clashes of the fifties and after. Later, when new archive materials became available, covering both of Kazan's main studios, Twentieth Century-Fox and Warner Bros., and subsequently his own papers, I was keen to revisit and try to demystify the director as author, and to track the key choices and collaborations, industrial constraints and opportunities. What relation did the legendary figure I remembered darting around his small office have to 'his' films?

This book is thus a study of the film work of Elia Kazan (from 1945 to 1976) in industrial, cultural and political contexts. It is inductive in approach, examining the director's role as part of the changing *process* of filmmaking, with particular regard to the transition between the studio era of the forties and the changed role of the studios, as predominantly financers and distributors of independently produced films, in the fifties.[2] Among the issues raised are the censorship conflicts of the fifties and early sixties, as audiences and attitudes changed, the Production Code Administration declined in effectiveness and the Legion of Decency fought a rearguard action. Two strands of interpretation dominate writing and thinking about Kazan, and they are explored through an analysis of the films, the circumstances of their production, and their reception. First is the view of Kazan as predominately an actor's director, and of his work in the cinema – for all its powerful and some would say revolutionary impact on screen acting – as essentially derivative of his role as the dominant figure in post-war American theatre. As such he pioneered the application of the Stanislavsky tradition to Broadway, changed notions of the stage director with his pro-active interpretations of landmark plays by Arthur Miller and Tennessee Williams, and co-founded the Actors Studio. Others have seen Kazan as an 'American studies' director whose work reflects changes and tensions in the national culture, an approach which inevitably involves consideration of his involvement in the infamous post-Second World War collision between Hollywood and the House Committee on Un-American Activities (HUAC). These and other notions of the filmmaker were most recently reviewed and refocused when he was controversially awarded a Life Achievement Award at the 1999 Academy Awards ceremony, and again following his death in 2003 at age 94.[3]

Of the formative experiences that the 35-year-old brought with him to Hollywood when he signed a seven picture contract at Twentieth Century-Fox, the most fundamental related to his family background. Kazan was in effect a second generation immigrant, having been born to Greek parents in Istanbul – then Constantinople – in 1909 and brought to New York at the age of four. It was Kazan's uncle who had been the first of the family to make the journey to America; his father's background had been in the central Anatolian town of Kayseri, while his better educated mother had grown up in Constantinople. In New York the young Kazan had grown up speaking Greek and Turkish, suspicious of the wider 'Anglo' culture and also of his father's expectation that he should, as the eldest son, join the family rug and carpet business ('The Persian Warehouse'). Kazan's autobiography gives an account of the developing 'conspiracy' in his early years between him and his mother, a relationship that led to him attending Williams College and graduating in 1930, just as the ripples of the Wall Street Crash were undermining his father's business.[4] Kazan then moved to Yale Drama School, waiting tables to support himself, before leaving early to become an apprentice at the newly formed Group Theatre.

What is apparent from accounts of Kazan's early involvement with the Group is his intense drive, his effort to be indispensable. His nickname of Gadget (or Gadg), first attached to him at Williams, reflected this versatility, and early on Kazan was an actor, stage manager and assistant press agent while he also strove to write plays. Group member Herb Ratner remembered that in that first summer Kazan 'was able, not only to design the sets, cut the wood, but also to put them up for a new show every week, which he did extremely well'.[5] In the middle years of the decade he also taught at the New Theatre League and directed for the first time for the Communist-supported Workers Laboratory Theatre, while his acting was recognised with the powerful response to his performance as the taxi driver Agate in the 1935 Group production of Clifford Odets' iconic strike play, *Waiting for Lefty*. In a letter of that year to Cheryl Crawford and Lee Strasberg, two of the Group's leaders, Kazan recalled 'swarming' over the 'whole organism' of the Group Theatre 'like Lupe Velez' – a Mexican-born actress then at the summit of her Hollywood career. He also wrote of the importance of politics to him at that time, explaining that he was finding out 'what it means to belong to a collective', and that he now found 'active meaning' in the slogan 'The Theatre is a weapon in the class struggle'.[6] (Kazan's 18-month membership of the Communist Party in the mid-thirties is discussed further in the chapter on his early fifties encounter with HUAC). Also evident from his hard won membership of the Group was his admiration for Harold Clurman, its founder and sole leader after Crawford and Strasberg resigned in 1936 and the theatre was reconstituted. Kazan, who was then his key lieutenant and executive, later recalled that he '<u>loved</u> Harold Clurman', and that the Group's founder 'was my teacher not only in the specific arts of the theatre but how to live a life in the arts'.[7] It was also from Clurman that Kazan adapted, albeit loosely and inconsistently, an approach to preparing and analysing dramatic texts by noting, in three columns on the blank pages opposite script pages, issues relating to character, sub-text and mood, and business.

Apart from his admiration for the Soviet filmmakers, in particular Eisenstein and Dovzhenko, Stanislavsky and his protégés at the Moscow Art Theatre were key influences on his work and indeed the work of everyone in the Group. Kazan's most important personal relationship, however, was with Molly Day Thacher, whom he married in 1932. Although Kazan threatened the marriage at various times – he later described being faithful to her in every sense except sexually – she remained a powerful professional and political influence on him until her sudden death in 1963.[8] As the granddaughter of the President of Yale University she was very much the Yankee to Kazan's immigrant: according to his mother it was Molly who 'brought us into America'.[9] She was an intellectual of the theatre, a tireless critic and editor who also worked as a play reader for the Group Theatre. In the late thirties it was Molly Kazan who was one of the first theatre people to champion the work of Tennessee Williams, while after the war she urged her husband to direct *A Streetcar Named Desire* for the stage, although her relationship with Williams later deteriorated following her criticism of *Camino Real*. She and her husband had two children before the war, Judy (1937) and Chris (1938), and two in the late forties, Nick (1946) and Katherine (1948). It was in the war years that Molly left her husband for a time when she became aware of his liaison with the actress Constance Dowling. In the later fifties Molly aspired to be a playwright, with her political play, *The Egghead* (1957), being her most successful work, while she also headed the Playwrights Unit within the Actors Studio for four years. Her own papers, also lodged at Wesleyan University, may well reveal more about the nature of her working relationship with her husband, when they are opened to scrutiny.

Reflecting his outsider status in terms of politics and ethnicity, Kazan as an actor specialised in gangster roles in stage productions of the late thirties, while he also made supporting performances in two Warner Bros. films, first as a poor kid turned gangster, in *City for Conquest* (1940), and then in the 1941 melodrama of crime and jazz, *Blues in the Night*. In preparing for his role alongside James Cagney in *City for Conquest*, Kazan noted that 'listening actively with your eyes' revealed your thinking and helped 'keep you alive'.[10] His last theatre performance was in *Five Alarm Waltz* in 1941, and the next year came his first Broadway success as a director with Thornton Wilder's *The Skin of Our Teeth*. Kazan's film work in the thirties related to experimental and documentary work in collaboration, in particular, with photographer and cameraman Ralph Steiner, although he also made Hollywood screen tests in 1937 when he worked briefly as an assistant to Lewis Milestone. Kazan acted in *Café Universal*, an anti-war short made by Steiner in 1933, and the next year he worked with Steiner again on an improvised, agit-prop two-reeler called *Pie in the Sky*, after the Joe Hill trade union song of that name. It was made by Nykino, the film branch of the Theatre of Action (previously the Workers Laboratory Theatre), and was shot, and in part improvised, on a rubbish dump on the outskirts of Long Island City. More witty and subversive than revolutionary, it was a satire on the organised religion and welfare services of the time. The film looks inventive now, as two vagrants, played by Kazan and Elman Koolish, use props from the city dump to act out the rich life that they can only dream about in Depression America. Kazan throws stones and wears his hat down over his eyes like a later New Wave 'rebel', and uses discarded objects, including an old film can, a mannequin ('Mae West') and the wreck of a car, to mime fantasies of middle-class life. Writing at the time in *New Theatre*, Ray Ludlow saw the film as exploring for the first time on the screen the acting technique of Stanislavsky and the Moscow Art Theatre, with reference both to the use of affective memory as a source of 'genuine and immediate emotion' and in particular to the actors who engaged with resonant objects (and other actors) rather than

Kazan and Ralph Steiner (behind the camera) in Tennessee, making *People of the Cumberland* (1937). Courtesy of the British Film Institute (BFI).

'playing to the audience'. Kazan's second practical experience of filmmaking was when he went with Steiner to Tennessee in 1937 to make a short documentary for Frontier Films, a unit that reflected the late thirties' Popular Front politics that brought together anti-fascist liberals and Communists. The result, *People of the Cumberland* (1937), captured the despair and poverty of the Depression South and showed how the Highlander Folk School could make a difference by teaching local people to organise themselves into unions and press for change. The film includes a short, dramatised sequence, shot at night, in which gangsters take revenge on the union organisers, but the ending is optimistic, demonstrating the growing confidence of 'the people', aided by New Deal programmes and in particular by the Tennessee Valley Authority.[11]

My own interest in Elia Kazan as a filmmaker began with the impact on me of *On the Waterfront* and *America America*, when I first saw them in the early sixties. Kazan's work seems, in David Thomson's phrase, to be 'vital to the

emotional reawakening of the fifties', and for me it was part of the liberating
experience of cinema experienced by those who were part of the post-Second
World War baby boom. Martin Scorsese, who with Robert DeNiro presented
the director with his 1999 award, has written of Kazan's films as extending 'the
limits of what was emotionally and psychologically possible', leading the way to
John Cassavetes and the later independent movement. In historical terms
Kazan was also one of a number of younger directors, often with thirties experience of New York theatre and politics, who began working in Hollywood in
the forties. Nicholas Ray, Jules Dassin, Abraham Polonsky, Orson Welles,
Joseph Losey, Robert Rossen, John Berry, Cy Endfield and others brought different perspectives on art and politics to a mainstream studio system that was
itself in transition. In the post-war years the studios incurred a number of
shocks, from the Paramount anti-trust case to the Congressional hearings and
the beginning of a decade-long decline in cinema attendances.[12] Welles's
Citizen Kane (1941) was perhaps the most dramatic example of the coming
together of the Hollywood studio machine and an artist with a distinct and individual set of concerns. Most of the others came west later and began directing
at the end of the war or after it, learning under line producers, but also developing their own practice. Conservatives in the film capital saw the influx of
such directors, together with the increasing impact of liberal and radical screenwriters, as threatening traditional notions of mainstream film entertainment.[13]

In a previous book I trace the work of these directors in the context of
changes both in the political climate and the industry. They were part of a
broader movement of writers and others who had been politicised in the
Depression years and who were associated in varying degrees with the American
Left. Recent research and writing has drawn more attention to the significance
of this group's work, especially in the later forties. Kazan, although long out of
the Communist Party, contributed to the innovation of this period with his
direction of two aesthetically conventional but outspoken (at the time) social
problem films at Twentieth Century-Fox, and of two 'semi-documentaries' at
the same studio.[14] *Boomerang!* is perhaps most politically distinctive, with the
director taking the often conservative form of the 'semi-documentary' or police
procedural and adding a sub-text that casts doubt on the democratic rhetoric
of the film's narration. Yet the onset of the Cold War and the hearings held by
HUAC changed the filmmaking climate and placed pressures on directors,
including Kazan, with past associations with the Communist Party. Of those
mentioned above Dassin, Losey, Berry and Endfield were blacklisted and eventually re-established themselves as filmmakers in Europe, while writer-director
Polonsky remained in America and was unable to work under his own name
until the mid-sixties. Kazan's friend Nicholas Ray escaped the blacklist, despite

Kazan, James Cagney and Frank McHugh, in *City for Conquest* (1940). Courtesy of BFI.

previous membership of the Communist Party, while Welles, who was never in the Party, nonetheless spent most of the fifties in Europe. The post-war vestiges of the Popular Front came to an end and a new liberal anti-Communism further split the old progressive movement of the late thirties and war years while incorporating some of its old concerns and rhetoric. Kazan's encounter with HUAC in early 1952, when he first declined to give names and then changed his mind, was to have a lifelong influence on his reputation and on some of his key artistic associations.

Immigrants were under particular pressure to affirm American values at the time. Lillian Hellman later referred to the vulnerability of the 'children of timid immigrants', while Tennessee Williams noted in relation to Kazan's cooperative testimony that his friend had been under great strain and felt 'quite guilty about it', but that ultimately he 'felt that it was a patriotic duty and so he did it'. To the French critic and filmmaker Bertrand Tavernier, writing much later, 'it was as if he wanted to become more American than the Americans and this is how he could do it'. Kazan had been out of the Party for 16 years and although he grossly exaggerated the cultural threat of domestic Communism in his ill-judged *New York Times* advertisement, his personal views (and in particular those of his wife) made it easier, after some debate with himself, friends and associates, and with anti-Communist intellectuals such as Sidney Hook, to sacrifice his previous distaste about testifying. After his testimony Kazan also looked for reassurance to liberal politicians of the day: Kazan's archive contains clippings, marked in red, of speeches by 1952 Presidential aspirant Adlai Stevenson concerning his belief in 'the nature of the Communist conspiracy abroad and at home'.[15] Michel Ciment, without defending Kazan's decision, called some years ago for an end to the baiting of him, and also argued that the director, far from being silent on the matter, had revealed his torments and uncertainties in his films. One of the best writers on that era, Thom Andersen, has concurred with David Thomson in criticising Kazan but pointing to the greater culpability of the studios (and later the talent agencies) that agreed, administered or acquiesced in the blacklist.[16]

Much of the early published material on the director was written by French critics. Roger Tailleur's study was published in two editions in 1966 and 1971, while Ciment's extended interview, *Kazan on Kazan*, came out in French and English editions in 1973. This last paperback always seemed to me to be the most revealing of a British Film Institute series of interviews that were an important part of that era's widening appreciation of cinema as an artistic and cultural form, while it was here also that Kazan revealed most clearly his ambivalence about his testimony. One of Tailleur's contributions was to emphasise the progression in Kazan's work, from the relative detachment of his studio films to his interpretation and adaptation of the work of others in the middle phase of this career, to the greater personal expression of the later work. Until Richard Schickel's sympathetic biography, Thomas Pauly had written the only book-length critical study of Kazan's work in both theatre and film, marshalling much evidence on his career and offering excellent critical assessments. Yet the book stresses the theatre work and gives relatively limited space to some of the director's mature film works, from *Baby Doll* and *A Face in the Crowd* to *Splendour in the Grass*, while completely ignoring *The Visitors*. In another book-length interview, conducted in 1971 but only published in 1999, the producer–director Jeff Young was effective in prompting Kazan to reflect on his own film directing techniques and practices. Other contributions to the critical literature on Kazan's film work include an analysis by Jim Kitses which stresses the recurring role of family tensions in the films, together with the tendency of auteur theory to neglect a director who avoided genre projects and engaged with major themes and currents in American life. Robin Wood also contributed a key criticism of the unevenness of Kazan's film work to a special issue of the British magazine *Movie*. Also encouraging to my own project was Lloyd Michaels's distilled critical survey, part of his invaluable guide to sources on the director: I note in particular his comment on the director's persistent exploration of the relationship between money and power.

Kazan himself wrote well and self-critically about his film work, in particular in his extraordinarily personal and detailed 800-page autobiography in 1988, while in the same year Ciment edited a sample of the collection of letters, notes and other materials that the director had donated to Wesleyan University.[17] The Wesleyan archive, which Schickel uses, provides a valuable insight into the director's working methods. Kazan's emphasis on casting, theme and especially character is reflected in his production notebooks and annotated scripts, together with the notion of his provoking or encouraging the expression by his actors of sub-textual needs and emotions and using the camera as a 'microscope' to reveal them. These materials also support the notion that Kazan increasingly tried to animate and ground his film stories by references to his own life and relationships. As he explained looking back on his film career: 'A more important thing is to find your relationship to the theme and decide that you are really telling a little piece of autobiography, no matter what it is about.'[18]

His early films at Twentieth Century-Fox provided him with an apprenticeship within a supportive if constraining studio environment. As vertically integrated production centres with extensive rosters of contracted crew members and actors, the studios were in decline. Darryl F. Zanuck himself supervised the development of Kazan's early film career while allowing him some autonomy, in particular in adapting for the screen the psychological and behavioural emphasis of his work with stage actors. John Garfield gives one of his most relaxed and effective screen performances in his role in *Gentleman's Agreement*, providing that film with most of its political bite. In addition the director was able to use the greater freedom of shooting on location, and the 'semi-documentary' form that Zanuck and Louis de Rochemont had introduced at the studio, to develop a more cinematic style. The two strands of Kazan's work – the intensely psychological, and that drawing more on documentary elements – were demonstrated in films at the turn of the decade that reflected the director's growing ambition: *A Streetcar Named Desire* (1951) and *Viva Zapata!* (1952).

It was however the success of *On the Waterfront* (1954), produced in New York by Sam Spiegel, which radically changed Kazan's prospects, enabling him to make films more independently. Kazan's new relationship with Budd Schulberg became a central one in his later life, and owed something I think to the greater confidence that the novelist and screenwriter had about the position that he had taken before the Committee in 1951. *On the Waterfront* was a work of collaboration between them, with Schulberg contributing expressive dialogue, a tight narrative structure and strong background authenticity, but the emotional power of the film beyond its 'social problem' context owes most to Kazan's clear insistence that it was centrally about the redemption of the Terry Malloy character, and to Marlon Brando's uniquely sensitive performance in this role (James Naremore writes of Brando's rhythms and gestures, displaying the tides of emotions beneath the talk).[19] The film provided the template for Kazan's subsequent production base in New York, from where he produced and directed a series of films for his own company, Newtown Productions. (Apart from *Wild River*, made under his original contract with Twentieth Century-Fox and shot entirely on location in Tennessee, all these films were financed and released by Warner Bros.) The chapters that follow provide a historical and contextual account of Kazan's complete film career, covering the 19 films that he directed, from *A Tree Grows in Brooklyn* (1945) to his personal and in part auto-biographical work of the sixties, to *The Last Tycoon* (1976), which turned out to be his last hurrah.

1

Kazan at Twentieth Century-Fox

It was early in 1944 that Elia Kazan, after having considered other studio offers, signed a non-exclusive, seven picture directing contract with Twentieth Century-Fox, a studio that had enjoyed spectacular profits during the war years, but which with other studios faced a number of problems in the immediate post-war period, not least because of the long-term decline in attendances and studio profits that set in early in 1947. The head of production at Fox was Darryl F. Zanuck, a writer turned executive who at Warner Bros. in the late twenties and early thirties had overseen the first sound film, *The Jazz Singer* (1927), and the early gangster cycle, including *Little Caesar* (1931) and *The Public Enemy* (1931). Overlooked for promotion, Zanuck had resigned from Warners and founded a new production company, Twentieth Century Films. When Twentieth Century-Fox was formed in 1935 from the merger of Fox Films and Twentieth Century Films, the 33-year-old Zanuck ran the studio, favouring nostalgic Americana in the thirties, producing *The Grapes of Wrath* in 1940, and calling in the war years for Hollywood to adapt its new found social responsibility to the post-war era. A registered Republican and the most significant non-Jewish studio head, Zanuck's social concerns were also reflected in his personal involvement in *Wilson* (1944), an idealistic and expensive recreation of President Woodrow Wilson's struggle for the League of Nations after the First World War, and in his ultimately unsuccessful effort at the end of the war to mount a production, 'One World', based on the ideas of 1944 Republican Presidential candidate Wendell Wilkie (at one point Zanuck had approached Kazan to direct the latter project).[1] Fox writer Philip Dunne later noted the studio was 'no place for an Auteur', given Zanuck's intense involvement with all stages of the production process, from script conferences to casting and editing.[2] John Ford was perhaps the exception to the rule, generally ignoring Zanuck's urgings that he quicken the pace of his films, although the studio head made significant changes to Ford's cut of *My Darling Clementine* (1946), Ford's last film under his studio contract. Kazan's work at Fox provided him with a film apprenticeship while he remained based for much of the period in New York, where he worked with Arthur Miller and Tennessee Williams on ground-breaking Broadway plays. During the time that he lived in Los Angeles, while working on *Gentleman's Agreement*, Kazan enjoyed working with Zanuck, but saw himself as something of an 'exile' in Hollywood.[3]

With no film experience except for his collaborative work in the mid-thirties with the Theatre of Action Film Unit, a brief spell as assistant to Lewis Milestone in 1937, and his work with Frontier Films, Kazan faced a steep learning curve as he directed the Fox adaptation of Betty Smith's semi-autobiographical and best-selling first novel of 1943, *A Tree Grows in Brooklyn* (1945). He was, as he later said, 'thrown into directing right from the New York stage'.[4] Kazan began work after the script was completed and the film was shot entirely on the Twentieth Century-Fox lot. He was aided by the film's producer, Louis D. Lighton, with whom he worked on the casting, and by cameraman Leon Shamroy, who advised on angles and close-ups. The completed film was well received by audiences and critics; it was one of the top moneymaking films of 1944–5 and also made the National Board of Review's ten-best films list for the year. To Bosley Crowther of the *New York Times*, discussing the shift from novel to film, 'the main and essential story of a little girl's painful, hopeful growth in a tenement home full of fancies and patient, wretched toil has been kept'. Manny Farber was more critical, appreciating the truth in the earlier part of the story, but finding the photography to be destructive, blanketing 'the poverty in lovely shadows and pearly sentimentality'. James Agee disliked the deadness of the sets and the too neatly 'tagged' characters, but felt nonetheless that the film represented, after the stereotypes of the war years, 'the respectable beginning of at least a return toward trying to represent human existence'.[5]

A Tree Grows in Brooklyn is a historical saga of family survival amid the poverty of a Brooklyn tenement of the early 1900s. Kazan found in Peggy Ann Gardner, as Francie, the young girl, and James Dunn, as her father, feelings and vulnerabilities that chimed with those of their characters. Singing waiter Johnny Nolan (Dunn) is full of charm, but his drinking and pipe dreams of success divert the family responsibilities on to his hard-working but emotionally rigid wife, Katie (Dorothy McGuire). She is well aware of her husband's vices but blind to his virtues, as well as to those of her cheerful and flirtatious sister Sissy (Joan Blondell). The sister's extra-marital relationships had concerned the Breen office, necessitating some script changes. When Katie insists that Francie leave school so that her younger brother Neeley can continue his education (a decision that makes a lasting impression on Francie), Johnny is upset and leaves home, and within a week he is found dead of alcoholism and pneumonia. In effect he has sacrificed himself so that his daughter can continue her education. Katie eventually sees her own shortcomings, in particular after Francie nurses her during the difficult birth of a third child, and the bond between mother and daughter is repaired. Francie returns to school and the film ends on a conventionally optimistic note, with Katie accepting a proposal of marriage from reliable and respectful local policeman McShane (Lloyd Nolan).

Kazan was a new cog in a disciplined, well-oiled studio machine that released 27 films in 1945. His work with Dunn and Garner was particularly recognised. Dunn gained an Academy Award as best supporting actor the next year, while Peggy Ann Garner was named the most promising newcomer. This work is particularly evident when Katie is painfully in labour and uncharacteristically vulnerable and fearful, in need for the first time of her daughter's love and nursing. The whole scene takes place during a downpour that has an aural and visual association with the mother's trauma and emotional release. The rain on the windows is reflected in a pattern of light on Katie's face as she lies back on her pillow. Afraid of death – a glimpse of the real fears that accompanied the lives of poor women in childbirth at the time of the story – Katie finds a new emotional register. As she lies in her bed in front of Francie, viewed as if through a veil of tears, the image suggests a sentimental variation on the iconic Dorothea Lange photograph, from 1936, of the 'Migrant Mother'.

On set, Kazan penned some 'personal notes of a rank beginner', edited by Kazan's sometime assistant on the film Nicholas Ray, and sent them to his wife and professional confidant Molly Day Thacher in New York. Ray, an old friend from the Theatre of Action days in New York, came west with Kazan, and made his own first film, *They Live By Night*, belatedly released by RKO in 1948. The notes construct an opposition between cinema and reality, on the one hand, and the 'illusion and unreality' of the stage, on the other. Kazan cites approvingly the notion of the Russian theatre director Vsevolod Meyerhold that dialogue was 'the decoration of action', but he also wanted to go further in film in discovering 'what's going on in the hearts and feelings of the characters'. He expressed a desire to provoke and photograph authentic behaviour from his actors, so that the dialogue becomes secondary to looks and behaviour that become 'pieces of real experience'.[6]

Despite being aware of the need to learn about the new medium, Kazan also analysed key characters and relationships in terms of the theatrical notion of a three act structure. In the first act Johnny and Katie are unaware that they have fallen out of love, in the second the couple realise that their relationship is dead, and finally Johnny turns to Francie, and Katie and Francie are reconciled.

In terms of themes Kazan was interested both in immigration – the drama is set around the time when his own immigrant family established itself in New York – and also in the young girl's emotional need for her father, an element that the director related to his own separation from his children in New York. It was at this time that Kazan also first referred to the work of other directors and notably to John Ford's ability to create depth within the film frame. During his forties sojourn at Twentieth Century-Fox, Kazan would run several of Ford's films, including *Young Mr Lincoln* (1939), and talk to the veteran director, in particular about his use of locations. In his notes on his first film, Kazan mentions various borrowings in terms of technique but also admits that Ford's work transcended technique: to Kazan 'the truth is FORD is a poet. His frames sing with feeling.'[7]

Perhaps this early feeling for Ford was a factor in Kazan's unlikely involvement with MGM's production of *The Sea of Grass* (1947), in 1946, although he did later recall thinking that he had 'made it' when he took the Super Chief out to Hollywood to work at this most renowned of studios. At MGM Kazan had no role in the casting and never met the screenwriters, Marguerite Roberts and Vincent Lawrence, who had adapted the 1937 Conrad Richter novel of – in the words of the *Motion Picture Digest* – 'infidelity and bastardy'. There are certainly political and environmental undertones in the epic conflict, set in the 1880s, between wealthy cattle baron Jim Brewton (Spencer Tracy), who affects a mystical commitment to the unfenced grasslands of the South West, and the homesteaders who want to settle on the land. Brice Chamberlain (Mervyn Douglas) represents these farmers and also has a relationship with Jim Brewton's wife, the Eastern socialite Lutie Cameron (Katherine Hepburn). Unsympathetic to her husband's attitudes towards the 'nesters', Cameron spends long periods away from her husband's ranch and has an illegitimate son with Chamberlain. The couple are separated for 20 years and during this time the son, Brock (Robert Walker), grows into a disturbed young man; it is only when he dies (shot when he escapes justice after killing a man during a card game) that Cameron returns west for the funeral and is improbably reconciled with her husband.

The Breen Office had been concerned at the woman's out-of-wedlock relationship and had repeatedly urged the studio to ensure that she was properly punished.[8] This punishment seems to take the form of Lutie Cameron admitting that her husband had been right about everything, including the unsuitability of the land for anything but grazing. In effect the conclusion shows an independent woman returning to domesticity, a theme with some relevance to immediate post-war American experience. Writer Marguerite Roberts was a leftist who was later blacklisted, while Tracy, Hepburn and Douglas were all prominent Hollywood liberals. To Roberts, a Western specialist, Kazan, despite his liberal politics, was a 'chauvinist', and favoured the Tracy character, although it is doubtful if the director had much opportunity to change a perspective that, under pressure from the Breen Office, was central to the script.[9] More fundamental to Kazan's evident frustration with the project was the studio's unwillingness to film on location, so that the vast grasslands, the 'sea of grass' of the title, appear only in the form of back projected footage, shot a year earlier in Nebraska.

Seeking to provide 'spines' for the main characters, Kazan saw Katie Cameron as an 'adventurer' and Col. Brewton as a 'fanatic'; yet these identities, and the pain of separation implied in the story, impinge little on the star performances of the two principals. Tracy was ill at ease with horses and makes an unlikely man of the West, while the Hepburn character is pegged as an MGM star by her succession of opulent costumes. A scene in which Brewton strolls into a room on his ranch, ostensibly after an arduous ride through a snow storm, seems particularly ludicrous in terms of Kazan's concern with capturing 'pieces of real experience'. The story does make references to the experience of the Depression, and Kazan noted that 'the nesters' should not be 1935 Dust-Bowlers but 'should have something hungry-eyed and desperate about them'. Purely in terms of the story there are echoes of *The Plow that Broke the Plains*, the Resettlement Administration sponsored documentary, directed by Pare Lorentz, of 1936. Yet in the film (described as a 'Woman's Drama' by the *Hollywood Reporter*), it is the Tracy figure and not the Government who conserves the land, although the film is also sympathetic to Chamberlain, who provides for the interests of the settlers.[10] To the extent that Lutie Cameron returns unconditionally to her husband the sexual politics of the film, together with the politics of the land, are ultimately resolved in his favour.

After this unhappy spell at MGM Kazan was happy to return to Fox, and the four additional films that he made there in the late forties were equally divided between two forms, the location shot 'semi-documentary', and the high budget, high prestige social problem film personally supervised by Zanuck. *Boomerang!* (1947) was made on location in Stamford, Connecticut in the autumn of 1946 and was produced by the former *March of Time* producer Louis de Rochemont, who had joined the studio in 1943, and was responsible for two successful films dealing with wartime espionage, *The House on 92nd Street* (1945) and *13 Rue Madeleine* (1947). Zanuck, who was always suspicious of documentary elements that were insufficiently enlivened by strong acting and dramatic values, felt that he had invented the 'semi-documentary' form in tough negotiations with de Rochemont, who favoured stories dealing with FBI and police technique and procedure. At the time the *Hollywood Reporter* saw Kazan's film as 'something of a novelty, in as much as not a foot of the feature was filmed in Hollywood, or in any studio, but all of it on location'.[11] With the squeeze on profits at the studio from 1947, the shortage of and increasing cost of studio space was to contribute to the wider attractiveness of location shooting. Products of this trend included Jules Dassin's *The Naked City* (1948), described at the time as risky and experimental by producer Mark Hellinger, and Robert Rossen's production of *All the King's Men* (1949) at Columbia Pictures. In terms of the origins of *Boomerang!*, de Rochemont had referred Kazan to a 1945 *Readers Digest* article, 'The Perfect Case', based on a 1924 incident in which an accused man was arrested but eventually acquitted through the efforts of prosecuting attorney Homer L. Cummings. Yet the producer's main contribution seems to have been related to the most conservative element of the film, the heavy-handed voice-over narration at the beginning and again at the end.

Location work crucially allowed inexperienced directors such as Kazan to work with a new freedom from studio thinking and supervision. He worked closely on the script with ex-journalist Richard Murphy, while he also had much greater influence over casting, bringing in New York stage actors whom he had worked with, including Lee J. Cobb, Karl Malden and Arthur Kennedy, as well as Ed Begley. In accordance with the semi-documentary form, Kazan used local people for 'bit' parts, as well as former Group Theatre colleagues Lewis Leverett and Herb Ratner, dialogue coach Guy Thomajan, and even his own uncle – and the inspiration for *America America* – Joe Kazan. The scenes of suspects being arbitrarily picked up, and of the falsely accused Waldron (Kennedy) being coerced into making a confession, are quite distinct from the textbook civics implied in the patriotic closing narration. One of the suspects, briefly seen in a police line-up, ill shaven and being manhandled by two cops, is playwright Arthur Miller, who Kazan was simultaneously working with in preparing the Broadway production of *All My Sons*, which opened in January 1947. Ed Begley (as Paul Harris, a corrupt businessman and public official) played the much larger but thematically related part of Joe Keller in the Miller play. When Kazan cooperated with the House Committee on Un-American Activities in his second 1952 testimony, he referred to *Boomerang!* as being based – as the closing narration records – on the life of Homer Cummings, later Attorney General of the United States:

> It tells how an initial miscarriage of justice was righted by the persistence and integrity of a young district attorney, who risked his career to save an innocent man. This shows the exact opposite of the Communist libels on America.[12]

In fact the ringing statement heard over the conclusion is all but irrelevant to what is revealed in the film as a whole, and the district attorney, played by Dana Andrews, is, although central to the plot, furthest from Kazan's notion of sub-textual acting for the movies. In the year that *Boomerang!* opened Kazan worked with Robert Lewis and Cheryl Crawford to establish the Actors Studio in New York as an institutional base for the training and development of professional actors. A non-commercial venture, it was born out of an attempt to recreate something of the work and spirit of the Group Theatre, and the initial roster of actors included future Kazan film performers Marlon Brando, Montgomery Clift, Mildred Dunnock, Karl Malden, Kim Hunter, Julie Harris, Patricia Neal and Eli Wallach. The director began taking the classes for beginners, working with them on exercises and improvisations and challenging their spontaneity and sensory awareness. He remained a key father figure at the Studio, except during his involvement with the Repertory Theatre of Lincoln Center from 1962 to 1965, although Lee Strasberg was introduced as a teacher in the late forties and became artistic director in 1951, becoming particularly associated with the notion of 'the Method'.[13]

Boomerang! begins with a 360 degree panorama of the centre of Stamford, Connecticut, and with a narration that reflects on Bridgetown, a supposedly typical American town. Kazan keeps the story moving quickly, as we see the reaction of local townspeople to the murder of a well-liked local clergyman. There is growing pressure on Chief of Police 'Robby' Robinson (Lee J. Cobb) to find the murderer, not least from the Reform Administration and rival machine politicians, both with an eye on their prospects in the forthcoming election. The sonorous narration contrasts in tone with the cynicism of many of the principals, notably Robinson and local journalist Dave Woods (Sam Levene). Robinson, sourly biting the end of his cigar, introduces a more hard-bitten tone from his first appearance. We see men being picked up and hauled in for questioning, before the unemployed Waldron (Arthur Kennedy) is brought in from Ohio on flimsy evidence as the major suspect. The central and most persuasive part of the film involves the persistent questioning of Waldron in a series of short, claustrophobic scenes. A war veteran who had been looking for work, he pleads his innocence but becomes increasingly alarmed and defeated. Kazan frames small groups of investigators, bearing down on the suspect, and after sustained interrogation, Waldron breaks down and signs a confession. Robinson, carrying the exhausted suspect over to a bed, comments: 'What a way to make a living'.

Thereafter the State's prosecuting attorney, Henry Harvey (Andrews), begins to have doubts about Waldron's guilt, much to the frustration of both Robinson and the town notables, who see a conviction as crucial to the result of the forthcoming election. One such notable is Public Works Commissioner Harris, a character seen by Kazan as a 'desperate man, but a good man', while an opposition party group, shown conspiratorially at a country and golf club, are equally happy to use Waldron as a pawn in their political ambitions. The suspect is menaced by a huddle of men in coats, hats and ties, so-called 'Friends of Father Lambert', a scene that hints at mob-like elements and self-interested cabals lurking behind the formal edifice of this average American town, beyond the democratic rhetoric of the opening narration. Building towards the more conventional climax, Harvey uses a number of devices to undermine the testimony of local people who are happy to point to Waldron's guilt, before proving via a courtroom demonstration that the suspect's gun could not have been the murder weapon. Waldron is acquitted and the narration tells us that the murderer was never found. Yet the film has hinted at the real murderer and in a coda a policeman is seen reading a newspaper report that this same man has died, apparently crashing his car after being chased by the police for speeding. Spectators are thus given more information than prosecutor Harvey, and the film's multiple perspectives question both its documentary claims and the reassurance of the closing 'voice of God' narration.[14]

In terms of theme, Kazan brought his own sense of the story's sub-text, a perspective that drew on his own immigrant and political background. He wrote at the time that the town had 'a huge conventional, business-man-like front', and that in this kind of society 'Everybody is desperate'. Perhaps drawing on his on-going discussions with Arthur Miller, Kazan prepared notes on the production in which he suggested that the 'show has to be a REVELATION of the ANATOMY of Bourgeois Society', with its characteristic emotions – including fear, worry, awkwardness, foolishness and the 'scramble for the almighty buck'. His contemporary comments on Miller's *All My Sons* indicate similar political assumptions, while he prompted himself to 'use this story to portray everything that you despise about life in New Rochelle', his parents' home town in the twenties. As for the women, Kazan saw them as 'so stuffy and so goddam empty', reflecting a spiritual vacuum of the town, made suddenly transparent by the opening murder.[15] Something of this social texture is in the completed film, from the scheming local power elites to the suspicious notables, newspapermen and police officials. Yet the narration, the role of Harvey and his wife (Jane Wyatt) and the closing trial are more conventional elements, while there is insufficient low key photography (mostly in the interrogation scenes) to consistently underline the pessimistic elements of the story and so place the film obviously in the work that post-war French critics first described as film noir. Raymond Borde and Etienne Chaumeton, however, in their pioneering mid-fifties book, did point to connections between the post-war semi-documentary films and their own notion of film noir. Writing in March 1947, James Agee hinted at these darker elements in speculating that *Boomerang!* might be 'the best American film of its year, barring only Chaplin's' (i.e. *Monsieur Verdoux*); he also noted that the performances were 'the most immaculate set of natura-listic performances I have seen in one movie'.[16]

The semi-documentary style has often been seen as politically conservative, especially following its use in the service of anti-Communism, at first in Twentieth Century-Fox's *The Iron Curtain* (1948), but the same studio's *Boomerang!* and *Call Northside 777* (Henry Hathaway, 1948) were well received at the time by the left-wing press. Herb Tank, in the Communist *Daily Worker*, referred to the photographic style of these two films as 'so much less glossy and high-lighted than the usual Hollywood output', while Kazan's film was seen as presenting 'a fairly accurate picture of the backstage manoeuvrings of small town politicians in their own interest'.[17] The film also shares some of the doubts about the applicability of democratic values to small town America exhibited in Frank Capra's last great (and then unappreciated) work, *It's a Wonderful Life* (1946). (Capra's extended 'happy ending' can in this sense be compared to the role of narration in *Boomerang!*) Crime films provided opportunities to a new generation of directors to push at established visual conventions and introduce oblique political comment. Behind its homily on professional integrity *Boomerang!* provides a sceptical view of local democracy and even the com-mitment of ordinary citizens to justice. Zanuck kept a beady eye on the rushes, but his interventions were restricted to requests by telegram for more protec-tion shots and close-ups. By the time that he supervised the final editing, in December 1946, Kazan was already in New York supervising rehearsals for *All My Sons*.

Having served a kind of apprenticeship at Fox, Kazan was next entrusted with the direction of one of Zanuck's personal, high budget social problem projects. While RKO had released *Crossfire* (1947) before *Gentleman's Agreement* (1948) opened, it was the prestigious Fox film, dealing with anti-Semitism in terms of middle-class evasions, silences and conspiracies, that was seen as especially daring, and that was most successful at the box office and at the following year's Academy Awards ceremony. The script, written by Moss Hart from Laura Z. Hobson's bestselling novel, makes several references to 'crackpot' approaches to anti-Semitism in which the main source of the prejudice is seen as a disturbed if not psychotic individual, like the returning veteran played by Robert Ryan in *Crossfire*. The Fox film, shot in the studio except for a few early sequences establishing the New York locale, recreates in language and atmos-phere the gentile world of the metropolitan and Eastern upper middle classes. Kazan, always sensitive to issues of class given his immigrant background and political training, noted that the script was 'in every detail and in every instance upper middle class'. As with his preparation for his previous film Kazan felt that the rich 'haven't much humor – only psychoses, ulcers and worries of all kinds', although here the anxiety relates to the problematic issue of anti-Semitism in post-war America.[18]

Phil Green (Gregory Peck) is a newcomer to this world, coming to New York from Los Angeles to work on a special assignment for the magazine *Smith's Weekly*. The first third of the two-hour film shows him struggling to find an angle for a series of articles on the subject of anti-Semitism. Finally he decides to pretend to be Jewish, and the tension of the film relates to the impact that this exercise, which he invests with an appropriate moral seriousness, has on his burgeoning relationship with a divorcee, Kathy Lacey (Dorothy McGuire), niece of the magazine's editor. As Green discovers for himself the various forms of bigotry and discrimination, the drama revolves around the question of whether Kathy's liberalism is part of the problem, or of the solution. However carefully the film observes the anti-Jewish prejudice of the day, it is also a love story, and the likely romantic resolution weakens the prospect that the lovers might at any stage fall out over the central political issue.

There are interesting, well-researched scenes which enable Green, along with the audience, to discover the nature of these kinds of gentleman's agreements. His secretary, Elaine Wales, played by June Havoc, is a Jew who denies her own Jewishness and seeks to defend her status by identifying with the prejudice against Jews in the society around her. Green also meets a Professor Lieberman (Sam Jaffe) at a party, so that he and we can learn about notions of race and religion, while a particularly effective scene shows the campaigning journalist getting a smooth brush off when he tries to register at a 'restricted' country hotel. This latter scene is particularly well handled by Kazan, as desk clerk and manager conspire to send Green on his way without stating openly that the hotel is closed to those of the 'Hebrew persuasion'. There are also repeated references to real anti-Semites and racists such as the evangelist Gerald L.K. Smith, the Mississippi Senator Theodore Bilbo, and the Mississippi Representative John Rankin. Bilbo had advocated deporting all African-Americans to Africa, and Rankin was a notorious anti-Semite who had been instrumental in the decision of the House Committee on Un-American Activities to investigate Hollywood. It was just after the film had opened in New York that Rankin thought to discredit a number of actors who had protested against the House Committee, including June Havoc, by revealing their original and more 'Jewish' names – in her case, Hovick.[19]

Despite these contemporary references the scenes that bring the film alive dramatically, and also give it some political punch, are those involving Jewish

'What did you do, Kathy?': John Garfield and Dorothy McGuire in *Gentleman's Agreement* (1948). Courtesy of BFI.

leading man John Garfield as Dave Goldman, a friend of Green who is newly out of the army. Garfield, Kazan's choice, underplays but produces a real power and authority during his limited screen time. It is Goldman, who is in uniform throughout, who turns angrily on a soldier who makes slurs about the record of Jews in the war, and it is the same character who finally gets through to Kathy (or so we are led to suppose), in a pivotal and climactic restaurant meeting in which he convinces her of the inadequacy of her polite, reticent form of liberalism, thinking the right thoughts but never rocking the boat by speaking up in public. As a recent commentary has suggested, the film both denies any difference between Jews and non-Jews while also associating Jews with what Kathy, in resisting the inconvenience of her boyfriend's work for her decorous family circle, calls 'shouting and nerves'.

Zanuck, who supervised every stage of the production, was adamant that the Kathy character was not anti-Semitic, and required Kazan to re-shoot an early dinner scene in which Zanuck explained to his director, 'she betrays herself so completely that it is difficult to know why Phil comes back to her'. Yet it is Green's constant return to Kathy, despite the evident weakness of her own conviction, which seems to compromise the film, certainly for modern audiences.

Kazan reported some of his frustrations on this subject at the time to Arthur Miller, whose novel dealing with anti-Semitism, *Focus*, had appeared in 1945. He explained that 'I'm constantly tightrope walking – I mean, how to make our leading lady instinctively anti-Semitic, like most of the Gentile people of the Goyish upper middle class, without making her an outright louse and without making her <u>aware</u> of her own anti-Semitism.'[20]

Zanuck worked with Moss Hart on the script from early 1947 before Kazan was brought in to conferences. Again, the director was keen to use the camera as an 'instrument of introspection', picking up 'tiny reactions', particularly crucial in a milieu in which the veneer of politeness is rarely broken. The director wrote at the time that it was the Jews who understandably make the 'noise and the fuss', as they have the job of 'breaking down what exists', the *'Gentleman's Agreement* to exclude the JEW'.[21] As the review in *Time* pointed out, the film 'contends that decent, intelligent people, who know better than to be anti-Semitic but take no militant steps to stamp out the social weed, are chiefly to blame for its hardy growth'. Elliot E. Cohen, editor of *Commentary*, praised the film's engagement with the 'good, wholesome liberal Kathies of the nation', with the 'inactively good' as well as the 'actively evil'.[22]

In marketing the film in October and November of 1947, Zanuck arranged a series of East Coast preview screenings with invited opinion leaders. It was at precisely this time that the House Committee's opening hearings on supposed Communist influence within the film industry were reaching their climax. The November 1946 elections had returned Republican majorities to both houses of Congress, while the ground for ideological conflict within the film capital had already been prepared by the founding in 1944 of the Motion Picture Alliance for the Preservation of American Ideals. Bitter industrial conflicts had polarised Hollywood politics in 1944–6, while the emergence of the Cold War and of President Truman's executive order of March 1947, instituting a loyalty programme for the executive branch, established a public image of domestic subversion within government. During the first year of J. Parnell Thomas's chairmanship of HUAC, 1947, the Committee developed a close relationship with the FBI, which had collected extensive information on Hollywood communism with the aid of numerous informers. Among the studio chiefs it was Jack Warner who stoked the fires of the anti-Communist crusade by providing the Committee, meeting covertly in Los Angeles in May 1947, with horror stories of Communists working at his studio. Warner repeated his testimony at the formal hearings in Washington, DC in October, alongside other 'friendly' witnesses. Of the 19 'unfriendly' witnesses called before the Committee, 13 were Jewish. Among the 'Hollywood Ten', those of the 19 who actually testified, Edward Dmytryk and Adrian Scott had been called before the

Committee because of their involvement as director and producer of *Crossfire* (1947), the first completed film attacking anti-Semitism. In a *Variety* ad published during the week when the unfriendly witnesses testified to the Committee, Kazan's name was listed among those protesting that any 'investigation into the political beliefs of the individual is contrary to the basic principles of our democracy', while he also wrote to Scott at the time offering his support. On 24 November the House of Representatives voted overwhelmingly for the citation of the Hollywood Ten for contempt of Congress, and this led to the declaration of key studio representatives, in the so-called Waldorf Statement, that they would not re-employ any of them until they had purged themselves of contempt and declared under oath that they were not Communists.[23] This document established the basis for the blacklist that gathered strength from 1950, following the failure of appeals to the Supreme Court.

Jack Warner in his testimony had told the House Committee how much he had hated *All My Sons*, and his comment on its director was that he was 'one of the mob. I pass him by but won't talk to him.' Throughout this period the editor, founder and publisher of the daily *Hollywood Reporter*, William Wilkerson, linked the decline in cinema attendances with the political divide revealed by the House Committee's hearings. Wilkerson blamed a new generation of serious minded writers, directors, producers and actors who felt that entertainment was not enough and who wanted the industry to become 'realistic': 'All life is a struggle, they said, and we must present it as such'. He welcomed the Waldorf Declaration as evidence of a desire to purge the industry of the so-called 'realists' and he looked forward to a new order of the day in which Hollywood would offer 'pictures that tell of happiness, contentment and promise'.[24]

The success of *Gentleman's Agreement* had led to a decision to go ahead with a film on the race issue, based on a bestselling novel, *Quality*, that had been purchased by the studio in 1946. The story of the completed film, released in November 1949, concerned Pinky, a young black woman who has 'passed' for white in the North and returns to see her grandmother in the Deep South. Aunt Dicey (Ethel Waters) works for the local matriarch, Miss Em (Ethel Barrymore), a cantankerous but principled figure, and the dramatic tension of the latter part of the film is prompted by the old woman's death-bed decision to reward Pinky's stoic nursing care by bequeathing her home and property to her. Since black people cannot inherit property under existing state law, the issue becomes the dual one of whether the legal challenge to Miss Em's bequest will succeed, and whether Pinky will return with her white boyfriend to a life of renewed 'passing' in the North, or embrace her black identity and use her inheritance to found a nursing school for local children.

Work on the script had been protracted. Zanuck had been concerned that the production might be associated with Harry Truman's civil rights platform during the 1948 election campaign, but Truman's unexpected victory in November seemed to indicate improved prospects for further public action – the President had desegregated the armed forces by executive order in July 1948 – and send a signal to Hollywood. In successive script conferences Zanuck had stressed that the film should be focussed not on the problem in general but on the personal adventures of the central protagonist. It was the liberal writer Philip Dunne who recast the story in the autumn of 1948, following National Association for the Advancement of Colored People (NAACP) criticism of an earlier Dudley Nichols script. Dunne had warned Zanuck that he would be attacked by 'the professional leftists' as much as by the 'professional negrophobes', and recommended that the emphasis of the story be placed on Pinky's decision to reject the option of passing as white. Kazan indicated to Zanuck that he was eager to direct the picture, but his East Coast commitments to *Death of a Salesman* led to the choice instead of John Ford. In March 1949, after the Miller play had opened and Ford had shot a week of *Pinky*, Zanuck appealed to Kazan to come west for six weeks to direct the film.[25] Ford had apparently lost a battle over shooting on location, with Zanuck insisting that it was made on the studio back-lot, while the director reportedly fell out with black actress Ethel Waters, who played Pinky's grandmother. Kazan, who soon agreed that the theme of the film was the need to be yourself and the necessity of pride in a milieu of injustice, inherited the existing casting, which crucially included the white actress Jeanne Crain as Pinky.

To the critic of *Time* magazine *Pinky* was the most skilful type of propaganda, avoiding crude and conventional labelling and leaving a 'strong impression that racial discrimination is not only unreasonable but evil'. Leo Mishkin of the *Morning Telegraph* praised the film but felt that 'you are always conscious that it is Jeanne Crain, a white girl, playing a part in a movie'. He suggested that the black actress Lena Horne would have been much stronger in the role, and decried the 'falsely, prettily happy ending', although he still saw the film as one of the few socially significant American pictures of the time. *Pinky* was released in November 1949, and to *Variety* it was the boldest of any of 'the three treatments so far on the subject of Negro discrimination in the United States'. Of the films that constituted the 1949 'race cycle' – *Lost Boundaries*, *Pinky*, *Home of the Brave* and *Intruder in the Dust* – Ralph Ellison felt that only the last named 'could be shown in Harlem without arousing unintended laughter'. To *New York Times* critic Bosley Crowther, *Pinky* provided a vivid and forceful exposure of 'certain cruelties and injustices', yet he detected residues of 'old mammy' sentiment and paternalism, and felt that its observation of

'Negroes', as well as whites, was 'largely limited to types that are nowadays far from average'.[26]

A very extensive set was built on the Twentieth Century-Fox back-lot for Aunt Dicey's home and the surrounding streets, while much of the rather talky 'action' takes place in Miss Em's home, and in the courtroom. Despite a script that increasingly focussed on the reactions and identity of one central character, Pinky Johnson, there is little sense of depth and expression in Jeanne Crain's performance, while the noble but beaten down Aunt Dicey character only rarely departs from the 'mammy' stereotype. Of the other black characters Jake Waters (Frederick O'Neill) is at least livelier, as when he casually picks up and eats a chicken leg on entering Aunt Dicey's shack. William Lundigan's wooden performance as Dr Thomas Adams, together with Pinky's evident whiteness, undermines the sense of an inter-racial marriage as an option.

In the end the film is shot through with the notion of liberal paternalism. Zanuck in particular, as with other politically controversial films, was concerned that the personal story was always predominant. As well as Miss Em's decision, other figures of liberal benevolence amid the local racism that is occasionally depicted are Pinky's defence counsel at the trial, and the judge. Both are characteristic of the Hollywood tradition of social problem pictures. Having said all this, and accepting the film's conceit, the film was certainly seen as packing a liberal punch in its time, in part by helping white audiences identify with the indignities suffered by Southern blacks. It became the third most commercially successful film of 1949. In theatrical and social terms, Pinky's climactic statement had, and has, an impact: she tells her white middle-class boyfriend that 'I'm a Negro, I can't forget it, I can't deny it. You can't live without pride.' The censor in Atlanta, where the picture made its Southern debut, commented that the picture would be 'painful to a great many Southerners' and would 'make them realise how unlovely their attitudes are'.[27]

In the later forties Kazan was also beginning to work on film projects that promised greater control and involvement. As early as 1944 he had mentioned the figure of the Mexican revolutionary leader Emiliano Zapata to Molly as a theme that suggested films of 'the calibre of the greatest Russian pictures'. In May 1948 he prompted Zanuck to write to John Steinbeck, and by June the novelist was meeting with the director and making research trips to Mexico, having agreed to write the script. Kazan took an active role in the scripting, responding to Steinbeck's extensive 1949 draft script and research notes, while at the same time he was discussing with Arthur Miller the playwright's interest in developing a 'Play for the Screen' based on his knowledge of the struggles of longshoremen in Brooklyn and the Italian community of Red Hook. Kazan responded with a series of comments and criticisms in May 1949, and also discussed the possibility of an independent production.[28]

Kazan was well aware of film work that offered alternatives to Hollywood. He endorsed Vittorio De Sica's *The Bicycle Thief* (*Bicycle Thieves*, 1948) for a flyer advertising the film's 1949 New York run, and given his New York roots he would have been particularly aware of the success of the Italian and other foreign films, playing in the city in a growing number of dedicated theatres. At the time he linked the American trend to shoot on location with the 'obviously natural and dramatically realistic effect attained in so many foreign-made films'.[29] Two 'neo-realist' films directed by Roberto Rossellini, *Paisà* (1946), which Kazan later cited as a profound influence, and *Open City* (*Rome Open City*, 1945), had both been shown in New York in 1948, and were celebrated in part for their location shooting and use of non-professionals. Contemporaries of Kazan also drew on documentary aesthetics in the late forties: Jules Dassin's *The Naked City* (1948), for example, explored disparities of wealth in New York City, although much of this element was removed when one of the film's writers, Albert Maltz – who Kazan also knew in the early thirties – was convicted of contempt of Congress as one of the Hollywood Ten.

As discussed before, Kazan had talked to John Ford and noted his advice, especially to get ideas for staging from his locations. It was with his next film for Fox, *Panic in the Streets* (1950), that he was to liberate himself from studio pressures, making the whole film, at the end of 1949 and the beginning of 1950, in New Orleans. Working again with Richard Murphy, who was with Kazan throughout, reworking a previous script, the director would shoot in a host of city and port locations and recruit scores of local people as actors. Shifting from the primacy of his 1947 nostrum – penned originally in his notes for the stage production of *A Streetcar Named Desire* – that 'Directing is turning Psychology into Behaviour', Kazan set himself the task of capturing as much of the real texture of the city as possible, emphasising external as much as internal keys to behaviour, staging in depth – using 28mm lenses – and employing longer takes. To Borde and Chaumeton, in their pioneering 1955 study, *Panic in the Streets* was notable for both cinematographer Joe MacDonald's 'dark, lustrous images' and for Kazan's shooting 'à la Rossellini'.[30]

The catalyst for the story is a gang shooting and the discovery by the city authorities that the victim, a recent immigrant, had pneumonic plague. A representative of the United States Heath Service, Dr Clinton Reed (Richard Widmark) – the character's name recalls the public health pioneer Walter Reed – is called in, and we see the friction between this 'outsider' and the local police captain (Tom Warren, played by Paul Douglas) in their 'race against time' to find the contacts of the dead man and therefore save the city and indeed the wider

national and global community. Parallel with the depiction of this emerging relationship are scenes of the New Orleans underworld, and in particular gang
leader Blackie (Jack Palance in his first screen role) and his rotund partner Fitch
(Zero Mostel, a stand-up comedian who had only one previous, wartime film
credit and would later be blacklisted). Reed, the underappreciated public
servant, is given a strong domestic context in scenes with his wife (Barbara Bel
Geddes) and young son, but in his public role he is prepared to be ruthless in
pursuit of what he sees as the public interest, in particular when a newspaper-
man is briefly arrested to stop him reporting the story. Reed and Warren
gradually develop an understanding, and together, in a climacteric chase in the
warehouses and jetties of the harbour, they track down their men.

Despite the director's desire to develop a broader visual repertoire, using the
conventions of the contemporary crime film, his production and script notes,
written at a time when the intention was to film in San Francisco, are revealing of his contemporary political thinking. Thematically Kazan wanted the new
film to be hard and cynical in mood, and to transcend its 'cops and robbers' origins by dealing with 'the Spectacle and the Technique of Democracy at Work!'
In preparing *Boomerang!* Kazan had thought in terms of the perspectives of the
Left, and when radical writer Walter Bernstein visited Kazan on location in New
Orleans he felt that the director 'seemed to share my politics'.[31] Yet in his 1949
notes the director went out of his way to quote passages from Arthur
Schlesinger Jr.'s book *The Vital Center*, which had been published earlier that
year. The period since the war, and particularly after Cold War politics became
the dominant public narrative in 1947, had seen the disintegration of the
Popular Front alliance between Communists and liberals and the emergence
of new liberal anti-Communist groupings. Spying cases, the advance of Soviet
influence in Eastern Europe, the Truman administration's purge of 'subver-
sives', and the Republican 'Reds under the bed' campaign after the 1948 election – all these developments were changing American political culture in the
late forties, even before the Soviet testing of an atomic bomb, the Communist
victory in China and, in 1950, the conviction of Alger Hiss, Senator Joseph
McCarthy's speeches and the beginning of the Korean war. Polls in late 1949
indicated that 68 per cent of the American public supported the banning of the
Communist Party. Harvard academic Schlesinger had been a founding member of Americans for Democratic Action in 1947, and his new book called for
a 'vital center' of liberal and radical but anti-Communist opinion. He referred
to liberals such as Arthur Miller, who attended the Cultural and Scientific
Council for World Peace at the Waldorf Astoria in New York in the spring of
1949, as 'native innocents and muddleheads' who were supporting a 'scheme
of totalitarian window dressing'.[32]

Kazan, in his preparatory notes for *Panic in the Streets*, quotes, and endorses in terms of the action of the film, a passage from the conclusion to Schlesinger's book, dealing with the fruitful nature of conflict and compromise in a democratic society. The director noted thematic epigrams for the film including 'Democracy at Work!' and 'Democracy vs. the Bug', while elsewhere he sees the planned story in terms of the notion that 'ordinary guys in ordinary spots can cope with real out-sized threats to the people's lives'. Kazan's quotation from the Schlesinger book ends as follows:

> The totalitarians regard the toleration of conflict as our central weakness. So it may appear to be in an age of anxiety. But we know it to be basically our central strength. The new radicalism derives its power from an acceptance of conflict – an acceptance combined with a determination to create a social framework where conflict issues, not in excessive anxiety, but in creativity.[33]

The use of this analysis by Kazan is indicative of something of his political thinking at the time, beyond his continued proletarian manner and identity with old friends from the thirties. The sentence immediately after the passage quoted distils the book's thesis that 'The center is vital: the center must hold'. In his notes at the time Kazan also refers to secondary themes, including the 'one world' notion, and the importance of the health service in society. In the film Dr Reed, arguing against the local newspaper editor's claim to represent the public interest, replies that: 'We're all in a community, the same one'. In support of the 'one world' notion the director deliberately used different nationalities in the local casting, and this is obvious in several scenes in the film, in particular on board a freighter and in several 'ethnic' restaurants. The debates in the film, between Washington doctor, local police chief and the press, are consistent with Schlesinger's notion, and while they pay tribute to New Deal public service (as Kazan intended), they also, as Peter Biskind suggests in his study of fifties film, catch something of the new sense of emergency associated with the Cold War politics of the time, and the belief of experts and professionals that they knew the public interest best.[34]

Panic in the Streets, however, is much more an entertainment than a political parable, although it draws – particularly in the elements of police procedure at the beginning, and the use of real professionals at the police morgue – on the semi-documentary tradition. Kazan felt that the cycle of Fox semi-documentary films, including his own *Boomerang!*, had become a 'formula', of 'cold action against brick backgrounds'. Instead he wanted to dig deeper into reality and to handle the people with a 'WARMER FEELING', and he achieves this in those parts of the film dealing with the domestic life of Dr Clinton Reed, of the US Public Health Service, and his wife. As in *Viva Zapata!* later (and even in *On the Waterfront*), Kazan identifies with the private man who has, or sees himself having, public responsibilities. Reed is seen as underappreciated (his painter neighbour has a better car and fewer bills), while the Nancy Reed character – played with some spirit by Bel Geddes, who like Mostel was to be black-listed in the fifties – in part anticipates another familiar motif of fifties drama in terms of her support for her husband and her creation of the home as a fortress or refuge from her husband's onerous public role. In what was to be a regular practice in the fifties, Kazan also used one of his Actors Studio class, calling Lenka Peterson down to New Orleans for the small but important part of Jeanette, the young woman who searches out Reed in a café, following his hiring hall call for information on the dead man.[35]

The film is notable for long takes and long shots, with far more of the action than in Kazan's previous films being in deep focus, with real street life visible through windows and doors. There are also complicated set-ups, many shot and lit at night. Most striking is the early extended sequence in which Kochak, the man who turns out to have been suffering from the plague, staggers across a railway track, alarmingly just missing a moving train, and is then cornered and shot by Blackie and his associates. This is an impressive feat of lighting and photography – by *My Darling Clementine* and *Call Northside 777* cinematographer Joe MacDonald – as well as direction. Kazan himself seems to appear in an early scene at the morgue, in the proletarian guise of a hospital cleaner, sweeping the floor. As with the earlier *Call Northside 777* there are some echoes of Italian neo-realism, particularly in a scene shot in a real longshoreman's hiring hall, and elsewhere in tenement homes, neighbourhood bars, and seedy rooming houses. A tracking and panning dolly shot in the dilapidated café (mentioned above) reveals a striking row of local faces, while the closing chase is distinctive in its use of space, in particular with a continuous 360 degree take of Blackie and his exhausted sidekick running along a warehouse roof, reversing and then dropping down through a skylight onto the coffee bags below.[36]

A *Time* review exploring such films noted that 'few directors can match Kazan at filling them with people whose behaviour seems equally authentic', while Lindsay Anderson praised the 'amazing naturalism' generated by the director's 'masterly control of detail'. Gavin Lambert felt *Panic in the Streets* to be the best of the films deriving from the American semi-documentary tradition, including *Kiss of Death* (1947) and *The Naked City* (1948); he enjoyed its acute observation but also noted that it was the final chase, 'flawlessly contrived' as it is, 'that reminds us that we have been watching a masterly entertainment and not a concentrated account of human beings in a particular crisis'.[37]

Kazan and cinematographer Joe MacDonald on location in New Orleans, *Panic in the Streets* (1950): Richard Widmark is bottom right. Courtesy of Wesleyan Cinema Archives.

Kazan's later autobiographical reflections provide some sense that he was at this time, as he attained major success in his work on both coasts, drifting away from the politics of those previously in his circle. As well as his use of Schlesinger's work he later mentioned his support for the Truman Doctrine in 1947, on the basis of his fears that Greece might go the same way as Eastern Europe.[38] In terms of work, Kazan, at the end of the decade, was pushing at the limits of his 'studio director' role at Fox, working with John Steinbeck and Arthur Miller on possible productions and creating a production company in

Richard Widmark and Lenka Peterson in *Panic in the Streets* (1950). Courtesy of BFI.

New York (in 1950) with a view to making films independently. His next realised film project was arguably a step in this direction. Despite initial reluctance he agreed to film his 1947 stage collaboration with Tennessee Williams for leading agent turned independent producer Charles Feldman, using the Warner Bros. studio to produce and distribute the film in what was to become a characteristic fifties procedure.

2

New Directions: *A Streetcar Named Desire* (1951)
and *Viva Zapata!* (1952)

Kazan's original intention was to follow *Panic in the Street* with his and Steinbeck's picture on Emiliano Zapata, but late in 1949, before he began shooting in New Orleans, he agreed to direct a film version of *A Streetcar Named Desire* for independent producer Charles Feldman, who purchased the rights in October and subsequently made an agreement with Warner Bros. Kazan originally declined to return to the Williams play, but was apparently persuaded by the playwright, and originally intended to 'open out' the play by filming in Mississippi and Louisiana. Feldman employed screenwriter Oscar Saul to write an adaptation, and early in 1950 Saul completed a script that began the drama in Belle Reve, the original family home of Blanche and Stella Dubois. Williams later worked on the screenplay, and Kazan changed his mind on his plans to shoot on location, deciding instead (except for the opening shots in New Orleans) to photograph the original play as closely as censorship problems would allow. Williams, who gained sole screenplay credit, felt that he and Kazan made a good combination, with the director's 'passion for organisation' and for 'seeing things in sharp focus' complementing his own work.[1]

The turn of the decade had seen Kazan considering making films independently. It was evident that Miller's 'Play for the Screen', *The Hook*, was unlikely to interest the major studios, although Columbia Pictures eventually made a commitment, mainly in the hope of securing Kazan's services for subsequent pictures. Even before tying up with Feldman, Kazan had briefly felt that an independent production might enable him to make an uncompromised film of the Williams play by bypassing the Production Code process.[2] William Wyler had also shown interest in a production at Paramount in 1949, and at the time Joseph Breen had drawn attention to three substantial problems of adapting the play for the screen: the 'sex perversion' (the homosexuality of Blanche's husband); the rape scene; and 'the experience of prostitution of Blanche'. In addition Kazan later told Jack Warner that 'old L.B. Mayer' came to New Haven, where the Williams play was running prior to its Broadway opening, and 'tried to influence me in his best and most persuasive manner to have a happy ending tacked on to the play and make Blanche the heavy'. Zanuck was also interested in the property and later claimed to have agreed a deal with Kazan before abandoning the idea when Fox President Spyros Skouras referred him to what he felt were insuperable censorship problems.[3]

Zanuck had been grateful to Kazan, in particular for taking over at short notice as director of *Pinky*. In June 1950 the studio and production chief wrote to the director Delmer Daves, pointing out that after making five successful films with him he did not claim that Kazan was 'the best director in the business', but felt that no director who had worked on the lot had given members of his crew as much authority and responsibility, and had responded so often to their recommendations.[4] Kazan continued working with Steinbeck on a project that was becoming politically more problematic, and for which Zanuck had still to approve a final script and agree a starting date. At the same time Miller was responding to Kazan's first draft criticisms of his proposed waterfront screenplay. Meanwhile in Hollywood, in early 1950, negotiations began between Warner, Feldman and the Breen Office in an attempt to clear the extensive censorship problems. With preparations under way for three films Kazan turned down the opportunity to direct Williams' next stage play, *The Rose Tattoo*.

It was in his notebook for the stage production, dated August 1947, that Kazan had originally set down the notion that 'direction finally consists of turning Psychology into Behaviour'. Crucially, he had justified a 'stylized' production because of the important relationship between the central character's 'inner life', her memories and emotions, and the events depicted in the play. Kazan saw the play, which Molly had initially urged him to direct, as a 'poetic tragedy' in which Blanche, 'an emblem of a dying civilisation', was confronted with Stanley, a figure who also had social resonance in terms of 'the basic animal cynicism of today'. Kazan and Williams maintained the close working relationship that they had developed in the extended period of rehearsal and textual revision before the play opened. Given his 1950 decision to translate the play as directly and honestly as possible into the film medium, the bulk of Kazan's extensive notes on character and theme in the Williams play also apply to the film.[5]

Kazan came to believe that the great merits of the work owed much to a claustrophobic atmosphere that was achieved on the stage. Influenced both by the realistic theatre of Stanislavsky and the greater theatricality of Meyerhold, Kazan had worked closely with designer Jo Mielziner on the 1947 production.[6] The subjective factor of Blanche's memories, the playing of past events on present behaviour, was seen as central to understanding her life and her eventual tragedy. This inner life had been represented on stage by music and various visual effects, with Blanche both wedded to the false ideals of the aristocratic tradition of the old South and also fearful of losing her attraction to men. She seeks protection and refuge in the New Orleans home of her sister Stella and her brother-in-law Stanley Kowalski. Kazan saw the Stanislavskian 'spine' of Blanche's character in terms of this desperate search for protection, while in his notes on the screenplay he describes her as an 'emotional parasite', trying to save herself, finally, through an alliance with Stanley's ex-wartime buddy and fellow poker player, Mitch.[7] In 1947 Kazan had described the play as a triangle in which Stella, with her desire to hang onto Stanley, was at the apex. He saw her as in a 'sensual stupor', distracted from the moral consequences of her unconditional love for her husband. The baby that she has during the course of the events of the drama only makes her more dependent on him, and the repetition at the end of the film of Stanley's 'Hey Stella' cry – as his wife for the second time seeks refuge in her neighbour's apartment at the top of the outside stairway – suggests that it may bring the same response (Stella's return to her husband) as it did after the poker game fracas earlier. Stanley is happy to preserve his existing life, his possessions and his comfortable way of life. A war veteran and salesman (he 'travels' for the plant that Mitch works for in a lowlier position in the machine shop), he was seen by Kazan as self-absorbed and unreflective, indifferent to everything bar his own pleasure, and the desire to protect his home and marriage.

It was producer Charles Feldman who insisted on at least one star, at a time when Marlon Brando had only worked on one film, Fred Zinnemann's *The Men* (1950). The result was that Vivien Leigh, who had played Blanche in the London production directed by her husband Laurence Olivier, replaced Jessica Tandy in the central role. The British star of *Gone with the Wind* was thus added to the company responsible for the successful and long running New York production, all of them – Brando as Stanley, Kim Hunter as Stella and Karl Malden as Mitch – founding members of the Actors Studio. In his 1950 notes Kazan, aware of Brando's power as well as his training as an actor, particularly outside of the Studio with Stella Adler, was insistent that the film production reveal more effectively than the play the emotion within Blanche, 'her suffering, her pain, her inner life'. Kim Hunter remembers that one of the factors that led Kazan to make the film was that he wanted to place the focus more on Blanche. He wanted to use what he called 'Subjective photography', using the camera to 'penetrate Blanche and then showing the SUBJECTIVIZED source of the emotion'. In particular he wanted to use the camera and music to reveal, to make present, this 'inner life', to craft 'a poem of the inner'. He also revealed his fear of presiding over a 'gab fest', and of making a 'melodrama', or 'tear jerker'. He wanted Blanche to be seen as intelligent, and as a woman with humour – 'Don't over do "insanity" at the beginning', he urged himself: 'You tell not the literal facts, as an observer might see them. You bring directly to the screen BLANCHE'S WORLD!'[8]

The first problem in achieving anything of this vision, for Kazan, Feldman and Jack Warner, was related to the substantial problems that the Williams play raised in terms of the Production Code. Feldman had made an early effort to ease some of these problems by urging that the rape of Blanche be excluded from the screenplay. Kazan responded fiercely to this notion in a letter to Jack Warner that implicitly challenged Feldman's prerogatives as producer, drawing on his own close relationship with Williams and asserting that Feldman had 'fucked up' the film production of *The Glass Menagerie*, released that year by Warners. To Kazan, who was impressed that the touring company of the Williams play was performing successfully in towns in the South that he had never heard of, Feldman was trying to 'bring the thing down to the taste HE THINKS the audience has'. In April 1950 the Breen office was still concerned with the 'inference of sex perversion', 'Blanche's nymphomania' and a rape that was 'both justified and unpunished'. Kazan had observed most of the early censorship negotiations from his New York home or his newly acquired property in Sandy Hook, Connecticut, but in terms of many preparations for the production he was acting essentially as the film's producer. He successfully lobbied for Dave Weisbart as 'cutter' – 'the one side of the business that I'm somewhat unsure about'. In fact, Kazan later wanted Wesibart given an associate producer credit on the basis of his extensive advice on set. Veteran art director Richard Day (also Kazan's choice, after some early consideration of Boris Aronson and Jo Mielziner) came out to see the director in New York, while Kazan successfully urged Warner to send costume designer Lucinda Ballard (who had worked on the New York stage production) to London to start work on Vivian Leigh's clothes.[9] Although Ballard was only credited for her work with Leigh, she also helped choose Brando's clothes, suggesting the shrinking and redesign of the baggy sweatshirts of the day into the gear that contributed to the actor's iconic impact.[10] Kazan also insisted, over studio resistance, on the signing on of Alex North to compose the music for the film. Kazan and North had both worked on the documentary *People of the Cumberland*, for Frontier Films, in 1937, but they did not develop a close working relationship until 1949, when North wrote the music for the stage production of *Death of a Salesman*. North, who like Kazan was based in New York, had mainly worked for the theatre and had not previously worked in Hollywood. For a film set in New Orleans, Kazan wanted a score that used jazz idioms and the director sent him to the city to gain experience of the indigenous music. North wrote a complex score which used a variety of chamber ensembles that were appropriate to the film's intimate character, and which became recognised as the first composed jazz score for a Hollywood film.[11]

Kazan thanked Warner for not making an issue of the costs to the studio of his not living in California. His letters to Warner began a long and important professional relationship and provide abundant evidence of the director's mastery of relaxed but effective argument, attention to detail, charm and flattery. Kazan's strength in his associations with Warner, Feldman and Joseph Breen lay in his special bond with Williams, whose own letters reveal a strong trust in his friend's ability to carry the fight for artistic integrity into the smoke-filled rooms. In this way Kazan often outflanked the ostensible producer, Charlie Feldman, and greeted his arguments with scepticism. On the question of the film's ending, and the requirement that Stanley be punished if any rape was to be permitted, Williams urged his artistic partner not to give any more ground than he had to, feeling that 'Stella's retreat up the stairs from Stanley is surely adequate punishment if it is handled firmly'. Feldman, however, wanted further trims to the script, not to mention a bizarre addition, which he believed would give a 'lift to the ending', in which Mitch's voice is heard suggesting that he will be waiting for Blanche to be released from the 'nut house'. Feldman fed this to Warner, hoping vainly that the mogul might sell it or something like it (as his own idea) to Kazan.[12]

Filming began in mid-August 1950 with the Breen Office still reserving its final position on the Code seal until it saw how the rape issue was to be dealt with. Several weeks into filming Kazan wrote to Joe Breen, confirming that he was happy to delete Blanche's reference to homosexuality. He also referred to cutting 'enormous hunks' out of a number of long speeches, especially those of Blanche. In a letter that is revealing about his aspirations and notion of film-making, Kazan reported to Warner that 'Now I'm down to beating the typewriter myself, which is the way Movies are made'. On the 'rape thing' he added that 'I've got sight of a real solution'. This crucial scene was due to be shot in the first week of October, and Jack Vizzard, who had joined the Production Code Administration (PCA) after leaving a Jesuit seminary, phoned the studio that week to try and find out what solution, if any, had been found. He urged the shooting of protection shots, clearly indicating the absence of a rape, so that they could be used should Kazan's preferred plan not be acceptable.[13] After the filming, as they awaited Breen's final judgement, Kazan underlined to Warner that as far as he was concerned the film was consistent with an agreement reached several months before in Warner's trophy room, in which Kazan had threatened to withdraw if the 'rape' was cut from the script, and where agreement had been reached that the rape could be included if it were 'done by suggestion and delicacy', and if Stanley was later 'punished' by being deprived of his wife's love. The agreement apparently included Breen, although Kazan notes that at several subsequent meetings 'Joe seemed to waver from this understanding'.[14]

Williams, probably on Kazan's prompting, wrote directly to Breen in late October, arguing that the 'rape of Blanche by Stanley is a pivotal, integral truth in the play, without which the play loses its meaning, which is the ravishment of the tender, the sensitive, the delicate by the savage and brutal forces in modern society. It is a poetic plea for comprehension.'[15] Williams and Kazan sacrificed a good deal of the more sexually explicit language of the play and the final negotiations took place in a flurry of communications on 2 November 1950, when agreement was reached on a form of words which suggested Stanley's final 'punishment' and Breen confirmed that the script was now consistent with the Production Code. After a conference between Breen and Kazan, Williams wired a suggested form of words in which Stella, talking to her baby, whispers: 'We're not going back in there. Not this time. We're never going back. Never Back. Never Back Again'. These were the words used when this scene was shot the next morning, although the closing sequence as shot, provoking audience memories of Stanley's previous cry for his wife's forgiveness, casts major doubt on the long-term nature of their separation. To Kazan, Joe Breen felt 'that he was letting us down very easy as far as the seal requirements went'.[16]

There followed an argument between Kazan and Warner, in which the director insisted on an 'Elia Kazan Production' credit on the picture. Warner resisted, reminding Kazan of the range of Feldman's work as producer, but the director asserted that he 'chose each artist working on the picture' and in other ways 'functioned as the producer on the picture'. Kazan also pitched to Warner on the 'advertising and exploitation' of the film, worrying that the ads were too lurid and common and urging Warner to give the film the 'Goldwyn treatment', which to him meant opening the film in New York at the Astor theatre.[17] Kazan drove with Alex North to a preview in Santa Barbara in February 1951, and small cutting changes were subsequently made. According to Feldman, preview cards were 70 per cent excellent, yet the producer felt that the audience was very restless and urged Warner to make further cuts following a New York preview.[18] There were more trims following a New Jersey preview in March, and the same month Kazan, Feldman and Williams met in New York and agreed on what they felt would be final cuts. The director, beginning his arduous two month stint of location work on *Viva Zapata!* in Texas in May, anticipated no further problems, and a release date in June or July was anticipated. In support of this belief trade and press showings took place in June, and favourable responses were reported. The reviewer for the *Hollywood Reporter* felt that the film would bring the artistry of the playwright to 'students, sophisticates and those interested in the drama', but felt that it would need 'specialised selling and exploitation', including 'long runs in the classic and art houses'. Kazan, however, had always been confident that the film's combination of art and frank sexual drama would have a broader appeal. Writing to Warner from Texas he referred to the *Hollywood Reporter*'s editor, noting that from 'thinly veiled hints to us in some of Billy Wilkerson's editorial remarks, I gather that his opinion is that STREETCAR is not the kind of picture he thinks the industry should be making'.[19]

In the next month, in July 1951, there were dramatic developments. The Legion of Decency, with Father Patrick Masterson taking the leading role, had concluded that the 'entire subject is undesirable' and indicated to Warners that unless there were further cuts they would give the film a 'C', or 'Condemned' classification, so advising their Catholic parishioners not to see it. The Legion had been created in 1934 as a Catholic pressure group concerned to press for the effective censorship of motion pictures. Without contacting Kazan, Warner authorised Jack Vizzard to go to New York to act as the studio's intermediary with the Legion. From there the PCA man reported to Breen that 'the prospect is very bleak indeed', and suggested that the problem was all the greater because Legion reviewers felt that the picture was both 'artistic' and 'so realistically done': had it been poorly done 'it wouldn't have been so worrisome'. In the light of this threat, and again behind his director's back, Warner sent Dave Weisbart, the film's editor, to New York, where Martin Quigley, a founding father of the Legion and co-author of the Production Code, was huddling with Vizzard with a view to agreeing cuts that would allow the film to gain a B rating. Out of their labours came around 12 cuts to key shots and sequences and to a number of lines of dialogue; overall the cuts amounted to three or four minutes of playing time.[20]

Kazan was worried by the silence, and lack of information, and wrote not to Warner but to his executive assistant Steve Trilling that 'The fact is SOMETHING is being done to my picture – I don't know what!' Kazan reported that he called Weisbart in New York, and that it was clear that the editor had been told not to tell him anything. He also told Trilling that Jack Vizzard, who had trained for the priesthood, was the 'wrong person to have sent to New York'. Fearing that the picture was being 'castrated', Kazan warned: 'If someone spits in my face, I will not say it's raining.' To Williams he even indicated a willingness to take his name off the picture. The director left off supervising the editing of *Viva Zapata!* at Fox and arranged to see Quigley in New York, asking to be sent a work print and all the cut material. Unable to influence events, Kazan particularly objected to the cuts in the sequence in which Stella, following the poker night fracas in which Stanley hit her, returns down the staircase to her now penitent husband. Kazan protested to Quigley that 'I have the most violent possible objection to the recutting of the staircase scene. This scene has been, in effect, redirected.' The director went public with an article on the whole incident in the *New York Times*, by which time the film, in its cut version, had finally opened – in September 1951. In a letter around this time Kazan told his friend Alex North that he was fed up with the 'manufacturing process in relation to pictures' and that his experiences had fed a 'determination again for the nth time to go out and make some pictures independently'.[21]

To Hollis Alpert the film was one of 'Hollywood's rare attempts to give the whole meaning and scope of an author's vision'; he also felt that it would take a 'singular obtuseness not to know what Blanche is referring to when she speaks of the unmanliness of her husband'. Bosley Crowther in the *New York Times* felt that 'Inner torments are seldom projected with such sensitivity and clarity on the screen', while John McCarten, in the *New Yorker*, praised the filmmakers for resisting the censors but criticised what he saw as an over insistent use of close-ups. There are echoes of this last point in Karel Reisz's *Sight and Sound* review; he felt that Brando combined 'frightening charm' and 'affecting moments of tender, infantile charm', yet found the visual qualities of the film – the dominance of medium and close shot – unadventurous and at odds with the stylised dialogue. Manny Farber was particularly critical, arguing that the film lacked the 'thoughtful, muted, three dimensional qualities of the play', and that it instead substituted melodrama – 'all clamor, climax, Kazan'. Elsewhere he complained about being caught in 'the middle of a psychological wrestling match', an impression that he associated with several 'art or mood' films ('Freud-Marx epics') of the time, including *A Place in the Sun* and *Sunset Boulevard* (both 1951). There are certainly echoes in Billy Wilder's film of the vulnerability of a certain kind of old Hollywood glamour. Other reactions were more predictable. Powerful columnist Hedda Hopper disliked the new breed of stars, including Brando and Montgomery Clift, and felt that the film was even more 'sordid' than the play. On the left, and writing after Kazan's appearances before the House Committee, John Howard Lawson, while reviewing *Viva Zapata!*, made a sideswipe at Brando's use of 'crude tricks and mannerisms' to depict a 'brutally inhuman "worker"'. The film certainly transcended the art theatre ghetto, and became the fifth top moneymaking film of 1951. As is discussed in the next chapter, it was a leading contender at the 1952 Academy Awards ceremony, where Vivien Leigh, Karl Malden, Kim Hunter and art director Richard Day all won awards.[22]

The film begins rather like many of the crime dramas of the time with the city at night, as Blanche arrives at New Orleans railway station. Stanley is an ambitious, fifties family man but acts also as the investigator, exploring the background of the interloper in his tight family circle. Laurence Jarvik has even drawn a parallel between the merciless hounding of Blanche by the gathering of evidence on her past and the sense that many artists of the time were feeling persecuted (or being persecuted) about their past political affiliations. Blanche's creator was certainly aware of these pressures, while Kazan also knew that his own background made him vulnerable to a possible blacklist given the continued calls for the studios to 'clean house' and for a renewed round of Congressional investigations (which actually recommenced in March 1951). It was while Kazan was filming *Streetcar* that Cecil B. DeMille and others in the Screen Directors Guild made the effort to unseat Joseph Mankiewicz as President of the Guild and institute a compulsory loyalty oath. Kazan, having supported Mankiewicz and opposed his recall, absented himself from the climactic vote, telling his friend that his past associations might be counterproductive for the cause.[23]

What is achieved with the film of *A Streetcar Named Desire* is ensemble work of a high order, the product of both extensive rehearsal and the long experience of most of the actors with their roles. If the emphasis was and is on Brando's performance in terms of the arrival of a major talent (Kazan later used the word genius), the performances never place emotional expressivity before the 'given circumstances' of the drama. Kazan set out to serve the play, while recognising the need to think through the ways in which it would work on audiences via the medium of film. Harry Stradling's camerawork supported the claustrophobic effect that was a product of the decision to play out so much of the action inside the French Quarter apartment. The framing of the four central characters, in medium and close shots, involves relatively limited camera movement, although this in part reflects the cramped, realistic set in which the characters seem trapped; the use of wide angle lenses would have defeated this effect by exaggerating the space.[24]

Kazan played on Leigh's 'Hollywood glamour' and her lack of a 'Method' training to accentuate the tensions and conflicts of the drama, and to complement the way in which the character of Blanche has a need to perform, and to maintain an outdated and false tradition. As Karl Malden argues, 'the movie is more about Tennessee's Blanche DuBois than the play'.[25] If Brando as Stanley is the more emotionally expressive presence, the centrality of Blanche in the film is established by the additional, opening scene in which she arrives in the city through a cloud of steam at the railway station. The constant presence of the past in Blanche's mind is suggested by Alex North's score, which uses different themes to point up her key memories and traumas, in particular those relating to Belle Reve and the suicide of her husband. When Blanche first encounters her brother-in-law, his question to her, 'You were married once, weren't you?', echoes on the soundtrack, while the camera closes in on Blanche's distress as she relives the past and the audience hears dance music and the gunshot with which her young husband killed himself. By this fairly conventional device, repeated at later points, Kazan maintains the traumatic past as an active factor in Blanche's desperation and decline. It is perhaps most active as an influence on the present during her poignantly brief engagement with Mitch on the pier. Her wit and education, and her bond with her sister, stave off her loneliness and vulnerability, until circumstances – the revelation of her past, the rejection by Mitch and finally the rape by Stanley – demolish her remaining defences. She is a woman who is never able to escape from the false illusions relating to her class and femininity.

Brando as Stanley is part collar-and-tied fifties salesman, part animal, part child. He is instinctive and real, unreflective and uncritical, possessed by no demons, except a violent temper when things don't go his way. Brando is a force of nature, from the moment his character ambles home and wanders around the apartment in his sweaty T-shirt. Brando tips no-one off to his villainy and is as unrepentant at the end as at the beginning. His occasional charm, his childlike need for his wife's love and reassurance, go at least some way to balance his insensitivity (the 'business' about the Napoleonic code) and violence. Few male actors were allowed to cry, as Stanley does when coming to terms with what he has done on the night of the poker game. Brando's grimace is without inhibition, on the perilous edge of being ludicrous. Kazan was happy with such moments of extreme expressiveness from his actors, and there is one from the tragicomic Mitch – as he shouts impatiently that he is 'Coming!' to his friend and oppressor Stanley – that foreshadows Malden's character in *Baby Doll*, Williams's second, more minor key film collaboration with Kazan. Stanley, despite his cruelty and brutishness, is given a rationale, a case for the defence. That case has to do with his ambition to succeed as a 100 per cent American who has risen from his working class, second generation immigrant background. Here, at the dawn of the fifties, is a vision of domesticity that is also shockingly passionate and carnal.

It was these qualities that alarmed the reviewers from the Legion of Decency and Jack Vizzard. When Stanley loses his temper on losing a poker hand, throwing the radio through a window and subsequently hitting his wife, he is 'cooled down' by his poker partners, who hold him under the shower. Next comes a moment when Stanley paces his hall, crying as he realises what he has done and what it might mean. It is the following scene, showing Stella's slow,

Kim Hunter and Marlon Brando: the staircase scene in *A Streetcar Named Desire* (1951). Courtesy of BFI.

somnolent descent of the outside staircase, in response to her husband's animal cry, that suggested to the Legion an all too raw and sexualised aspect of the husband-wife relationship. As Vizzard explained to Breen at the time, the would-be censors wanted to create a much simpler story of a devoted wife who goes back to her husband 'to cook his hamburgers, mend his socks, or whatever you will'.[26] They wanted to cut the 'very sexy "register" on the countenance of Stella' and the jazz score accompanying it. Stella here may be the drugged ('narcotized') character mentioned in Kazan's 1947 notes, but her descent seems also to contain an element of deliberate taunting of her husband, waiting on his knees at the foot of the stairs. She seems aware of controlling and delaying, by the slow pace of her descent, an inevitable and highly sexual climax of forgiveness and redemption. Thus the overall scheme – the jazz score, together with the director's stretching of 'real' time – was disrupted by the substitution of a more conventional musical track and the excision of several of the closer and more expressive shots of Stella on the staircase.

Other scenes excised by Warners at the behest of the Legion also removed something distinctive about Kazan's contribution. Two further cuts followed the staircase scene discussed above. First, when Blanche follows Stella down the stairs, she is shown looking from the courtyard into the apartment, presumably at her sister and Stanley beginning their love-making. This disappeared from the 1951 release, as did part of the subsequent scene, of the morning after, when Blanche discovers her sister still in bed. The Legion may have been influenced by Kim Hunter's apparent nakedness under the bed sheet as much as by her happy, sleepy, sleepless revelation that on their wedding night Stanley had broken all the light-bulbs and that she had been 'sort of thrilled by it'. Without close shots and this dialogue the scene is weakened and has less impact on Blanche and audiences alike. Finally in the Legion's de-eroticisation of the film is the sequence that shows Blanche in a chair, just before the arrival of the bill collector, moving her body and hand in ways that suggest masturbation. She has just revealed to her sister the desperation of her desire, the conflict between her sense of herself and the need that she has for the 'last chance' relationship with Mitch. Additionally, on the rape scene, the main preoccupation of the Breen office, the Legion cut several immediately preceding elements, in particular Stanley's line, 'Well maybe you wouldn't be bad to interfere with', and two close shots of an excited Stanley advancing on Blanche. The rape itself survived in the suggested form that Kazan had devised, with Stanley struggling to overpower Blanche ('Lets have a little roughhouse') until her flailing arm, holding a broken bottle, smashes the mirror and reveals a closing, fading image of her head tilted back, resistance at an end.

The rendering of the brutish yet all too human figure of Stanley was both powerful and uncomfortable. Mary McCarthy, who had seen the play as inflating and sensationalising a 'wonderful little comic epic', which she called the 'Struggle for the Bathroom', later wrote of a 'new theatrical style in which aberrant characters appeared as normative national types'. McCarthy wrote of Stanley as 'a sub-human member of the lower urban middle class', and of Kazan as the 'whip-cracking ring-master of this school of brutes'. Such views suggest the distaste with which some critics, concerned in the new Cold War era with American role models, regarded Brando's 'Method' performance.[27] While Blanche is at the centre of both play and film, it was the role of Stanley that attracted the broadest attention, in part because, as played, it departed most from conventional Hollywood traditions of performance and of villainy. In his opening scene Brando constructs and inhabits a notion of realism that Vivien Leigh, as the 'wounded Butterfly', struggles to compete with, for all Kazan's efforts to present her world.[28] In the end it is the no less tragic figure of Stella who remains alone with Stanley in his realist realm. She is locked into a relationship with an abusive man who she loves and who loves her. Despite the Production Code dialogue to the contrary, she has no way out.

There is an additional scene, not in the play, that is set in the plant where Stanley and Mitch work. The scene supplies no information not better revealed by the later 'birthday supper' scene and it breaks too suddenly the rather touching moment of optimism, underscored by Alex North with a barely perceptible phrase from *Gone with the Wind*, when Blanche and Mitch embrace during their night out by the lake. Mitch's desperate need is also demonstrated by his wordless nods in answer to Blanche's queries about whether he loves his mother. He too loses out, and his life is likely to continue to revolve around bowling and playing poker with Stanley. Perhaps later scenes over-determine Blanche's decline (her regress to her role as Southern Belle and Mitch's merciless exposure of her prior to the rape). Kazan may have been aware of this when he exhorted himself, in his script: 'In the last few shots try to get the elliptical speed that Rossellini sometimes gets in his climaxes. So it goes always a little faster than the audience is prepared for.'[29] *A Streetcar Named Desire* remains a filmed play and one that took Kazan back towards his theatrical roots and away from his more cinematic work on location. Yet Kazan took a challenging drama to a wider audience. The characters struggle for survival like insects in a Disney documentary of the time, while the sexual passions, Stella's in particular, become more evident in the footage restored to the film after 40 years.

If *A Streetcar Named Desire* was concerned with psychology, Kazan tried in his next film, what he called his 'Mexican horse epic', to move to a more external perspective on his characters. In 1950 Kazan defined his cinematic ambitions in terms of the invention of 'whatever style (visual) necessary to bring out of these stories (not scripts) the concealed and real emotion that is there'.[30] With *Viva Zapata!*, Kazan was again subject to Darryl F. Zanuck's overall supervision and final control over editing, although the location shooting, and his own close relationship with John Steinbeck as writer, was consistent with the director's striving for greater independence. It was Molly who had encouraged Kazan to work with John Steinbeck, some time before the two families became near neighbours in New York City in the late forties. Steinbeck had made trips to Mexico since the thirties and written the script for a 1941 documentary set in Mexico, *The Forgotten Village*. Directed by Herbert Kline, who Molly Kazan had known through the magazine *New Theatre*, the film dealt in part with problems of progress and the environment in a small Mexican village. In the late thirties MGM had planned a film on the legendary figure of the Mexican Revolution, Emiliano Zapata (1879–1919), drawing on books and treatments by writer Edgcumb Pinchon. The screenwriter Lester Cole became involved when this project was revived after the war, but soon after he became one of the Hollywood Ten in 1947 MGM abandoned the project and the rights were purchased by Fox. An enthusiastic Zanuck, responding to Kazan's interest, concluded that MGM had abandoned the picture because of the possible reaction of the Catholic Church and the Mexican Government, although he also was himself wary of the subject, taking the view that the Mexican rebel's 'philosophy was of course very close to what we call communism'.[31]

Steinbeck, who spoke fluent Spanish, embarked on a period of extensive research in Mexico in 1948, interviewing witnesses and compiling a substantial dossier and initial script on the revolutionary leader. Intending from the start to make the film in Mexico, Kazan accompanied Steinbeck on a visit to Cuernavaca in November 1949, around which time the studio arranged for writer Jules Buck to help Steinbeck turn his draft into a more conventional screenplay.[32] Steinbeck's early work indicated that the plan was to give the story the 'quality of folklore', with Zapata as a universal symbol of resistance to oppression. In writing that dates from 1949, from both writer and director, one can see central themes and perspectives on Zapata's adult life that remain in the final shooting scripts of 1951 and the completed film. To Steinbeck: 'Collectivisation can come from both directions – from the extreme left and from the extreme right – and the life of Emiliano Zapata is a symbol of the individual standing out against collectivisation of either side.' His initial narrative dealt with the period 1909–19, from the emergence of Zapata as a leader of the rural poor of Morleos, a state in south central Mexico, to his assassination as part of a plot arranged by the then President of Mexico, Venustiano Carranza. Much of it relates to the early part of that period, during which the Zapatistas fought with the northern leader Francisco I. Madero for the overthrow of long-term President Diaz, and then against the military leader General Huerta. Zapata's personal life is given extensive treatment, detailing his closeness with his brother Eufemia and his courtship above his station of Josefa, daughter of a middle-class merchant. Steinbeck pays little attention to the political ideas associated with the historical figure of Zapata and more to his personal incorruptibility and relationship to the people. At one point in Steinbeck's early narrative a follower asks Zapata how the constant fighting will end, and he replies: 'I don't know. For us, probably badly. For the future, there is a chance.'[33]

In a treatment dating from October 1949, Kazan also uses motifs that remain present in the completed film. The director was interested in Zapata's legendary status in Mexico, but also in his relationship to power; he suggested that 'When Zapata left the Capitol, or rather abandoned it, he was in effect committing suicide. I believe he knew it.' In the film this moment divides the success of Zapata's campaigns, up until the meeting with Pancho Villa, and the later scenes of struggle, leading to his death. It also points up a sub-theme of Zapata's fear that his mission would be corrupted. The director also traced the last act as a 'Judas story' and sketched an idea for the assassination scene in which 'half a hundred hidden rifles pumped lead into Zapata's body'. Kazan suggested to Zanuck that in the 'third act he WINS, not thru himself, but thru creating a strong people, thru creating an armed and aware democracy, out of which new leaders (Cardenas) will rise'.[34] Thus many of the themes of the film are present in early treatments and drafts and one can exaggerate the impact of the political changes made much later, during the editing process. Early scripts consistently end with some reference to Zapata's legacy, either in terms of policies promoting the welfare of the country people and their traditional land rights, or in terms of legend. This at one point was to be expressed in terms of a traditional Mexican narrative ballad or corrida; in the April 1950 script the following lyrics are suggested:

> And so he was not dead because
> No one was beaten any more
> And no one dared to steal the land again
> And the crops grew freely
> And the people were not afraid
> And so he is alive

Prior to his involvement with *A Streetcar Named Desire*, Alex North had responded to Kazan's request that he write a musical score for the Mexican film based on indigenous music. North knew Mexico well and had lived there for a year just before the war. Their plan to use a corrida, however, was dropped sometime after December 1950, apparently because it was felt that it became repetitive.[35]

In terms of the distinction in the film between natural leaders and professional revolutionaries, this idea can be found in Steinbeck's earlier novels and screenplays, including *In Dubious Battle* and *The Grapes of Wrath*. The first of these, although sympathetic to a strike, is critical of a ruthless, professional revolutionary for whom ends are more important than means, while *The Grapes of Wrath*, Steinbeck's most famous novel and the last of his books to gain any significant praise from left-wing critics, broadly articulates and celebrates a classically American form of Jeffersonian populism. Steinbeck had never been a Marxist or a Communist, although that had not stopped the FBI showing some interest in his political associations and in a post-war visit he made to the Soviet Union. Zanuck, grateful to Kazan for his role in saving *Pinky*, was happy to let such a prestigious novelist work initially 'on spec' and to guide the preparation of the script, and only later did he become concerned with issues of political interpretation.[36] Steinbeck first worked with Buck, and then, in early 1950, with Kazan, with the director wielding the typewriter as he had on occasion during the preparation of A Streetcar Named Desire. What did emerge was very much a view of Zapata not only as a fighter for the land rights of the people of Morelos but also as a leader who is aware of and generally resistant to the personal corruptions implicit in revolution and military struggle, elements that dominate the last part of both script and film. The limitations of the finished film are in part a product of the problem of representing coherently the complexity of the Mexican revolution that is the context of Zapata's life (the film covers events from 1909 to 1919, including his emergence as a leader, the fall of President Diaz, the regimes of Madero and General Huerta, and Zapata's death). The last five years of Zapata's life, following Huerta's fall in 1914, pose particular problems of emphasis and compression for the filmmakers. The other difficulty relates to the imprecise fit between two themes: the worth and necessity of political, agrarian revolt, and the corruption seen as implicit in such action and the power it brings.

Alongside the historically-based figures – the sketches of Madero and Huerta are particularly effective – Steinbeck introduced a series of new characters designed to reveal the leader's relationships with power. Perhaps the most important of these were Pablo (a close, long-term associate who is later shot by Zapata for consorting with the enemy) and Bicho (finally called Fernando Aguirre), an opportunist and professional revolutionary. Ironically it is Fernando who, on first meeting Zapata, articulates the difference between the Diaz dictatorship and the American tradition of elections and of providing sanctuary for refugees. Zapata is from the beginning distinguished both from the military and political dictators of Mexico, the 'strong men' of the Right, and from the notion of revolution associated in 1950 with Marxist theory and Soviet practice. Yet successive scripts maintain an enthusiasm for Zapata's agrarian radicalism, and this and its visual enhancement under Kazan's direction is one of the more remarkable aspects of the film's 1952 release. The director later argued that from the beginning he and Steinbeck had a desire, only partly conscious, to express 'our feelings of being left and progressive, but at the same time anti-Stalinist'. The notion of a metaphoric reference to the Russian Revolution, to a Kerensky-type Madero, and to Fernando as a 'Commie revolutionary', emerged more strongly in the final shooting script of May 1951.[37]

Before then Zanuck had expressed himself delighted with the screenplay of April 1950 and to the extent that he had criticisms at this stage they reflected less a fear of political controversy than the possibility that 'we are trying to make an art or "mood" picture', a tendency that he associated with John Ford on a bad day.[38] The developing political sub-text of the project may also have owed something to a May 1950 visit to Cuernavaca made by both director and novelist to talk to Steinbeck's friend, the Mexican cinematographer Gabriel Figueroa. Figueroa, who was also president of the Syndicate of Film Technicians and Workers, had photographed Ford's *The Fugitive* (1947) and the Mexican made *The Pearl* (1948), for which Steinbeck had written the initial script. There is evidence that at the time Kazan wanted Figueroa to work on his film, although at their meeting the cinematographer expressed dislike of the script and warned that, as it stood, permission to film in Mexican locations was unlikely. The filmmakers still had hopes of working in Mexico, but developed contingency plans to film in Texas. After the film was made Steinbeck and Kazan felt that they had detected Communist Party machinations as explaining Figueroa's consultations on the script during their visit. Steinbeck felt that the 'party line was everywhere' on their trip, while Kazan felt that left-wingers in Mexico 'thought we were not making our hero an undeviating enough character'. In August 1950, with Kazan just about to begin the filming of *Streetcar*, all seemed to be in a state of readiness, although Zanuck had made no commitment to a starting date for the film.[39]

The end of 1950 and the beginning of 1951 saw increased political pressures on Hollywood and Kazan was concerned about the prospects both for his Mexican film and another film project based on *The Hook*, a screenplay by Arthur Miller. In December, following Congressional elections dominated by claims of Communist conspiracies in the State Department and elsewhere, Zanuck, in a memorandum to Kazan and Steinbeck, seemed suddenly much more concerned about the political reception of the Mexican film. The studio head, who was always concerned to leaven art or message with strong elements of entertainment, felt that the treatment of Zapata's life in the screenplay suggested that they had 'inadvertently told a story of pure frustration', and that audiences (and professional anti-Communists) might associate Zapata's struggle with communism: 'I hope people don't get the impression that we are advocating revolt or civil war as the only means to peace.' He felt that certain speeches 'might be interpreted by the Communists to claim that we are subtly working for them' and was concerned that 'people don't get the impression that we are advocating revolt or civil war as the only means to peace'. He even asked whether this was the right time to film the story of a 'Mexican revolutionary hero'.[40] In the New Year, Fox and Warners both passed on Kazan and Miller's proposed waterfront story, and while Harry Cohn at Columbia Pictures committed to the project, political discussions about the script finally led Miller to withdraw in February 1951. (Discussion of this project, its abandonment and its relationship to Kazan's later waterfront film with Budd Schulberg is found in Chapter 4.)

At a conference with Zanuck early in 1951 Kazan became aware that the studio head and producer was coming under some pressure to cancel the Zapata project. The direct effect was a strengthening of the character of Bicho as a 'professional Commie', the term used by Kazan in notes on the February script. Zanuck, resisting advice within his studio, gave the project the go-ahead, but wanted to balance the sympathy for a revolutionary leader with a more explicitly anti-Stalinist motif. Yet this theme was never central to the script as a whole; as has been pointed out: 'opposition to communism, while present in every stage, was never more than a secondary or tertiary sub-theme'. To Richard Slotkin it was 'important to both Kazan and Steinbeck to separate their rejection of communism from repudiation of the commitment to social justice, which they had once associated with the left'.[41]

Filming took place on the Texas border from May to July 1951 and thereafter Zanuck exercised his normal editing prerogatives during a fraught political period. American troops were dying in Korea, while prominent spying cases had encouraged a national panic over domestic as well as international communism. In March 1951 the House Committee on Un-American Activities (HUAC) had resumed its hearings on communism in the film industry, while the FBI developed plans to arrest some 12,000 Communists in the event of a war with the Soviet Union. In this atmosphere Kazan was conscious that his political associations – his 18 month Communist Party membership in the mid-thirties – made him vulnerable, while Zanuck, suggesting additional lines about a strong man making a weak people (spoken by Zapata near to his death), felt that they were 'a direct punch on the nose to Stalin and his Communists in the Kremlin', not to mention the Fascist dictators.[42]

Letters exchanged between Kazan and Alex North give some sense of the progress of the project. Reading the shooting script North felt that Darryl Zanuck was 'the "strong man" in this version'. He also commented that it seemed to him to be a 'post Korean War version with all the not too subtle innuendoes', and noted that the repeating of the 'circling the name' business, first by Diaz and then Zapata, reminded him of the end of All About Eve (1950). The use of related conceits in the two films – Zapata's realisation that he is aping the earlier behaviour of President Diaz, and (in the Mankiewicz film) the Anne Baxter character's realisation that a new young fan is mirroring her own social climbing – suggest an inevitable cycle that precludes real change. Despite his reservations about the script and the loss of 'those scenes that seemed to give Z. more dimension', North expressed his confidence that Kazan would do a 'truthful and artful (not arty) job'. North also reminded Kazan of the substantial national resentment in Mexico against America and asked him not to interpret this as Communist antagonism. Wishing that Kazan was in town for the previews, North warned his friend that he had a hunch that Zanuck was 'losing a tiny bit of confidence'. Kazan, on first seeing the picture, felt that North's score was 'first class', although he added that he felt that 'it was all played too g.d. low by the mixer', and that it was 'placed behind the picture as if it were musak'. Coming as it was, not too long after the complicity of Warners in the additional cuts in *A Streetcar Named Desire*, Kazan told North that he was 'getting a little annoyed with big studio processing' and hoped that his new New York-based company might be the way forward. Yet the composer, whose personal and working relationship with Kazan would be ended by the director's testimony to HUAC, still felt that the film had 'guts and realism rarely found out here' and that 'I may still have differences with the historical approach but not with the treatment'.[43]

Preoccupied as he was with the New York censorship struggle over *A Streetcar Named Desire*, in September and October 1951 Kazan seemed frustrated with some of Zanuck's 'experiments' with the editing of *Viva Zapata!* Making a number of cuts in Kazan's absence, Zanuck screened the film for head of production Ray Klune, who had argued against going ahead with the film earlier in the year. In a telegram Kazan pleaded with Zanuck to leave in two cut sequences, in particular more of a speech by the Old General in the Presidential palace, just before Zapata leaves Mexico City to go home. This was probably a reference to the character's suggestion to Fernando and others in power that 'somewhere, sometime, we must start building for peace' and that 'unless the purpose is peace, the road is endless, the journey empty'. Zanuck had been worried that the use of the word 'peace' might be suggestive of 'Red' propaganda in the political climate of the time and he got his way: this was the word, he told Kazan, that 'the Soviets had adopted as their own'. Yet by January 1952 Kazan was writing to Zanuck, asking him to refer anyone who doubted the 'politics of our picture' to the character of Fernando, the figure who recruits and follows Zapata but finally betrays him (and Madero), shifting his allegiance to those with more power. In the film Fernando declares himself to be 'a friend to no-one and to nothing except logic', a reference to the supposedly scientific nature of the beliefs of Russian revolutionaries, although he is mainly presented as an opportunist, determined to end up on the right side. While Fernando's part and role is, as discussed previously, a subsidiary theme in the film, to the studio and to Kazan at the time – with the director facing his HUAC appearances – this element was given great prominence. Although Kazan saw attacks from the extreme right, from those 'who say the picture is class angled', he argued at this time that the film was 'not only pro-democratic, but it is specifically, strongly and uncontrovertibly anti-Communist'.[44]

In the early fifties the studios came under increasing pressure from various
anti-Communist groups. Zanuck replied robustly to a charge from the Catholic
War Veterans organisation that three actors in *Viva Zapata!* had affiliations with
subversive or 'Communistic' organisations. *Counterattack*, circulated to studios
and others by an organisation called American Business Consultants, also
referred in a February 1952 issue to the apparent left-wing associations of
Zanuck, Kazan and others involved in *Viva Zapata!* The film was completed but
unreleased by the time that Kazan first appeared before the House Un-
American Activities Committee, in January 1952. As is discussed in the next
chapter, he answered questions on his own Communist Party membership, but
refused to give the names of others. The film was released in February and in
a letter in the *Saturday Review of Literature* in early April, Kazan discussed how
the 'political tensions of the present time bore down on us – John Steinbeck,
and Darryl Zanuck and me – as we thought about and shaped a historical
picture'. He pointed out the significance of the 'Communist mentality' of the
Fernando character, and referred to Zapata as 'a man of individual conscience',
who led his people 'out of bondage and did not betray them'. A week later Kazan
appeared again before HUAC, as is discussed elsewhere, and identified eight
former members of the Group Theatre as previous members of the Communist
Party. He also supplied the Committee with a self-serving account of his career
and productions, a list that ended with a reference to *Viva Zapata!* as an 'anti-
Communist picture'.[45]

Yet as is suggested by a number of commentators, including Slotkin and
Jonathan Schoenwald, such perspectives misrepresented the film. The enlarge-
ment of the role of Fernando reflected the political pressures of the time, but
the film as a whole, as Dan Georgakas argued in a later debate with Peter
Biskind, was and is much more than a phenomenon of the Cold War.[46] The
episodes of the first hour of the film sympathetically present the growth of justified agrarian revolt and Zapata's emergence as a popular leader. As elsewhere
in Kazan films there is tension between the protagonist's private life – in this
case Zapata's desire to court Josefa (Jean Peters) – and the broader politics, but
his instinctive response to injustice makes him a natural rebel and a leader. It
is Zapata who emerges from the group at the beginning, in Diaz's state room,
to engage directly with the President. It is Zapata the man of action who rides
to the rescue as country people try to establish their land rights and who acts
on impulse when he sees injustice, whether it is a hungry child being beaten
for eating horse feed or the farmer Innocente being pulled along by the local
police to his execution. In a long, wordless sequence Kazan shows a partial
resolution of the dialectic between Zapata as private and public person, as his
brother uses the sound of stones, knocked together, to signal to the people

Kazan and Brando: the capture and release of Zapata, in *Viva Zapata!* (1952). Courtesy of BFI.

that Zapata needs their help. It is now he who is being pulled along with hands tied behind his back and with a rope around his neck. Alex North's music takes over from the sound of the stones as the column proceeds, building momentum as a stream of local people descend from the hills in support of their leader, until the officers recognise the new power of the people and acquiesce in Zapata's release. Zapata's look suggests that he is both grateful at regaining his freedom (directly from the people) but also aware that this is the beginning of the end of his private life. The scene reaches its climax with Zapata reunited with his white horse (from Diego Rivera's 1929 fresco) and with his brother Eufemio (Anthony Quinn). Urged by Fernando to cut the telegraph wires, Eufemio hesitates a moment as a captain warns that this act would mean 'rebellion', before Zapata gives the order. The cutting of the wires is one of the more stirring if unlikely – in 1952 – revolutionary moments in American cinema. The whole scene, played virtually without dialogue, reflects the influence of a moment in Eisenstein's *Alexander Nevsky* (1938), in which peasants seem to emerge from land and river, from the earth itself, to stand behind Alexander as the new defender of the nation. Less precisely, there is also a nod towards the more expressionistic sequence in *Battleship Potemkin* (1925), in which unending streams of people emerge to pay homage to the martyr Vaculinchuk in Odessa.

Kazan later argued that he did not think that Steinbeck, Buck or himself had completely 'cracked' the script. Yet, drawing on his work on *Panic in the Streets*, Kazan as filmmaker transcends rather than merely serves his script, whatever his input into the latter. The episodic structure, moving from one sequence to the next, bypassing intervening events, departs from the seamless progression of the classical Hollywood model, although at times it obscures elements of the story's development. In notes on his copy of the screenplay Kazan urged himself not to be too sequential and to start the beginning of each sequence with a dramatic leap to a close shot, only then following this with an establishing shot.[47] This notion of jumping from 'crag to crag' of the story owes something, at least in intention, to Rossellini's work and in particular *Paisà*. No attempt is made to age the characters to represent the ten-year span to which the film's events correspond. In fact, Kazan largely bypasses psychological realism and presents instead a more impressionistic study of an extraordinary central figure and his relationship with the people. Kazan encouraged the actor to hide his inner emotions and feelings. On the cover of the final shooting script Kazan wrote: 'Keep people doing and saying things that unmask Brando.' In the previous script version Kazan noted that Zapata was an Indian, 'half animal, half mystic', a proud and fierce man who loved the people of Morelos. He is both chieftain and peasant, although the film's historically inaccurate depiction of him as illiterate undermines the former role.[48] Kazan plays here on Brando's masking of his vulnerabilities, and it is only with the death of his brother that the actor is given time and space to improvise, as the grief stricken leader entwines himself with his dead brother's body.

Other scenes sketch externally Zapata's emerging public role. Early on Fernando Aguirre is introduced as a minute figure in a huge canyon, searching (on behalf of Francisco Madero) for this already mythical 'leader' of the south. The sequence identifies Zapata with the land, and with his tight group of companions, as they squat close to the barren earth and out of the wind. Working for the third time with cinematographer Joe MacDonald, Kazan also used deep focus photography, flooding interiors with light and stopping down the lens to link and set up oppositions between foreground and exterior, Zapata's personal life and his public vocation. MacDonald had accompanied Kazan on trips to the American side of the Rio Grande, scouting for interior and exterior locations, including those around the plaza of the former Mexican village of Roma, Texas.[49] In the house of his would-be father-in-law Zapata engages in a mannered process of courting, exchanging arch proverbs with Josefa (Jean Peters), while we see Zapata's band of followers in a bar across the street, in perfect focus. Similarly from the bar, from where Eufemio provides a bemused and cynical commentary on his brother's emotional obsession, we see inside the Espejo home. Zapata, wearing a double sash of bullets, is linked even in this private moment to his broader destiny. As he proposes, Pablo rushes across to the open window to tell him the news of the flight of Diaz from the capital and the country.

Kazan drew on historical photographs dating from the Mexican Revolution itself, notably the re-enacted group picture taken in the Presidential palace, showing the delegations of a reluctant Zapata and an enthusiastic Pancho Villa, celebrating their apparent victory. Also in the palace is the scene in which Zapata demonstrates to the hapless Madero, by the use of the new leader's watch and his ever present rifle, how power follows military advantage. Zapata's charade, handing Madero his rifle and only then returning the President's timepiece, seems in retrospect to illustrate the notion of another agrarian leader, Mao Tse-tung, that power grows out of the barrel of a gun.[50] Frank Silvera, looking much like the real General Huerta, contributes a short, effective cameo as the military leader who has Madero shot, in a nightmarish night-time sequence.

There is much in the film that raises real political dilemmas about authority, military discipline and guerrilla warfare. Women play a key role in the guerrilla attack on a military garrison, in a scene that prefigures those in that sixties classic of political cinema, Gillo Pontecorvo's *Battle of Algiers* (1966). A woman leads a small column of mourners, while others lay gunpowder trails, place baskets of explosive (disguised as eggs) by the garrison walls and then set off the explosion that allows Zapata's men to take the fort. Madero (Harold Gordon, one of a number of New York actors) is represented as an honest man, although he is weak politically, and misjudges Zapata by trying to placate him with the gift of a ranch. Yet Steinbeck also gives him arguments – 'Before you can do anything by law you must first *have* law' – that highlight the limits of populist movements, however honestly led. In presenting a conflict between dictatorship, quasi-socialist provincial populism, and a weak liberalism, Kazan and Steinbeck also use the non-historical character of Fernando to suggest a metaphor between Mexico and the highly resonant – especially in 1952 – revolution that created the Soviet Union. But visually, as Jeremy Butler has argued, the film counters this notion with a stirring portrait of Zapata and the people he represents.[51] To Kazan the country people at the beginning have the lethargy of black Americans in the South at the time, waiting for the moment that leadership would bring them to active life. This interesting observation, at the beginning of the decade that would see the birth of the civil rights movement

and of Martin Luther King's leadership, is one that helps to give some substance
to the notion, referred to in the film, that the slow growth of popular involvement is as telling an indicator of social and political change as the role of
any leader.[52]

The later scenes cover impressionistically the complicated sequence of
events after the fall of Huerta, during which Mexico's revolutionary leaders
failed to make common cause. Zapata, lolling in the President's chair but making it clear that he is not President, circles the name of a petitioner with his
pen, in ways that remind him of Diaz's circling of Zapata's name in the opening scene. This scene is structurally important, but Zapata's leaving of the capital seems to suggest a renunciation of power that he and his people had
struggled so much to achieve. Indeed this is the point of the parable of the rifle,
played out earlier in the Presidential chamber by Zapata with Madero. Nor is
the return of the lands to the country people in Moreleos, something that
is referred to, shown visually. Instead, following Zapata's own, uncharacteristic
awareness of his own potential for corruption, a series of scenes indicate the
moral dilemmas of military leadership in a long guerrilla campaign. Zapata
orders the execution of a Zapatista, executes Pablo for consorting with the
enemy, and then confronts his brother, who has exploited the power he has
gained through the struggle. Here the meaning of the film at this stage relies
more on rhetoric, with longish speeches by Pablo ('Can a good thing come from
a bad act?') and Zapata ('a strong people is the only lasting strength'). These
scenes nonetheless suggest something of the chaos and betrayal of the time, as
suggested in a contemporary novel such as Mariano Azuela's *The Underdogs*.[53]
Zapata is on the march again, risking his life to capture a cache of arms that
will aid the cause, but the sense of real achievements for the people is displaced
on to a sense of the leader's martyrdom and his use to subsequent generations
as an ideal or myth.

With the latter scenes painting a darker, more ambiguous view of the nature
of sustained political struggle, Kazan ends with a powerfully cinematic scene.
Zapata is persuaded to visit a general who has apparently deserted from the
enemy, and who is offering armaments and ammunition. Josefa is finally given
a scene of some substance – the wedding night scene is the film's weakest – as
she pleads in vain for her husband to stay home. Her life has become precisely
what her father predicted and she alone among the characters seems aged by
the hardships of military struggle; dressed in black, she looks as if she is in
mourning already. The next day, Zapata is inspecting the ammunition and a
General indicates a walled courtyard containing his white horse, which he previously gave to a young boy as a reward. Zapata walks over and has a few
moments with the horse, which is wary. We see General Guajardo backing off

and giving a signal, following which the horse rears and – from above – rifle-men shoot down at Zapata from all sides. The horse escapes and Fernando – almost hysterical – rushes towards the camera, shouting for someone to shoot it. Meanwhile the volley continues, and we look up at the parapets where the men fire from four sides. Zapata's crouched body is ripped by bullets, and the body twitches and is then still. The fusillade is far more than that necessary to kill a man, and there are echoes of this myth in popular sixties' counter-cultural cinema, including *Bonnie and Clyde* (1967) and *Butch Cassidy and the Sundance Kid* (1969).[54]

Thereafter a long shot shows horsemen dump Zapata's body like a sack of potatoes on the stone slab by the well, in the town plaza. The women advance, creating stark shadows in the sun, and attend to him. The water seems to flow directly from Zapata's body. Women come to nurse and tend to the body, while men (including Lazaro) say that he is not dead, that if 'we ever need him again he'll be back'. They look up and we cut to an end title shot of the white horse in the mountains, symbolising the continuing spirit of rebellion. Lazaro, a foot soldier since the beginning, dismisses notions that Zapata is not a man, but says he will come if they need him again. The white horse in the mountains is too trite and familiar (and cursory) an image to carry much independent weight, although this notion in the concluding scenes (including Fernando's attempt to capture the horse) does link with the filmmakers' intentions. As Kazan wrote prominently on the title page of his February 1951 script, 'A legend is the cre-ation of the need of the people who create it.'[55]

The *Hollywood Reporter* felt that the film had 'many of the qualities of the documentary without being oppressive'. Hollis Alpert in the *Saturday Review* saw it as a 'misfire', too slow, at times obscure, and with the director uncom-fortable in the 'Western' locale and form. Alpert's review did however provoke a series of interesting responses in the magazine, not least from Kazan. Laura Z. Hobson defended the film and the relevance of Steinbeck's key lines, while Kazan reiterated his and Steinbeck's belief that Zapata's refusal to make him-self president or caudillo, after the meeting with Villa, was historically grounded and part of their unwillingness to make Zapata a 'poster figure' for the Communists. Visually Kazan also defended what he saw as a lack of conven-tional romance: 'no Madonnas, no filter clouds, no horizon silhouettes!' Bosley Crowther was enthusiastic, drawing attention to the film's vivid presentation of 'social injustice and unbalance in a primitive and misgoverned land'. Yet at the time, and in particular in the light of Kazan's testimony, many saw the film as conservative in its implications for the possibility of successful popular revolt. To John Howard Lawson: 'If power is an absolute source of corruption, if it must be renounced by every honest leader, the people are doomed to eternal submission.' To the reviewer for the *Daily Worker* the film was an attack on revolution and showed how every 'leader fails the peasant masses'.[56]

Yet John Womack Jr., author of a definitive biography of Zapata, found the film to have 'distorted certain events and characters, some grossly', but he also concluded that 'it quickly and vividly develops a portrayal of Zapata, the villagers, and the nature of their relations and movement that I find still subtle, powerful and true'. Womack also remembers it in terms of a sense of 'Zapata's integrity, his suspicion of all outsiders, his absolute sense of responsibility to his local people'. He also reports that the Mexican novelist and man of letters Carlos Fuentes spoke highly of the film. The element of anti-communism, exaggerated at the time of the film's release by Kazan and Zanuck for their own purposes, was nonetheless rooted in the experiences of director and writer. Yet, as Georgakas argued a quarter of a century later, at a time more sympathetic to indigenous social movements, the film actually opposes notions of the inevitable corruption of leaders and presents Zapata as 'a man from the masses who serves their cause with unswerving dedication in spite of every temptation and hardship'.[57] In a longer perspective the Fernando character, a product in part of contemporary political pressures, seems a reasonable if unfocussed comment on the exploitation of popular revolutions by opportunistic leaders. In an era when Joseph McCarthy and others were using the Communist scare to promote their own agenda of conservative populism, the film provides visual imagery that strikingly reflects a more progressive, grass roots populist vision. The film contains thematic inconsistencies and an ambitious episodic structure which also fails to impose an overall aesthetic unity. Yet as director Kazan turns from the closed theatrical space and intense psychological drama of *A Streetcar Named Desire* to produce some of his most visually eloquent cinema.

3

Elia Kazan and the House Committee on Un-American Activities

The House Committee on Un-American Activities (HUAC) was established in 1938 and became a Standing Committee of the House of Representatives in 1945. As was discussed in Chapter 1, it was in October 1947 that the Committee held formal hearings in Washington on the film industry, providing a forum for various industry conservatives and some studio heads to testify as to what they saw as Communist influence on the industry. The refusal of the so-called 'Hollywood Ten' to answer questions on their Communist affiliations at these hearings led to their being cited for contempt of Congress by the House of Representatives. On the same day representatives of the major studios signed the Waldorf Declaration, pledging that they would not in future employ Communists. This essentially instituted a blacklist, although its full implementation would have to wait nearly three years until 1950 for the Supreme Court to decline to review an appeal on behalf of the Ten.[1]

Senator Joseph McCarthy's February 1950 speech in Wheeling, West Virginia – in which he began his campaign against Communists in the State Department – came in the immediate wake of the conviction of Alger Hiss, the former State Department official who had been accused by HUAC of passing secrets to a Communist spy ring and was now beginning a five-year sentence for perjury. To the cultural historian Richard Pells the conviction of Hiss 'lent credence to the theory that all communists should be regarded as potential foreign agents'. Under the Internal Security Act, which became law in September 1950, Communist and Communist front organisations were required to register with the government, while the next year the Supreme Court upheld the convictions of the Communist Party leadership, further legitimating the FBI's anti-Communist crusade.[2] By the time that HUAC reopened its hearings on Hollywood, in March 1951, the country was in the grip of a national panic over what was seen as the international and domestic threat of Communism.

For the 1951–2 Congress a new Chairman of the House Committee, the Georgia Democrat John S. Wood, was appointed to succeed J. Parnell Thomas, who was serving a prison term for corruption. The Committee also had a new director of research, one Raphael I. Nixon, an ex-FBI man not to be confused with future President Richard Nixon, whose membership of the Committee had ended following his election to the Senate in November 1950. Rather than the failed strategy of investigating supposed communist propaganda in film, Raphael Nixon felt that the Party's 'prestige, position and money' in Hollywood was a better angle of enquiry.[3] Given the fate of those who had invoked the First Amendment in 1947, those unwilling to cooperate with the Committee by naming names were now advised to invoke the Fifth Amendment against self-incrimination. The Supreme Court, in its decision in *Rogers v. U.S.* in 1950, had decided that witnesses who admitted present or past Party membership could not subsequently refuse to answer questions about the membership of others. In addition a number of anti-Communist organisations and groups stoked the flames, supplying Committee and studios alike with information about the left wing associations of Hollywood personnel. Despite the new hearings, in December 1951 the American Legion published an article by the fellow traveller turned anti-Communist J.B. Matthews, asking 'Did the Movies Really Clean House?' The overwhelming majority of those summoned to appear before the House Committee between 1951 and 1953 either admitted that they had been party members and revealed the names of such members they had known, or pleaded the Fifth Amendment, with the latter course leading to blacklisting by the major studios. Over 300 film artists were so blacklisted and were denied employment in the industry, while others were greylisted and found it difficult to find regular work.[4]

Kazan had a brush with the new climate of concern and hysteria about communism in early 1951, when he and Arthur Miller pitched their proposed project on the New York waterfront to Columbia Pictures. Kazan had already discussed it with Zanuck and Skouras at Fox, describing it as 'out of the general run of motion pictures', but also as a project that he was very enthusiastic about and determined to make into 'a very exciting picture'. Skouras disliked it and Kazan doubted if Zanuck would be interested either, or even whether he should be. Warner Bros. also passed on the project, but Harry Cohn at Columbia was more receptive, agreeing to make the film in an attempt to attract Kazan to the studio. Cohn then referred the script to Roy Brewer, the anti-Communist head of the International Alliance of Theatrical Stage Employees (IATSE), and to the FBI, and the result was forceful advice that the hoodlums in the script be associated with Communism. Kazan and Miller's accounts differ slightly, although it is clear that Miller withdrew from the project as a result of the changes being demanded. Kazan seemed to feel that he could finesse the script problems, as he was to some extent doing with Steinbeck and Zanuck on *Viva Zapata!*, and he was annoyed at Miller's withdrawal at a time when budgets for the picture had already been prepared. To Miller, there was no possibility of proceeding with the project as planned.[5]

By 1952 Kazan's name had become attractive to a Committee that was as interested in publicity as in the Communist Party. Kazan had told friends that, if called before the Committee, he would make clear his own membership of the Party but refuse to name names. As expected he received a subpoena from the House Committee, calling him to appear before an 'executive session' in Washington DC on 14 January 1952. Kazan had an initial, pre-lunch meeting with the Committee's director of research, who assured him that the special status of the session meant that what he said would remain confidential. Nixon asked him to reconsider his decision to withhold names, seeking to influence him by giving him transcripts, for perusal over lunch, of the cooperative testimonies (dating from April and May 1951) of director Edward Dmytryk and writers Budd Schulberg and Richard Collins.[6] Schulberg, who Kazan did not yet know, had stressed the evils of Stalinism in the Soviet Union, together with the way American Communist officials had treated him as a novelist during his period in the Party in the late thirties. He later claimed to have been a 'premature anti-Stalinist' by testifying as he did. Dmytryk, one of the Hollywood Ten, had changed his position after serving a one year prison sentence, while Collins spoke of being afraid that 'in the event of a war with the Soviet Union I would be considered a friend of the Soviet Union'.[7]

The House Committee met at 2pm in room 226 of the Old House Building to hear Kazan's testimony. Francis E. Walter (Democrat, Pennsylvania), a future Committee Chairman, presided, and also present were Clyde Doyle (Democrat – California), James B. Frazier Jr. (Democrat – Tennessee) and Bernard W. Kearney (Republican – New York). Kazan also remembers Harold Velde (Republican – Illinois) as present for a time, as congressmen entered and exited the committee room.[8] Raphael Nixon asked the bulk of the questions during the session. As the transcript makes clear, Kazan made no bones about his own membership of the Communist Party, in a unit (he used the word cell) associated with the Group Theatre. Kazan had been a member of that theatre from 1932 (a year after its formation) till its demise in 1940 and he testified that he had been a member of the Party from approximately July 1934 to January 1936. At the time Kazan was highly politicised and took his membership seriously, meeting the officials on 12th Street, the Party's headquarters, and making speeches on current issues. In his testimony he cited *The Coming Struggle for Power*, a book by the British Marxist John Strachey that was first published in

1933, as an influence on his radicalisation. In a 1935 letter to Cheryl Crawford and Lee Strasberg – Kazan was seeking permission to take a two-week break – the feverish 'activity' that he reported, combining politics and theatre, included work on the play *Dimitroff*, which he had written and produced (for the New Theatre League) with fellow Group member Art Smith and which had been published in *New Masses* in 1934. The play had dramatised the release by mass pressure of a working-class hero, falsely accused of setting the Reichstag on fire in 1933.[9]

In his January 1952 testimony Kazan discussed the Group Theatre and the independent, non-Communist credentials of the three directors: Crawford and Strasberg, and the Group's key leader throughout its existence, Harold Clurman. He referred to the Communist Party's unit in the Group in the mid-thirties as containing nine members apart from himself, in the overall company of around 30. Kazan remembered being instructed, as an elected representative of the Group actors, to urge the 'democratisation' of the way the Group made decisions. The Communist Party official who coached him on the Party's desire for such changes was V.J. Jerome, the national Party official responsible for dealing with artists and with cultural affairs. Kazan described how he alone voted against Jerome's 'instructions' in the actors committee and how he was then called to account at a meeting at which he was castigated by an outsider, an organiser for the Auto Workers Union. This humiliating meeting with the 'Man from Detroit', also discussed in a diary entry cited in his autobiography, precipitated his immediate resignation from the Party. Wendy Smith, in her authoritative account of the Group Theatre, judges Kazan's account to be 'broadly true', although she feels that Kazan may have taken longer than he claims to leave the Party, and she also notes that the Party exploited as much as instituted divisions within the Group at this time. Kazan was to give much importance to this case later, when he saw it as part of the Communist Party's general interference with the arts in America. It was in 1935 that the Party's Popular Front policy was instituted, thus blurring for a time (until the Nazi-Soviet Pact) the distinction between Communists and liberals in support of broad anti-fascist goals.[10] The non-aggression pact, and the American Communist Party's sudden belief, following the shift in Soviet policy, in the moral equivalence of both sides in what was now called an 'imperialist war', was a shock to liberals and many radicals alike. Kazan had remained supportive of the Soviet Union since he left the Party, but there is evidence that the Pact of August 1939 had an impact on his political perspective. At the time Kazan and his playwright friend Robert Ardrey baited Kermit Bloomgarden (the Group's business manager) on his stance of 'standing pat' with the new official Communist Party line.[11]

Kazan explicitly disavowed the use of any constitutional immunity, including that of the Fifth Amendment, in his first encounter with HUAC in 1952. When asked to name members of the Group Theatre Communist unit he rested his unwillingness to identify them on grounds of 'personal conscience'. When asked to explain this notion by Kearney, he referred to fears that anyone he mentioned might not be able to work in 'radio, movies, and television'. He added that if it 'weren't for that employment thing, I might feel differently about it'. Towards the end of the interview Kazan became even more specific: 'God knows, I think you should investigate, and what you are doing is right. But I feel, myself, if this were known, if this were an open meeting, I would be out of a job, so to speak.' Kazan here clearly thinks that the fact that his meeting is an executive session, i.e. a secret session, gave him at least the possibility of avoiding the alternative of giving names or taking the Fifth Amendment. Kazan may also have had in mind planned discussions with Jack Warner in which the studio head, pleased with the success of *A Streetcar Named Desire*, was keen to sign up the director and Tennessee Williams to a new project.[12]

Apart from asking about the members of the Group Theatre's Communist Party unit, the Committee ran a series of other names past Kazan. The Committee's pursuit of celebrity was indicated by its intense and continuing interest in John Garfield, a sometime member of the Group Theatre who had been a Hollywood star since the impact of his performance in *Four Daughters*, for Warner Bros., in 1938. Never a member of the Party, Garfield had involved himself in numerous left wing causes and his answers failed to satisfy the Committee on his appearance of 23 April 1951. Following that appearance his film work had dried up, and the actor was contemplating a press 'confession' (of his associations with Communist fronts) when he died of a heart attack in May 1952.[13] Kazan responded that he could not remember, but that Garfield was not a member at the time he was a member, up until 1936. He did not respond to a series of other names that were put to him, although he replied at greater length when prompted on Andrew Overgaard, a union official and Communist who attended Group Theatre sessions.

Kazan was particularly careful in responding to a question on the playwright and screenwriter John Howard Lawson. The director had worked as assistant stage director on a Theatre Guild production of Lawson's *The Pure in Heart* in 1931. In the nearest he came to identifying or confirming anyone's membership at the January hearing, apart from the officials Jerome and Overgaard, he testified that he did not know Lawson as a Communist, but suspected it in 1937. He referred to a new play 'which I thought was straight Party line'. Lawson had joined the Communist Party in 1936 and had gone on to become, as would have been well known to Committee members and Kazan alike, the key leader of the Hollywood Communist Party from 1937 to his imprisonment, as one of the Hollywood Ten, in 1950.[14] The play that Kazan refers to, and which was rejected by the Group Theatre, was *Marching Song* (first performed in 1937). Kazan would have known through his wife of Lawson's (and the Party's) role in the demise of the magazine *New Theatre and Film* in 1937. This is one of the examples of Communist Party interference in the arts that Kazan reveals in his autobiography as being a factor in his final decision to name names in his second appearance before HUAC. The other cases, involving Lawson and/or V.J. Jerome, included Budd Schulberg's problems with the Party over his novel *What Makes Sammy Run*, in the late thirties, and the pressure exerted on Albert Maltz, Kazan's friend in the early thirties, to renounce his *New Masses* article in 1946.[15]

Kazan was excused after just 45 minutes, having neither 'named names' nor taken the Fifth Amendment. There was no question of Kazan being cited for contempt at the end of the hearing, despite his refusal to give names. He remembers that Nixon told him after the meeting that some Committee members wanted him to be called again, but in the immediate aftermath of the meeting, with no proceedings or minutes made public, there seemed a possibility that the matter might go no further.[16] But this was always unlikely, in particular given the role played by the press and anti-Communist pressure groups in the operation of the blacklist. A number of such organisations exploited and expanded the blacklist in the early fifties for a mixture of commercial and ideological motives. For example, American Business Consultants, formed in 1947 by ex-FBI men, marketed books and newsletters, in particular *Red Channels* (1950) and *Counterattack*, to employers and advertisers interested in the leftist connections of those in the entertainment industry. An edition of *Counterattack* of 12 February 1952 focussed on the left-wing associations of Kazan and others involved with *Viva Zapata!*[17] (The anti-communist motif in that film, and Kazan's public reference to it in April 1952, a week before his second Congressional testimony, is discussed in Chapter 2.)

As it was, the fact of Kazan's appearance, and crucially his unwillingness to give names, was leaked to the Hollywood press. In the *Hollywood Reporter* trade paper of 19 March 1952 there was a one-sentence report on Kazan's Committee appearance in Mike Connolly's daily 'Rambling Reporter' gossip column. Connolly was the most venomously anti-Communist of the Hollywood columnists, regularly using terms such as 'vermin', 'rat' and 'scummie' in his writing; Hollywood Ten member Dalton Trumbo called him 'HUAC's staunchest friend'. The complete reference to Kazan in Connolly's column was as follows: 'Elia Kazan, subpoenaed for the Un-American Activities session, confirmed Commie membership but refused to supply any new evidence on his old pals from the Group Theatre days, among them, John Garfield.'[18] As studio head of Twentieth Century-Fox, Darryl F. Zanuck immediately protested to the paper's founder and publisher William R. Wilkerson. Wilkerson had been an especially enthusiastic supporter of the 1947 Waldorf Declaration, seeing it as an opportunity for the industry to 'clean house'. He had been particularly hostile to what he saw as a new generation of serious minded writers, directors and others whose commitment to realism threatened the Hollywood norm of 'pure entertainment'. Wilkerson told Zanuck that he had received the testimony from Congressman Harold H. Velde of Illinois. The gossip column item was all the more powerful, coming as it did the day before the Academy Award ceremony, held on 20 March, at which *A Streetcar Named Desire* was a leading contender for the Best Picture and Best Director awards. All this at a time when the studios still feared that films with which Communists or unrepentant ex-Communists were associated might be picketed.[19]

In his autobiography Kazan noted the impact of the leaked report on the heads of Twentieth Century-Fox. Kazan was still contracted (non-exclusively) to Fox, where Darryl F. Zanuck had generally opposed the blacklist and, within the limits of his autonomy within the corporation, worked to resist its effects. In cases where he had fired writers who had fallen foul of the Committee it was generally under direct instruction from the East Coast office, and in particular from the fiercely anti-communist President of the studio, Spyros Skouras. Skouras had been born in Greece in 1893, had come to America at the age of 17 and had worked himself up through the exhibition side of the business, becoming President of Twentieth Century-Fox in 1942. Arthur Miller once described Skouras as Kazan's 'friend, boss and godfather', and while Kazan was hostile to most of the industry norms and perspectives that Skouras represented, there was a link between the two men based on their common Greek heritage. They had visited Greece together in November 1951 and had talked to the Queen about the possibility of the director making a film there with John Steinbeck on a Greek theme.[20]

Kazan recounts that Zanuck advised him to name names and asked him who he was protecting. With the leak, Kazan was aware that no middle way strategy was possible, and that he would be required to appear again before the Committee (Wilkerson had told Zanuck that this would be the case). With Kazan in Hollywood for the Academy Awards it seemed clear to him that he would not have a future in the industry unless he fully cooperated with the Committee. There are even suggestions that the leak might have affected the decisions of the Academy. Kazan's *A Streetcar Named Desire* (1951), up for 12 awards, the highest number of any of the nominees, lost out on the key awards and picked up only four, including those for Best Actress (Vivian Leigh),

Best Supporting Actor (Karl Malden) and Best Supporting Actress (Kim Hunter, soon to be blacklisted herself). The surprise winner was *An American in Paris*. Evidently surprised to beat the Kazan film, and George Stevens' *A Place in the Sun*, MGM ran an ad in the following week's *Variety* in which MGM lion is shown bashfully accepting the award, saying 'Honestly, I was just standing in the sun waiting for a streetcar'.[21]

In his 1988 autobiography Kazan agonises about his memories of that period. Kermit Bloomgarden remembered Kazan telling him that he had been to Washington and met with J. Edgar Hoover and Skouras, although it seems doubtful if this meeting, urged on Kazan by Skouras, actually took place. To his friend John Steinbeck, who supported his ultimate decision, 'this Congress thing tore him to pieces'. Kazan recounts his discussions with Arthur Miller, Lillian Hellman and others, but it is clear that the most important influence was his wife, Molly Day Thacher Kazan. From Yankee stock that contrasted with Elia Kazan's immigrant origins, she was a powerful professional influence on her husband for 30 years. He later saw her as 'my talisman of success and my measure of merit'. She had developed a strong anti-Communist critique in the early fifties, saw testifying as a patriotic duty, and later wrote a play (discussed more fully later in this chapter) which reads in part as a wife's questioning of her husband's naivete about domestic communism. Yet beyond all this, and the pressures that immigrants felt at the time to assert their American identity, a factor that he also recognised in later writings, Kazan was most concerned by the threat to his career in films. After years of silence on the issue Kazan wrote in his autobiography that 'I began to measure the weight and the worth of what I was giving up, my career in films, which I was surrendering for a cause I didn't believe in'. He added: 'What I'd done was correct, but was it right?'[22]

Before his second testimony Kazan also consulted with two intellectual figures in the contemporary debate on Communism and anti-Communism, Sidney Hook and Bertram D. Wolfe. Kazan later talked of meeting Hook and also of being influenced and inspired by the pamphlet edition of the philosopher and anti-Stalinist activist's renowned early fifties work, 'Heresy No, Conspiracy Yes', reading it twice during what Kazan called some 'very bewildering days'. Versions of Hook's piece date from 1951, and the American Committee for the Cultural Freedom (ACCF) published it as a pamphlet the next year. Kazan wrote to Hook that:

> The very fact that there are liberals and leftists who are actively anti-communist makes some sense of the chaos for me. (You may well ask: Where the hell have you been all this time? My answer wouldn't be satisfactory.)

Hook, an ex-Marxist philosophy professor at New York University and the first chairman of the ACCF following its creation in 1951, explained in the pamphlet (later a book) why he thought that liberals did not have to defend the civil liberties of Communists, making a distinction between heresies, subject to free debate, and conspiracies that thrived on secrecy. In a sentence that the director quoted in his letter, Hook argued that 'If the conspiratorial purposes of Communist party teachers is glossed over by ritualistic liberals as a heresy, then all heresy comes under fire'. Kazan argued that liberals like him were painfully waking up, and that he was discovering how 'hide-bound and bigoted and self-blindfolded are the great mass of New York's intellectual set'. Kazan also met with Wolfe, a founding member of the American Communist Party, at a time when he was a leading anti-Communist attached to the State Department-run Voice of America in New York. Kazan, working in Germany on *Man on a Tightrope* in September 1952, thanked Wolfe for his help in 'bad days', while much later Wolfe, in a letter to the director, referred to the 'period when you were under fire from the Communists and came to the Voice of America to take me to a Greek restaurant'.[23]

Faced with the prospect of being blacklisted in film, although not in the theatre, Kazan requested that the Committee reopen his executive hearing, and appeared before it again on 10 April 1952. Only one Committee member, Representative Francis E. Walter, was present, along with the Committee's counsel, Frank S. Tavenner and Raphael Nixon. Kazan simply presented a prepared statement, together with a sworn affidavit. In the first part of this he revised his earlier testimony, naming eight members of the Group Theatre. Those identified as members of the Communist Party unit within the Group in the mid-thirties were actors Tony Kraber, Lewis Leverett, J. Edward Bromberg, Phoebe Brand, Morris Carnovsky, Paula Miller (later Paula Strasberg) and Art Smith, as well as the playwright Clifford Odets. Odets, the rising star of the Group in the mid-thirties, with his productions of *Waiting for Lefty* and *Awake and Sing*, had agreed with Kazan that they would name each other, and he indeed named Kazan at his Committee appearance a month later, on 19–20 May. The affidavit proceeds to deal with various affiliations and associations raised by the Committee earlier, and then to provide a blandly annotated list of all of his theatrical and film productions. *Boomerang!*, for example, is referred to as 'the exact opposite of the Communist libels on America', *Gentleman's Agreement* as in the 'healthy American tradition' of showing Americans 'exploring a problem and tackling a solution', and *Viva Zapata!* as 'an anti-Communist picture'. He went so far in the affidavit as to assure the Committee that he had not voted for Henry Wallace for President at the 1948 election. The testimony was published the next day and lengthy summaries appeared in newspapers on

12 April 1952. The same day Kazan published a paid advertisement in the *New York Times*, written by his wife, urging others to name names. He argued that those in possession of the facts concerning 'a dangerous and alien conspiracy' had an obligation to let the facts be known 'to the public or to the appropriate Government agency'.[24]

In Molly Kazan's play *The Egghead*, which was directed by Hume Cronyn and ran for nine performances in New York in 1957, the author repeats some of the arguments in the 1952 *New York Times* ad, and develops others relating to the need to challenge Communism in a democracy. The play deals with a University professor and his wife who argue about an ex-student of his who has been invited to speak at a seminar. There are accusations that the intended speaker, Perry Hall, who is black, is a covert Communist industrial organiser, but the professor, suspecting police state tactics, refuses to answer the FBI's questions about him. The wife has a different view, and her argument, that 'There weren't any witches but there are you know-whats', implicitly challenges the metaphor of Arthur Miller's 1953 play *The Crucible*, while she also asks if her husband would equally protect a Nazi or member of the Ku Klux Klan. Miller had himself been cited for contempt of Congress following a 1956 HUAC passport hearing at which the Committee had produced an unsigned party card in his name as evidence. In the play Hall conveniently asserts his support and work for the Soviet system, and the remaining mechanics of the drama are designed to vindicate the wife's judgement and to present her husband as – in the words of an FBI investigator in the play – a 'soft-boiled liberal', dangerous to himself and the country. In the last line of the manuscript version of the play the husband addresses his wife: 'Sally, you're my salvation'. The play certainly indicates something of the strength of Molly Kazan's opinion on the issue during the fifties.[25]

When asked in 1980 if the HUAC episode had influenced *On the Waterfront*, Kazan replied that it had 'influenced my whole life'. Former friends cut themselves off. Jules Dassin later commented: 'I loved Kazan, I loved Odets, and this still hurts'. Arthur Miller projects his memories of his disrupted friendship with Kazan onto characters in his play *After the Fall*, which Kazan directed in 1964. An editorial in *The Nation* concluded that Kazan's statement indicated that a 'man must want to make moving pictures very much indeed to be so willing to degrade himself in public'. In contrast Arthur Schlesinger Jr., public intellectual of the new anti-Communist liberalism proclaimed in his 1949 book *The Vital Center*, commented in a newspaper column that he found Kazan's statement to be 'a reasonable and dignified document'. More recently, Thomas Pauly has argued – in my view convincingly – that the testimony:

was not the action of one driven by motives that were purely selfish or monetary, but rather that of a man who, after intense soul-searching, came to believe that a decisive stand was necessary and that reluctance to speak out on Communism increased its current threat.

William Fitelson, Kazan's lawyer during this period, later expressed the view that the director's testimony 'was a matter of conscience and is so regarded by your true friends'.[26]

Whatever the mix of reasons for it, Kazan's sudden decision, and in particular his *New York Times* notice, came as a huge shock to friends and acquaintances in Hollywood, New York and elsewhere. Many at the Actors Studio were outraged, while key working relationships were ended. Jules Dassin, who remembers that the two of them 'grew up together', has argued that 'twenty-four hours before Kazan went before the Committee he called all his friends – we were all there in a group – to say "They think they'll make me talk! Never, I won't do it."' The blacklisted musician Larry Adler remembered a tearful Kazan buying tickets for a recital on the day his testimony was reported, shouting at him 'Larry, you've just got to lick those bastards!' Most attention has been given to the break with Miller, but a friendship and working relationship even more irrevocably ended at this time was that with the composer Alex North. North had been a Communist Party member early in his life, and was strongly influenced in his political thinking by his brother, Joseph North, who was the editor of the Communist cultural magazine *New Masses*. Tennessee Williams, John Steinbeck and journalist, screenwriter and Adlai Stevenson speechwriter Robert Sherwood (author of the new *Man on a Tightrope* screenplay) were supportive of Kazan's 'stand'. On the title page of his copy of Sherwood's July 1952 script Kazan inscribed the names of three friends who opposed his decision, 'Art, Lillian, Kermit' (i.e. Arthur Miller, Lillian Hellman and Kermit Bloomgarden). Under the names he wrote as follows:

> I ask myself, as I must, is it really the liberties that they're worried about? Did they worry about the infringements of the Nazi's liberties as they do (now) those of the Communists? I don't believe they are representing themselves honestly.[27]

A substantial body of literature has since dealt with the whole issue of the blacklist and the role played by friendly witnesses such as Kazan. In particular Victor Navasky's 1980 book, *Naming Names*, revived public awareness of the phenomenon, and also established a perspective on the period in terms of a clear moral distinction between those who cooperated with HUAC and those who resisted it. To Navasky, Kazan was an iconic informer in a system of 'degradation ceremonies', even though he had more industry clout than most, and could certainly have continued to work in the theatre. This perspective recognises the appearances of Kazan and others as essentially ritualistic, since in the great majority of cases the FBI and other blacklisting organisations already had records of those who were or had been Communists. Of those named by Kazan who had film careers, J. Edward Bromberg had appeared in over 50 films, the last in 1950. He had appeared before HUAC and taken the Fifth Amendment in June 1951 and had died of a heart attack in London in December at the age of 47 while waiting to appear in a stage production of a Dalton Trumbo play, *The Biggest Thief in Town*. Morris Carnovsky also had no credits after 1950, and Art Smith (with whom Kazan had written the play *Dimitroff* in 1934) had only three film appearances in 1951 and 1952, after a total of 26 in the period 1947–50. It is certainly poignant to see Smith's roles in Dassin's *Brute Force* (1947) and in Nicholas Ray's *In a Lonely Place* (1950), the latter of which makes oblique reference to the blacklist.[28]

For all the valuable evidence that Navasky provides, he arguably placed insufficient weight on how individuals viewed the Party at the time, and when or if they had left it, questions that arguably led those called before the Committee to see the moral calculus differently. The great majority of friendly witnesses had broken with the Communist Party some years before, while the witnesses who remained silent were in the main Communist Party members, or felt close to it, when they testified. Disenchantment with the Party, in personal terms, or in terms of an understanding of the national or international context, was thus a factor in the ultimate decision made by some witnesses to 'cooperate' with the Committee, despite a moral presumption against so doing. Paul Jarrico, a blacklisted screenwriter who remained a leading member of the Hollywood section of the Communist Party until after the Khrushchev speech of 1956, made a similar point, arguing as follows: 'For those who were generally pissed off at the party but reluctant to name names, the choice must have been difficult. For a person like me, a true blue red, the choice was easy.'[29]

The first part of Jarrico's division seems to closely fit Kazan's circumstance in 1952. A few directors, who did not like screenwriters have the option of working through fronts, made the decision to leave America for Europe in the early fifties, thus escaping the blacklist and in some cases the Committee. Dassin, whose own membership of the Communist Party had been in the late thirties, re-established his film career with some difficulty in Europe (along with Joseph Losey, John Berry and Cy Endfield). To Dassin, the bottom line on his former friend was that he had become 'an ally and accomplice to an infamous committee which shamed the nation'. (He resisted later efforts by Kazan to make contact with him on his visits to Greece.) This debate was particularly prominent in 1999 when Kazan was awarded his Life Achievement award at the Academy Award Ceremony of that year. The discussions produced light as well as heat: the affair has at least, in an age of much historical ignorance, encouraged serious debate about the past and questioned overly schematic notions – on both sides – of that period's supposed heroes and villains.[30]

Following the April testimony Kazan was not immediately restored to favour in Hollywood. He had begun the decade with plans of working on distinctive film projects with writers including John Steinbeck, Arthur Miller and Tennessee Williams. In April 1952 talks with Warners on a proposed new project with Williams were put on hold and pressure was exerted on Kazan by Twentieth Century-Fox to undertake a film with an anti-Communist theme as part of his overall rehabilitation. A week after Kazan's second testimony Zanuck wrote to him, pointing out that he had talked to Skouras about 'the present situation', that they were both eager 'to have you make a picture now', and that 'I would confidentially very much like to have you do MAN ON A TIGHTROPE'. Zanuck had previously urged the director to make *The Snows of Kilimanjaro*, but Kazan agreed instead to the German film, and its proposed director Henry Hathaway was reassigned.[31] As usual Kazan worked hard in preparing for the film, a contemporary story about a circus escaping from Czechoslovakia to the West, and making it as authentic as possible. He argued strongly and successfully that the film be made on location and spent five months in Europe, from June to November 1952, including an extended period on location in Bavaria. The long period away may also have suited Kazan, given the trauma of the period before and just after his Committee appearances.

Kazan also read up on material on Eastern Europe, including documents from the International Rescue Committee (which had Sidney Hook and Kazan's lawyer Bill Fitelson on its Board of Directors). Bertram Wolfe, with whom he had discussed the issue of his testimony, also sent him a paper that he had presented at the Waldorf Conference in Defence of Free Culture, held in New York in March 1952 under the auspices of the ACCF. The ACCF had been established in 1951 as an affiliate of the European-based Congress for Cultural Freedom, set up in Berlin the previous year. The Committee, which brought together 'leaders of the American cultural community', presented itself as rallying intellectual opinion against 'all forms of totalitarianism, especially Communism – the greatest present threat to democratic communities'. Wolfe's paper referred to Shostakovich, Meyerhold and Eisenstein amongst others on 'the long and tragic list of the heroes of culture that the total state has martyred'. At some point after his testimony Kazan became an ACCF member, although apart from his *New York Times* advertisement his only other public discussion of contemporary politics was in a lecture at Harvard University in May 1952. Referring to the issue much debated in ACCF circles at the time, Kazan there suggested that a man 'may not be a Communist, but he does not want to be called a McCarthyite either'. Perhaps more crucially he was also reported as noting that if a man refuses to reveal his position he shows a lack of faith in his country.[32]

For all his apparent enthusiasm for working on location on the new film, this was a retreat from Kazan's increasingly personal involvement in his film projects. He largely inherited the script, by Pulitzer Prize-winning writer, playwright and screenwriter (and Roosevelt and Adlai Stevenson speechwriter) Robert Sherwood, from a book based on a real incident of 1950. There is evidence of Molly Kazan's interest in the political issues raised by the script, and in the appropriateness of a circus as a symbol for issues of freedom and liberty behind the Iron Curtain. In the wake of the Soviet-backed Communist coup of February 1948 in Czechoslovakia a number of groups and individuals had escaped to the West via the boundary with Bavaria, including the Circus Brumbach, which appears as itself in the film. Yet Zanuck was concerned about what he saw as contemporary resistance by the public to films about politics, including anti-communism, and he opposed explicit political references in the script. Kazan was unhappy with the screenplay dramatically, and later told John Steinbeck that he had made the mistake of letting by 'two no good love stories that didn't tie in'. There was also friction between director and producer during the production: Zanuck complained of work being behind schedule and over budget, and referred to an excessive number of 'takes and angles' that made Kazan 'my representative in a contest with both George Stevens and Willie Wyler'.[33]

Man on a Tightrope (1953) recounts the story of a third-rate Czech circus and of the political interference that finally prompts its manager, Karel Cernik (Fredric March), to take the company on a dash to cross into the American zone of Germany. The key relationships are those between Cernik and his second wife Zama (Gloria Grahame), and his daughter Teresa and a young man who also wants to reach West Germany to search for his father. These relationships are never very convincing, and were further weakened when Zanuck subsequently cut 20 minutes from the early part of the picture. Kazan does try to stress the individuality, eccentricity and cosmopolitanism of the itinerant performers while the use of a real circus – the Circus Brumbach – contributes a reasonable sense of surface realism. To Sherwood this was the 'littlest' and not the greatest show on Earth, a reference to Cecil B. DeMille's Academy Award winning 1952 film. Zanuck's fear of having the film branded by critics as political or historical, assumed to be box office poison in 1953, led to it lacking any significant context relating to the politics of Soviet-occupied Czechoslovakia. More than ever, Zanuck argued, people are 'going to the theatre to escape lectures, propaganda, politics and the constant talk-talk-talk which they get on TV and the radio'. He felt that *Viva Zapata!* had been so branded, and doubted whether *The Snake Pit* (1948), *Gentleman's Agreement* or *The Grapes of Wrath* would be successful if released in the contemporary climate.[34]

A rare allusion to the political context comes with Cernik's reference to both Nazi and Soviet occupations and to Jan Masaryk and Edvard Beneš, symbols of the lost tradition of Czech democracy. At one point Sherwood had argued for a foreword which provided background on the Czechs as 'passionate fighters for freedom', but as released the film, while avoiding the heavy-handedness of some Cold War propaganda, lacks much sense of political context, save perhaps a brief scene of some passing trucks carrying what seem to be political prisoners. There are other motifs that seem to reflect Kazan's involvement in the casting, including the role of Cernik's mother as a totem of the independent fortitude of the circus people, and the ridiculous if touching lion tamer (Alex D'Arcy). Occasionally the relentless plotting subsides to allow a glimpse of ordinary circus life: the knife thrower practising with a nonchalant partner who is still having her breakfast. Yet the emphasis is on Cernik, his interrogations by the political authorities (notably and most effectively with the bureaucrat Fesker, played by Hollywood right-winger Adolphe Menjou), and on his final decision to escape political interference and take the whole circus to the West. The circus crosses the border and Cernik dies as his mission is completed, something that Kazan and Sherwood had insisted upon, but the result is further to reduce the film's box office prospects, since March as Cernik was virtually the only character of substance. Despite Zanuck's cuts the film was a commercial failure, and to Skouras it lacked 'mass appeal'.[35]

Kazan's subsequent writings have revealed a sense of guilt and anxiety about his testimony. He told Ciment in 1973 that 'I don't think there is anything in my life towards which I have more ambivalence, because, obviously, there's something disgusting about giving other people's names'. He was also concerned with the way his friend Clifford Odets was a much lesser figure after his testimony. Talking to Jeff Young, Kazan felt that 'what I did was the better of two mean alternatives', while in his autobiography Kazan recorded a diary entry of the time in which he noted that 'I know I've done something wrong'. His dreams of meeting Tony Kraber again, and his contemplation of Kraber's note of sympathy following Molly's death, bubble up in the autobiography, disrupting its overall tone of assurance. After 1952 Kazan had to rebuild working relationships and was no longer the blue-eyed boy of either Hollywood or Broadway. He later argued that after testifying 'they cut my directing salary in half'. Furthermore, he now felt that *Viva Zapata!* had not matched his hopes, that three of his last four films had disappointed at the box-office, and that *Man on a Tightrope* had been a disaster. In the theatre too, his successes of the late forties had not been repeated; *Flight into Egypt*, which ran for 46 performances in 1952, and *Camino Real* (60 performances in 1953), had both lost money and been unappreciated by critics.[36] In addition, Kazan's close relationship with Arthur Miller had been shattered for the foreseeable future. There was to be further frustration and struggle before, in New York rather than Hollywood, his fortunes changed.

4

After his testimony Kazan had lost some of his key creative relationships, including those with Arthur Miller and Kermit Bloomgarden. By the summer of 1952 Miller was at work on *The Crucible*, a play that would make pointed reference to contemporary informers in the historical context of the Salem witch trials. Before this, in the spring, Kazan had contacted the writer Budd Schulberg, urged to do so by his wife. To Schulberg, Molly Kazan had 'enormous' influence on her husband's testimony, while drama critic Eric Bentley remembers her as having a 'great intellectual domination' over her husband. (Arthur Miller later wrote of the importance of her analytic skills to Kazan's more poetic talent).[1] Kazan and his wife visited Schulberg at his Pennsylvania home, and so began a professional association and friendship that would last the director's lifetime. Politically, it was significant that Schulberg had also cooperated with the House Committee on Un-American Activities. He had appeared at his own request soon after the Committee's hearings into Hollywood Communism had recommenced, and after he had been named by the writer Richard Collins. He testified on 23 May 1951 as to the pressure exerted on him by the Party in relation to his first novel, *What Makes Sammy Run*, while he later characterised his position at the time as that of a 'premature anti-Stalinist'. In his testimony he spoke of Soviet artists who had been shot and silenced at the end of the thirties and of his efforts, as part of the postwar organisation Friends for Intellectual Freedom (with Arthur Koestler, John Dos Passos and others), to raise funds to help beleaguered Soviet writers. Finally at the session he had given or confirmed the names of 13 members of the Communist Party group to which he belonged.[2]

A novelist and sometime screenwriter, Schulberg was the son of one of the early pioneers of motion pictures, B.P. Schulberg. He had been born in New York but raised in Hollywood, where his father was a Paramount executive and a producer in the twenties and thirties. The young Schulberg had worked as a writer at Paramount but gained critical recognition with the publication of his first novel in 1941. It was the criticism of *What Makes Sammy Run* (prior to publication) by senior Hollywood Communists – John Howard Lawson and V.J. Jerome in particular – that led him to leave the Party after a three-year membership. During the war he served in the United States Navy and was a member of John Ford's documentary unit, while later he gathered photographic evidence of war crimes for the Nuremberg trials. After completing his post-war novels *The Harder they Fall* (1947) and *The Disenchanted* (1950) – the latter based on his encounter with F. Scott Fitzgerald during their time together in Dartmouth writing the film *Winter Carnival* (1939) – Schulberg researched and wrote a script about the New York waterfront for a film that was to be directed by Robert Sidomak for Columbia Pictures, but which was never made. This 1951 screenplay was inspired by Malcolm Johnson's Pulitzer prize-winning articles for the *New York Sun* and featured a crusading investigative journalist modelled on Johnson, as well as early prototypes of the Terry Malloy and Father Barry characters.

The story of the genesis of *On the Waterfront* also requires further reference to *The Hook*, Arthur Miller's ill-fated screenplay, which Kazan was to direct in early 1951. In the late forties the playwright lived in Brooklyn Heights and became intrigued by the circumstances of the death of a rebel longshoreman in the Italian–American community of Red Hook, and by the wider issues of waterfront corruption in all the New York harbours, as documented by Johnson and other journalists. By May 1949 Miller had produced a first draft screenplay, subtitled 'A Play for the Screen', and he, Kazan and Kermit Bloomgarden, formerly business manager for the Group Theatre, and producer of two post-war plays that Kazan directed, *Deep Are the Roots* (1945) and Miller's *Death of a Salesman* (1949), explored the possibilities of collaborating on an independently produced film.[3] The first draft story concerned Marty Ferrara, a 34-year-old hatch boss and Italian immigrant, and his emerging leadership of a rank and file effort to combat the crime and corruption of the union and waterfront power structure. Miller drew a complex picture of longshoremen, hiring bosses, hoodlums, stevedores and ship-owners. Extended, rather 'talky' scenes depict meetings and conclaves, discussions of 'fascism' and 'fink contracts', efforts to detach intimidated immigrants from their ties to the corrupt union leadership, and ultimately a limited move towards rank and file support for union democracy.[4]

Kazan's major criticism, to a playwright who had little experience in writing for film, was that the draft contained too many speeches, especially from a lawyer character who he called 'a bore of the first water'. (Against a script line about starving kids Kazan wrote: 'Show! Don't tell this.') Elsewhere he noted that some of the speeches and scenes of labour 'solidarity' reminded him of the Theatre Union rhetoric of the thirties. He and Miller had discussed Italian neo-realism as a visual key for the project, and Kazan referred positively to scenes in the Miller script that he saw as suggestive of De Sica's *Bicycle Thieves*. He also felt that his friend was chasing too many themes, including the contrary pressures on Marty, the role of gangsters, and both racial and immigrant identities as they influenced the broader fight for the men's allegiance. Instead he recommended that there be a greater focus on the central character and that audiences learn about the problems of the waterfront directly through this figure's experience. There must, he felt, 'be a concrete issue that presses on MARTY and from which he cannot escape'. Miller responded to these criticisms, and in the January 1951 script that Columbia Pictures intended producing, prior to the political involvement that led Miller to withdraw, there were key changes. The lawyer character and the racial issue were excluded, and there was a clearer focus on Marty's life – on the waterfront and at home – and on the related struggle for a more democratic union.[5]

This later script begins with a narration which dedicates the work to those men who were fighting to bring the democratic practices of other unions to the waterfront, a reference that evokes the wartime Popular Front and pro-labour films such as *Action on the North Atlantic* (1943). More cinematic scenes immediately demonstrate the iniquities of the waterfront system and awaken Marty politically. The first dramatises the shape-up system of hiring labour, which was still used on the East Coast although it had been replaced by the use of hiring halls in the West Coast harbours, as well as in New Orleans, as demonstrated by a scene in *Panic in the Streets*. Under this system the men gathered twice a day to seek work and mob-dominated hiring bosses often picked the men on the basis of their willingness to kickback part of their wages. Miller's shape-up scene ends with two remaining work counters being thrown in the air, provoking a desperate free-for-all from the waiting longshoremen. There follows a scene in the hold of a ship that is being unloaded. The local union leader and the owner of the stevedoring company have colluded to speed up the winching process and as a result an 'accident' occurs, with a load of cargo falling and killing a longshoreman. Both scenes push Marty Ferrara towards leadership of a small band who want waterfront change.

When Ferrara protests against a 'fink contract' he is denied work, and the economic implications for his wife and family are demonstrated. Marty and his wife Therese have their electricity cut off and their couch and television repossessed, while the pressures on him also extend to his son. Sub-themes include the way union leaders use 'muscle' to defend their power and the fears of some immigrant workers that change may threaten their work prospects and livelihoods. Out of desperation Marty puts himself forward for election to the union presidency, and the climax charts a limited move towards rank and file solidarity as a prerequisite for reform. Marty addresses the men (in English and Italian) about his experience of Fascism in Italy and about the fascism that he now finds on the waterfront in America. The script suggests that it is the American-born men, many with war service, who are more prepared to stand up against the powers that be than their first generation immigrant fathers. The union leaders attempt to rig an election, which Marty nonetheless loses, while they also try to buy him off by making him a union delegate. Marty refuses the help of a gangster and decides to 'fight clean', while the death of a veteran long-shoreman's son, a victim of the snapping of an overloaded cable, leads to a con-clusion in which a growing body of men are shown as ready to follow Marty's leadership.[6] It is a complex narrative, but one that captures the particularly Italian context of the Brooklyn waterfront, something that Miller was to revisit in his later play, A View from the Bridge (1955). It is difficult to speculate on what kind of film Kazan could or would have produced from it at Columbia Pictures, even without the intervention of Roy Brewer and the FBI, as discussed in the previous chapter.

Budd Schulberg denies that he ever saw any of Miller's scripts, so any influ-ence of the Miller script on Schulberg's is likely to have come through Kazan.[7] There are some echoes of the Miller work in On the Waterfront, apart from those that reflect the related subject and sources, and it might be that the director introduced them in later script discussions, or when planning his filming. Both scripts include shape-up scenes in which men scramble for counters, but both writers drew here on Johnson's accounts.[8] Miller's script refers to a car which 'mounts a sidewalk behind Marty, who is running for his life ahead of it. After a number of yards Marty darts into a doorway.' This might have inspired the dis-tinctive scene that Kazan devised in On the Waterfront, and which is not in Schulberg's script, in which a truck pursues Terry and Edie down an alley at night, leading to the discovery of Charley's body (another scene absent from the script). Miller's screenplay also includes a scene between Marty and his wife, set by some children's swings, and one in which Marty descends a gangway to the pier, with the men watching from the rail. Yet Kazan also used a swing in Baby Doll and for all that he may have borrowed several motifs, integrating them into his and Schulberg's very different narrative structure, the view of one com-mentator that Miller's screenplay was 'pillaged' seems grossly exaggerated. As Leo Braudy has recently noted, the two scripts have 'little in common in either plot or atmosphere', while Terry Malloy and Marty Ferrara are very different as central characters.[9] In particular, individual testimony, inspired by the 1952 hearings of the New York Crime Commission, subsequent to Miller's work, is never a motif in the Miller scripts, while the Terry Malloy character is a distinctive creation, and there is no equivalent to the Father Barry role in the final Miller script. One writer – this comparison has encouraged some polemical commentaries – goes so far as to describe *The Hook* as a 'quintessentially Stalinist composition', and while this phrase seems more like an attempt to label Miller's politics at the time, there is certainly more of a 'thirties' feel to Miller's screenplay, and something of the spirit and form of Clifford Odets's play, *Waiting for Lefty*.[10] (If anything, with its concern for the gentler side of its protagonist, *On the Waterfront* is closer to *Golden Boy*.) The emphasis in the Miller script on meetings and votes would have been difficult to dramatise in a Hollywood system for which collective action was rarely a narrative option.

When they met at the novelist's Pennsylvania farm Schulberg and Kazan discussed the case of the Trenton Six, a miscarriage of justice case that seemed to echo aspects of the Scottsboro trial in the thirties, but Kazan expressed particular interest in the writer's script on the New York waterfront for the project abandoned in 1951. In their discussions Schulberg and Kazan moved towards an agreement that the director would respect the final screenplay as he would a play for the stage, while the writer would respect the director's authority on set and location. Such an arrangement, and in particular the director's respect for the script, followed Broadway practice. Arthur Miller, commenting on the excitement of his own collaboration with Kazan in the late forties, noted that the director 'both revered the text, and tested it every ten seconds'.[11] Schulberg began working on the new script while Kazan was in Germany in the latter part of 1952 making *Man on a Tightrope*, and he became increasingly committed to the cause of the 'guys who said no to industrial feudalism', and also to a key 'waterfront priest', Father John Corridan of the Xavier Labor School, who saw reform on the docks as a moral and religious cause. In comparison with the dedication in Miller's script, many of Schulberg's screenplays began with a tribute both to the longshoremen and to the 'Waterfront priests who serve God by serving men'.[12]

There is no doubt that Schulberg's script was based on an intense identification with the cause of the New York longshoremen. There had been several post-war wildcat strikes against union approved contracts, while the early fifties saw investigations into waterfront crime that highlighted the corruption of the union, the International Longshoreman's Association (ILA). Governor Thomas Dewey established a New York Crime Commission in 1951, and Schulberg remembers Father John Corridan, the model for the Father Barry character, telling the waterfront insurgents that the 'only way to break this whole thing was to testify, to speak up'. The writer attended all 40 days of the heavily reported public hearings, beginning in November 1952, and later argued that

'life was writing the end of our film'. The motif of individual longshoremen testifying became central to a broader notion of collective revolt in his scripts,
while he also published several pieces on waterfront conditions and the Crime
Commission, including one in the *New York Times* in December 1952. By this
time Kazan had returned from Germany and the two men held regular meetings, in Pennsylvania and in Manhattan, to discuss character and theme within
a screenplay then titled *The Golden Warriors*. Early in 1953 a treatment was
submitted for comment to Darryl F. Zanuck at Twentieth Century-Fox.[13]

Meanwhile Kazan planned other projects. Before leaving for Europe he told
John Steinbeck that he was going to speak to Zanuck about the possibility of
using *East of Eden* as a basis for a film, while Tennessee Williams was working
on an early version of what would eventually become *Baby Doll*. Contracts were
signed with Warner Bros. for both projects in the first quarter of 1953, while
Kazan also returned to the stage that year with productions of *Camino Real* (in
March) and the much more successful *Tea and Sympathy*, in September.[14] At
this stage Kazan was confident that his waterfront project with Schulberg would
be ideal for Twentieth Century-Fox. Zanuck had several meetings with the
writer in February, but although the production head was attracted by the story,
industry conditions, and in particular the continuing decline in film attendances, led him to be cautious. The studio's sceptical attitude to films dealing
with social and political issues was not untypical of the industry at the time;
the number of such films being produced was much reduced from the late forties, and few such topics were being considered as of 1953. To Zanuck *Viva
Zapata!*, Kazan's last released film for the company, was not the kind of film that
people wanted to see at a time when, as he saw it, they were seeking escape
from the alarming political stories dominating the media.[15] Kazan's status at Fox
was to be further diminished by the commercial failure of *Man on a Tightrope*
(released in March 1953), despite Zanuck's involvement and extensive cutting
of Kazan's final version. On the proposed new film Zanuck was also looking over
his shoulder at Fox President Sypros Skouras in New York, particularly given
that Kazan and Schulberg were proposing an unusual profit participation deal
for the waterfront picture. Beyond all this, Marlon Brando, now a star, could
not at this stage be guaranteed for the proposed film, while Zanuck also feared
that the State Department, which in 1953 was actively working in Hollywood
suggesting 'improvements' in films, might advise against foreign distribution,
given that the film could be seen as indicating general rather than exceptional
corruption in American labour relations.[16]

Zanuck also had substantial criticisms of the script itself. Even at the high
point of 'semi-documentary' in the later forties, Zanuck had been concerned
that the treatment of social or political issues in such films might overbalance

the more conventional Hollywood attractions of story, spectacle and stars. In addition, at this stage the Terry Malloy character in Schulberg's script, an ex-boxer who eventually opposes waterfront corruption, had a son, something that Zanuck felt was likely to domesticate the character in a way that could harm the potential box office. For all this uncertainty, the company listed the film in March and April as one that it expected to make, and it was something of a shock when Kazan and Schulberg went out together to Los Angeles in May, only to be told by Zanuck that he did not like the project, and that the company would not make it. Feeling that Schulberg had adopted a number of his script suggestions, Zanuck was later annoyed by what he saw as the writer's suggestion that he had lacked the courage to back the project. In retrospect he felt that the advent of CinemaScope had been crucial to the studio's decision, although Kazan, in his autobiography, is cynical of this explanation.[17] The precise responsibility for Twentieth Century-Fox's rejection of the project is difficult to assign, although Schulberg remembered a 'handshake deal' with Skouras, who also later claimed that he had done a deal with Kazan but that others at the studio – presumably Zanuck – had reneged on it while he was away. Two years later, when Kazan offered Zanuck *A Face in the Crowd*, the producer replied that he wanted no further association with Schulberg.[18]

The other Hollywood studios, including Warner Bros., all rejected the *Waterfront* script in the wake of the decision by Fox, and thus Kazan and Schulberg were desperate when they had an unexpected opportunity to pitch their story to independent producer Sam Spiegel, in May 1953. Spiegel, who agreed to produce the film, at first for United Artists release, had been born in what was then Austria–Hungary, lived in Palestine in the twenties, become a fugitive from Berlin in 1933, and lived for spells in Vienna, London, Paris and Mexico City before settling in Hollywood in 1939. Kazan remembered him as a very bright man, and added incidentally that in Los Angeles he had 'run a house for men who wanted to meet women who were not their wives'. In 1948 Spiegel had founded Horizon Productions with John Huston and they had a major success with *The African Queen* (1951) before the director left the partnership. The producer's most recent production, *Melba* (directed by Lewis Milestone), had been a box office disaster on its release in 1953. For this New York-based venture Spiegel demanded a tightening of the script and Schulberg felt, as one revision followed another in the summer and autumn of 1953, that some of the 'broader canvas' of his waterfront study was being sacrificed on the altar of 'relentless storytelling'. The continuity line of the screenplay was reconstructed in October following 'Spiegel–Kazan suggestions', and Kazan, as he had done before, worked hard to keep his writer on board when his producer pushed hard for cuts or changes that his partner found unacceptable.[19]

Schulberg insisted, for example, that a key speech by Father Barry, following the murder of a rebel longshoreman in a ship's hold, be preserved in its entirety. The effect of this period of revision was certainly to diminish the roles of some of the other insurgent longshoremen (including Joey Doyle, and the black long-shoreman, Luke), and to focus more and more on the particular experience of Terry Malloy.[20] Kazan had seen the part as ideal for Marlon Brando, but the actor initially declined the part because of the director's testimony, and Frank Sinatra was hired for the central role. Only when Spiegel used his considerable powers of persuasion to get Brando to change his mind did the producer secure financing for his production from Columbia Pictures; a budget of $800,000 and a lean, 35-day shooting schedule were agreed, with production commencing in the bitter cold of the Hoboken docks in late November 1953.

The long struggle to make the film strengthened what was an unusual col-laboration between screenwriter and director. The script supplies a rich ver-nacular for the world of the waterfront. Schulberg knew the fight game and as boys he and his best friend Maurice Rapf had shared a pigeon loft. He writes of cheese-eaters, canaries, D&D longshoremen, and memorably of the gulf between 'being a contender' and a 'one-way ticket to Palookaville'. Kazan had undoubtedly contributed to the story, but Schulberg also involved himself in choosing the locations, walking around with Kazan and sharing his very con-siderable knowledge of the waterfront. A number of scenes that were scripted for tenement interiors were actually played outside, on the roof, on the pier and in a believable, artfully composite park. It was also writer who introduced direc-tor both to the Rev. John Corridan and to longshoremen who were standing up for democratic unionism. In particular, Tony Mike De Vincenzo, a pier boss who had led strikes against the corrupt ILA leadership and also testified to the real Waterfront Crime Commission, was to have a powerful influence on Kazan's conception of the Terry Malloy character. Schulberg recalls being in New York during most of the shooting, through the winter of 1953–4, and that he and the director would 'talk every morning early, and sometimes the night before', with Kazan describing to him 'how he planned to shoot it'.

Given this distinctive creative relationship, it is important to assess the evi-dence of Kazan's particularly strong commitment, less to the documentary back-ground of the screenplay (Schulberg certainly hoped that the release of the film might actually affect the outcome of a crucial union election) than to a spine of the story defined in terms of Terry Malloy's regaining of his lost sense of dignity and self-worth. Kazan's production notebook for the film, which he began in June 1953, provides characteristic information on theme and character, and places particular emphasis on the central figure, his inner conflict and his redemption. Kazan notes that 'this is a psychological study of a man between 2 loyalties, make both loyalties strong and affecting'. Under the heading of 'theme', Kazan writes: 'The Motion Picture is about one thing only: a Young man who has let his dignity slip away, regains it!' The director's advice to Brando, in the form of a careful letter written in November 1953, sums up the development of the Terry Malloy character as follows: 'A Bum becomes a man. That's it.'[21] It was Kazan who committed himself to the subjective focus on Terry's story. As he writes on the first right hand page of his annotated script, with the first three lines in red ink:

> PHOTOGRAPH
> *the Inner Experience*
> Of TERRY
> Don't be objective! This is not a
>   Documentary
> Be Subjective, Be Terry

In his notebook he adds: 'Photograph the inner experience of Terry & that's all!'[22] In this sense Kazan edges the film away from its sociological context, and the completed film furthers this social psychological context by exploiting Brando's extraordinary ability to convey, through gesture and body language as well as through his distinctively fractured delivery of the lines, an inner journey through machismo, guilt, vulnerability, love and confusion towards some kind of rebirth. On Brando's acting Kazan said later that you 'knew what was happening to him emotionally because it registered in the way he moved his body and used his face'.

In terms of the later interpretation of the film as a metaphoric defence of its creators' appearances before HUAC, it needs to be stressed that Budd Schulberg has always denied any such intention and complained that the dominance of this reading in academic circles trivialises the work and 'marginalises the actual longshoremen who took their life in their hands, to get up and testify'. To Kazan, on the other hand, it was true that 'as I worked more and more on that the fuel for it, the energy for it, came from the feeling that I was talking about myself'.[23] He also wrote in his autobiography that he doubted 'that Budd was affected as personally as I was by the parallel of Tony Mike's story'. Referring in particular to the culling of Terry's pigeons following his testimony, and to his subsequent confrontation with Johnny Friendly, in which he shouts that he is 'glad what I done', Kazan notes that the 'transference of emotion from my own experience to the screen is the merit of those scenes'. Yet Schulberg has praised Brando's work in the film as the 'performance of his life', and has never suggested that Kazan reneged on his agreement to respect the script.

There is little in Kazan's contemporary papers, and nothing in his letter to Brando on the Terry Malloy role, that specifically relates to a parallel with the testimony before HUAC. The nearest that Kazan comes in his production notebook to embracing a wider political theme is a reference to a parallel between the depiction of the mob and its terror to Communism, and his note that 'The Biggest loyalty a man has is to all the people, which in a Democracy, is the state. The Biggest obligation a man has is to be a citizen.'[24]

In terms of casting, Kazan, having finally secured Brando's services, again turned to the New York-based Actors Studio for his other key actors and a number of the smaller parts. From this source he recruited Karl Malden, who had acted with Lee J. Cobb and Kazan in the 1937 Group Theatre production of *Golden Boy*, and Rod Steiger, who had made only one previous screen appearance. Malden had stuck with his friend following the director's testimony and had urged Brando to continue his association with Kazan, while Cobb had given his own 'friendly' testimony to HUAC in June 1953. 21-year-old Eva Marie Saint, who had a year's television experience, was also in the Actors Studio, and was chosen for her first film role following an audition there. Some ex-boxers were used, as well as many real longshoremen, and for those with speaking parts there were three run-throughs at the Actors Studio, before filming began.[25]

The film's story begins with Terry's complicity in the murder of Joey Doyle. Earlier versions had developed the Doyle character more fully, but here he is briefly glimpsed through a tenement window as Terry, doing a favour for union boss Johnny Friendly, lures him onto the roof. The waterfront priest, Father Barry, and the dead man's sister, Edie Doyle, are introduced as the convent educated young woman, leaning over her brother's body, demands to know 'who killed my brother'. Terry Malloy's loneliness – Kazan stressed his identity as an orphan – is indicated in the contrast between his solitariness on the roof, accompanied only by the boy gang members who idolise him, and the key relationships in the Local, with his elder brother Charley and with Johnny Friendly, his patron and the surrogate father who used to take him to ball games. Terry becomes conscious of Edie for the first time at a shape-up at which he secures a work counter for her long-suffering father, and thereafter their relationship develops in a park, where they walk together, by his roof-top pigeon coup, and then in a bar. Slowly his feelings for her, his desire for a different life, emerges from beneath the veneer of toughness. Another aspect of Terry's character is revealed to Glover, an investigator from the Crime Commission, who draws out the ex-boxer's resentment at losing out on a 'title shot' so that some 'pals' could win a 'lousy bet'. His shift of stance is suggested when 'Kayo' Dugan (a role based on a real waterfront figure known to Schulberg, Arthur Brown) is

'They always said I was a bum': Terry Malloy to Edie Doyle following the killing of his pigeons. Eva Marie Saint and Marlon Brando in *On the Waterfront* (1954). Courtesy of BFI.

murdered in the hold, and soon after when Edie brings Terry the dead man's jacket (it was previously Joey Doyle's). Terry 'confesses' his role in Joey's death to Father Barry (who has articulated his view of waterfront corruption in a speech made over Dugan's body) and Edie, but he is not yet ready to respond to the Crime Commission subpoena. In a cab ride, Charley understands for the first time the depth of his brother's alienation, and is unable to convince him to accept the mob's attempt to buy him off. With his relationship with Edie restored, Terry then discovers his brother's dead body and commits himself to 'take it out on their skulls', only for Father Barry to convert this sentiment into a willingness to 'really hurt Johnny Friendly' by testifying to the Crime Commission. After his testimony some of his 'friends' ignore him and Tommy, the young gang member on the roof, kills his birds. While Edie seemingly loses faith, Terry goes down to the waterfront to 'get his rights', demonstrating to the rest of the men in the process that he is prepared to physically confront both Friendly and his waterfront muscle men ('He fights just like he used to'). Badly beaten, Terry is prompted by Father Barry to demonstrate further courage to the men by 'walking', or staggering, back to work.

Marlon Brando in *On the Waterfront* is both part of the ensemble while also the film's central focus for emotional identification. The work in finding locations roots Brando as Malloy in a graphic and believable sense of place, an environment and a 'world' that was startling to audiences unused to such documentary realism. Lee Rogow, one of a host of reviewers who were impressed by Brando's performance, also referred to the film as a 'documentary on the docks', and saw the film as breaking through 'the subtle filter which has previously shielded American lenses from the harsh light of reality'. The early scene in the back room in Johnny Friendly's bar reveals Terry's dependent relationships with Friendly and his brother Charley in the world of work, while he is next seen in his own space on the tenement roof, alone but for his pigeons and boy members of the waterfront gang, the 'Golden Warriors', that he founded. Role, performance and use of objects (his birds and their eggs, for example) reveal a tender, vulnerable side to Terry's masculinity that was unusual in the cinema of the time. In his November letter to Brando, Kazan had written of the combination in the character of primitivism and gentleness, of 'false swagger and painful self-doubt'. A British critic, responding to the film's 1962 re-release, referred to the way it soared 'from documentary to a series of brilliantly universal occasions', yet he was not alone in also seeing Brando as a 'fantastic presence' and 'a hugely unreal apparition'. The French writer Roger Tailleur also wrote of the 'sacred monstrosity of Marlon Brando' and the 'open wound' of toughness and vulnerability that he brought to the part, while the German film director Volker Schlöndorff, who saw the film first as a 16-year-old, remembers that at 'that age we are all kind of bisexual, and probably I was in love with him, unbeknownst to myself!' Recalling his first viewing as a 'punch in the stomach', he feels that the central performance now looks 'quite mannered and very daring'.[26]

An example of this behaviour and body language that is both naturalistic and baroque comes in an early scene in which Terry asserts his solidarity with the waterfront code of behaviour by giving short shift to the enquiries of the Crime Commission investigators. He is amongst a group of fellow workers, but far from stressing oneness with them, the staging, and Brando's exaggerated turn to his right to address the investigator's sidekick, his 'girlfriend', suggest the opposite. Perhaps the most discussed 'Method' scene is introduced by a tracking shot of Terry and Edie in the park, leading to the moment when Edie drops a glove and Terry, perched on a swing, plays with it and tries it on, suggesting both an intimacy and an awkward experimentation – the glove is too tight – with a different view of life. According to Eva Marie Saint she dropped the glove in rehearsal and Kazan asked Brando to repeat his subsequent improvisation for the camera. In the renowned cab scene it was Brando, by all accounts, who invented the 'caressing' gesture with which he pushes away the gun that his brother draws on him. What has become a 'classic' scene was born out of improvisation in the face of budgetary limitations. Without any back-projection facilities the space, the back seat of the cab, seems more oppressively enclosed, with Boris Kaufman's lighting serving both realism and the heightened state of the brothers' relationship, as Terry reveals both the depth of his resentment (his failed American dream) and his awareness of the implications of his 'decision' for his brother. This is something of a love scene, as both men reveal their emotions, Charley by drawing the gun and then collapsing back when it is brushed aside, and Terry by his sighing reaction, his bathetic expression of the word 'Wow'. The directorial and editing choices between master shot, two shots favouring each actor, and singles (which Steiger played to 'dialogue coach' and Kazan crew regular Guy Thomajan after Brando left to attend a session with his analyst) may be relatively conventional, but Kazan wanted the close-ups to capture the thought processes and feelings, and few other directors would have encouraged and expected such emotional expressivity in such a scene.

Elsewhere Terry is often 'favoured', as when Edie brings her brother's jacket to him on the roof, at night. Terry is stretched out on a ledge at the bottom of the frame, so that the figure of Edie approaching at the top of the frame almost seems to be part of Terry's subconscious. Brando's gestures can be seen as naturalistic and at the same time strange and distinctive. Discovering his brother's body, hung up on a hook against the wall, Terry drapes the dead man's arms around himself as he lifts him free, recalling the similar 'business' between the brothers in *Viva Zapata!* When Terry discovers the slaughter of his pigeons, he stands by his coup, waving one arm at Edie, to warn her, ward her off, and hide his private anguish. At the very least Kazan permitted such invention, and may at times have engineered it, and he also provided Terry with key point of view shots, emphasising moments of crisis or decision. When he and Edie are chased by the truck, and escape through a doorway, time seems to stand still for a moment as we share Terry's view of the vehicle passing, revealing to him and us the stricken figure of Charley. Elsewhere, Terry throws a beer glass at a framed photograph of Johnny Friendly pictured with a waterfront boss, after he has been persuaded by Father Barry to testify to the Crime Commission. The director, who often used such framed photographs and portraits in his films to underscore key relationships or memories, closes the scene with Terry's point of view shot of the smashed picture. One could also mention Terry's subjective view of the warehouse as he makes his staggering walk back to work, a shot suggested by the cinematographer James Wong Howe when Kazan asked him for advice on the shooting of the final scene.[27]

Perhaps most powerful in dramatising Terry's consciousness is the scene in which Terry responds to Tommy's slaughter of his pigeons, following his Crime Commission testimony. Crouched down, he looks forward and to the right and we see a shot, held for some time, of a liner moving south down the Hudson River, with Manhattan and the Empire State Building in the background. Not only does this show us a rare lyrical aspect of Terry's environment, and make Edie's suggestion that he retreat inland to a 'farm' all the more ludicrous, but it allows Terry time to decide on his final, dangerous course of action. Sam B. Girgus suggests that the ship is leaving New York for Europe and links Terry Malloy's new found commitment to fight for his rights as an American with Kazan's own rejection of elements of his past, his communist politics linked with his immigrant status.[28] Yet it was after the release of On the Waterfront that Kazan was to make his first return visit to Turkey to search for his 'discarded self' (his own phrase), a meditation that led eventually to the film about his own family's immigrant journey, America America (1963).

Terry's redemption results from his guilt, but also his developing relationship with Edie. Such love stories, cutting against a broader theme, recur in Kazan's later films. In marginal notes on his script Kazan sees the convent trained Edie as an 'Absolutist' who is gradually humanised as she falls for a 'bum', a remark that is typical of his conception of men and women, and perhaps of his own marriage. It is Edie's vow to discover who killed her brother that makes her the 'investigator' of the drama, despite the local code of silence and her father's warning. Twice she visits Terry on his roof, where he shows her his pigeons, waiting, in the director's expression, for her to 'admit him to the human race'. When she makes a second, night-time visit, delivering 'Kayo' Dugan's jacket, Kazan noted on his script that she was being 'sexually reckless'. Kazan charts the emotional undertow of the script and spurs his actors, encouraging in particular their expressive use of objects. Edie and Terry connect physically, from her efforts to wrest her father's work tab from Terry at the shape-up ('it's been nice wrestling with you') to the reverie at the wedding party they stray into – the only oblique reference to the motif of marriage. The tension generated is finally released by Terry's breaking open her door, and their subsequent, passionate embrace. Thereafter, as Jeffrey Chown has demonstrated, Edie is a more conventional figure, as she suggests that she and Terry leave the waterfront and then passively observes (with Father Barry) his final 'walk'.[29]

Although Sam Spiegel made some key decisions, including the selection of Leonard Bernstein to write the music, for the most part he stayed out of the intense cold during shooting, in a plush suite at the St. Regis Hotel in Manhattan. To Kazan this helped him bond with his cast and with a crew that included first assistant director Charles Maguire, costume designer Anna Hill

Johnstone and others who would become regulars in Kazan's independent productions. The choice of the 35-year-old Bernstein was intended to add marquee value, reflecting the producer's uncertainly about the commercial prospects of the completed but unreleased film. At the time Bernstein had an international reputation as Assistant Conductor of the New York Philharmonic, and he stayed in Los Angeles to oversee the dubbing himself and even played jazz piano for the scene where Terry takes Edie for a drink in a bar. The use of the solo French horn version of the central theme over the opening credits immediately strikes a distinctive note for the film, and although Kazan later complained of those elements of the score that pitched the film into operatic mode, there is no doubt of its power and lyricism, particularly in the scenes on the roof, but also as Terry discovers his murdered brother.[30]

In prompting himself in his notebook on the visual style of the picture Kazan made a reference to Ben Shahn, who had been given a first retrospective exhibition at the Museum of Modern Art in New York in 1947. Shahn had been committed to the use of art as a social instrument and had produced posters and paintings for labour unions and government agencies, remaining a 'champion of the poor and oppressed' in the changing political currents of the fifties.[31] The influence of stark and simple graphic design to make a social point is perhaps evident in the shape-up scene, shot from behind the all-powerful hiring boss, and in the added scene (designed to indicate a broader and corporate web of corruption) in which a Mr Big figure (based on William J. McCormick, President of the Penn Stevedoring Co.) watches Terry's testimony on television and distances himself from Johnny Friendly. The 'look' of the film is most distinctive in the scenes on the roof, the mess of slopes, chimneys, skylights, aerials and shacks. We see Terry casually accessing the roof from a window, climbing ladders, and generally criss-crossing his private domain. There is a sense of confinement in the wire of the pigeon coups, yet also a sense of Terry's sanctuary, as he tends his birds and shadow-boxes his way through life.

In terms of the visuals, Kazan's key decision was to choose Boris Kaufman (1906–80) as his cinematographer. Kaufman was the Polish-born brother of Dziga Vertov and Mikhail Kaufman, both of them members of the Soviet Kino-Pravda film group. He had worked with Jean Vigo on his films of the thirties and on documentaries after coming to America in 1942, and was recommended to Kazan by the documentary filmmaker Willard Van Dyke. Kazan remembers that, prompted by Kaufman, 'we'd try to talk as artists, not as men paid to manufacture entertainment, and not as technicians with mechanical problems'. Kaufman lured the director into a more artistic practice than he was used to:

I'd be surprised at how much there was to talk about and how much there was to be gained by this slightly off-center conversation. Ignoring all pressures of efficiency, he'd coax me through a ritual of discovery and by the end of the day I'd realise how much in his debt I was.

While Kaufman remembered that his director could be violent and tender, and that both styles were present in the film, Kazan recalled his cameraman's gift of lyricism, making 'a tragic poem in greys of the rooftops and alleys of Hoboken, New Jersey'.[32] Kaufman's high contrast lighting in the night scene in the alley contrasts with his use of overcast skies and long harbour vistas, and the more morally ambivalent, low contrast scenes, softened and clouded by the use of smoke pots. To the *Time* reviewer, seldom has the 'brick implacability of a workingman's neighbourhood stood staring in such an honest light – the tenement phalanx, the sad little parks, the ugly churches'. In the scenes on the roof, in particular, there is a cluttered, off-kilter world that was certainly miles away from the brave new suburban world of fifties Hollywood and America, while the pokey interiors are real Hoboken tenement rooms. According to Sam Spiegel the Venice festival chairman told him that *On the Waterfront* was the 'first Italian film made in America'. The film won a Silver Prize, along with Kurosawa's *Seven Samurai*, Moguchi's *Sansho the Bailiff* and Fellini's *La Strada*, at the 1954 Venice Film Festival, as well as a Grand Prix from an association of European Catholic Film Institutes.[33]

The ending has always been the most controversial sequence of the film, both politically and aesthetically. The British critic Lindsay Anderson saw Terry's climactic 'walk' to work, engineered by Father Barry, as unconsciously fascist, in terms of the men's transfer of allegiance to a new leader. It was the last act of the screenplay that Zanuck had felt needed most work, and debates on the ending continued until the last day of shooting. In terms of his relationship with Kazan, Schulberg remembers that 'if we had any argument it was on the very last day'. The final shooting script had Terry Malloy dying after being beaten up by Friendly's mob, following his testimony to the Crime Commission, and Schulberg is on record as preferring this ending, in which the men are inspired to 'take over in his name, so there is victory in death'. The Terry Malloy character also dies at the end of the novel that Schulberg subsequently wrote. However, the writer also remembers the ending being kept open when filming of the final scene commenced, presumably under pressure from Spiegel, and recalls that of the three of them it was the producer who was most vocal in pushing for as 'happy' and as 'Hollywood' an ending as possible, fearing that 'killing Brando off would not be good for box office'. Given his own strong preference, Schulberg remembers Kazan breaking the impasse by suggesting that Malloy be beaten up so that he is near death at the end. The director, talking later about criticisms of the film's ending, added that 'Schulberg didn't like my ending either'.[34]

Kazan's understanding of the climax was that the men are cautiously impressed by Terry's encounter with Friendly, while still suspicious of him. They are generally passive observers, before they edge forward once Terry has staggered to the warehouse doorway. There is certainly an uncertainty in the dynamics of the film's conclusion, although some commentators, for example John M. Smith, have countered Anderson's perspective with the notion that when Terry recovers his respect he 'is granted the awakening respect of the dockers, so that his personal victory becomes social'. Schulberg was 'bothered' by the shot of Karl Malden and Eva Marie Saint, with their 'self-satisfied smiles', as their characters watch Malloy 'lead' the men to work:

> I think that it is one of the few mistakes that Gadg made in the film, because if you accept the fact that he was dreadfully beaten up, and could even die, obviously they would be concerned. The look on their faces is what Spiegel wanted. Spiegel wanted a happy ending.[35]

The writer also felt that a change in the editing, or a stronger visual emphasis on Johnny Friendly's defiant shout to the men ('I'll be back', and 'I'll remember every last one of you'), would have undercut the sense of facile resolution that many see in the final scene. However, the last shot of the film is of the lowering of the iron door of the warehouse, and this casts some doubt on what has been achieved, outside of Terry's personal redemption. In the real life of the New York waterfront the Crime Commission investigation did not lead to any immediate reform apart from the ending of the shape-up. Schulberg remained concerned about the future of the rebels, including Arthur Brown and de Vincenzo, when the ILA narrowly clung on to power in a December 1953 ballot against a new American Federation of Labour (AFL) union.

On the Waterfront was one of the top 20 moneymaking films of 1954 and swept the board at the 1955 Academy Awards ceremony. Its strong and distinctive sense of working class place was combined with a powerful, even relentless narrative drive. Kazan pioneered with Schulberg a respectful association between director and writer, while also working closely and cooperatively with actors to emphasise sub-textual feelings, the space *between* words. The *New York Times* review found the film to be 'an uncommonly powerful, exciting and imaginative use of the screen by gifted professionals'. Among later critical views, Peter Biskind saw Terry Malloy as manipulated by church and state,

although such a reading seems to underplay the power and persuasiveness of
Terry Malloy as written, acted and directed. In contrast Michael Denning discusses the film in terms of the continuing impact of the thirties and forties
traditions of what he calls 'ghetto pastorals and proletarian thrillers, a combination of the proletarian avant-garde of Kazan and the Hollywood Popular Front
of Schulberg'.[36]

Kazan and Schulberg had both beaten the system and, in the sweep of
Academy Awards for their film in 1955, been victorious within it. Feeling mis-
treated by the Hollywood film industry that had rejected the film, they both
celebrated at a party at Chang's restaurant in New York rather than attending
the official Awards event. Kazan had bounced back from his weakest point (after
his HUAC testimony and the critical and commercial failure of *Man on a
Tightrope*) and was now on course to produce his own films, at first at Warner
Bros. and then – following the independent model of *On the Waterfront* – for
his own New York-based production company. For all the admiration for Kazan's
work on *A Streetcar Named Desire*, it was *On the Waterfront* that introduced
him to a new sense of himself as a film artist, as indicated by his remarks about
working with Boris Kaufman. The film also had a powerful and continuing resonance in the emerging culture of international cinema. Even Lindsay
Anderson's critical polemic was recognition of this impact, while baby boomers
were to be stirred by Terry Malloy as an anti-conformist far more than is recognised in Biskind's analysis of him as a conformist cheerleader for church and
state. In a much more minor key there is a similar defying of group pressures
by the Ernest Borgnine character at the end of the next year's *Marty* (1955).
With the 'gift of Brando', Kazan and Schulberg had fashioned a powerful parable of identity, and Lloyd Michaels rightly argues that the film is 'not, after all,
an allegory justifying informing or even an expose of labour racketeering but
rather the story of an inarticulate, undirected human being's struggle for personal dignity'. Perhaps this is also what Nicholas Ray was getting at when he
commented that the film was less about the waterfront than it was 'Kazan's
translation of "To be or not to be"'.[37] Yet the effectiveness of this existential
element relies also on Schulberg's blueprint, his context, including his own passionate feeling for John Corridan and the insurgent longshoremen. *On the
Waterfront* is classically a collaborative film, but Kazan and Brando help to push
it out of its time, towards American myth.

5

Producer–Director: *East of Eden* (1955) and *Baby Doll* (1956)

Warner Bros. reflected the wider transformation of the political economy of Hollywood in the early fifties, quickly adapting itself to the end of the old studio system of vertically integrated production, distribution and exhibition. Its profits had been higher than those of any other studio in 1950, mainly a result of cuts in personnel, while by the next year it had lost its theatres (as a result of the anti-trust action), together with most of the contracted stars that helped give the studio its distinctive profile in the thirties and forties. Alfred Hitchcock had signed a deal in 1949 to produce and direct at the studio, and other financing agreements for independent companies followed. By 1956 the studio advanced over $25 million to independent producers, compared to $1.5 million in 1946, and also became heavily involved in the production of television series.[1]

In the first half of 1953, well before the success of *On the Waterfront* transformed his prestige and market position, Kazan had signed contracts to direct two films for Warner Bros. Warner was keen to sign up the director and Tennessee Williams again, although scripting and Code problems meant a long delay until what was eventually called *Baby Doll* came before the cameras, as the first production of Kazan's Newtown production company, in late 1955. He had considered an offer from Warners when he had first come to Hollywood, and his relationship with Jack Warner remained cordial despite the cuts imposed by the Legion of Decency on *A Streetcar Named Desire*. Jack was the youngest of four brothers and the only one of the Polish immigrant family to be born in North America, in Ontario in 1892. The family had been in the moving pictures business from the early years of the century and Warner Bros. Pictures, founded in 1923, had become one of the major five studios by the early thirties. Jack Warner was ultimately responsible for the choice of stories, casting, budgeting and final approval, although he delegated many key responsibilities to line producers, and particularly to Hal Wallis during the thirties and the war years. He retained corporate control into the sixties, although his direct involvement in the filmmaking process declined.[2]

Steinbeck and Kazan also remained close after *Viva Zapata!*, and the writer's long and dynastic California story, *East of Eden*, had become the nation's best-selling novel by the end of 1952. Kazan had originally thought of making the film as part of his Twentieth Century-Fox contract, telling Zanuck in Munich that he was interested in the first third and the last third of the novel, with Nunnally Johnson, who had adapted *The Grapes of Wrath*, as the probable writer.[3] On returning from Germany, however, Kazan, who was discussing the new Tennessee Williams project with Warner, found him to be highly receptive to a deal on the Steinbeck book. The contract signed on 23 January 1953 provided Kazan, as producer and director, with control over the 'final cut' unless the head of the studio felt that changes were needed following two previews. Kazan was to be paid $125,000 and to receive 25 per cent of the net receipts, in return for directing the picture from Steinbeck's screenplay and in accordance with the Production Code, although he later negotiated a cash payment in place of his percentage. Thus the shift away from Twentieth Century-Fox, to whom Kazan owed one more picture, came before the falling out over the Waterfront project and the cutting, and commercial failure, of *Man on a Tightrope*. Zanuck was annoyed to lose this 'hot' property, and Kazan was to return to the studio (to make *Wild River*) only after Zanuck had resigned from his post as Head of Production to become an independent producer, based in Paris, in 1956.[4]

East of Eden was to be shot on location in California and on the sound stages and back lot sets of the Warner Bros. studio. It was to be Kazan's first film in colour and in the new CinemaScope process, with an aspect ratio of 1: 2.66 (1: 2.35 allowing for optical sound recording). Twentieth Century-Fox had first purchased and developed the system and from February 1952 they had concentrated their slate of productions on stories that would enhance the new widescreen process. Warners and other studios leased the process, and *East of Eden* was to be one of its first productions using the new technology. Kazan's first colour film was also to be made in Warner Color, one of the early one strip Eastmancolor processes that replaced the three-strip Technicolor system in the early fifties.[5]

Steinbeck and Kazan were close friends and so despite the novelist's eminence and the status of the book, the director had fewer problems than he had earlier with Robert Sherwood, who he had found over-protective about his screenplay. Steinbeck was happy for Kazan to use only the last section of the novel, Chapters 39–55, since it was the story of Cal and his relationship with his father that meant most to the director (Kazan felt that Zanuck had been more interested in the first part of the novel). Working with Steinbeck he became concerned about structuring the material, and for that reason he contacted another playwright friend, Paul Osborn, in April 1953, before he turned his main attentions to *On the Waterfront*. Kazan felt that he needed a 'first rate constructionist' and that as producer as well as director it was now his responsibility to ensure that the 'planning stage' of the film went well. Steinbeck was hurt for a time that the director had turned to another writer, but Kazan felt that Osborn, with his 'immense drive towards simplification', would help provide greater dramatic shape and 'singleness'.[6] At the time Kazan was conscious of the deficiencies of his recent work in this respect. In particular he felt that *Viva Zapata!*, for all its merits, had been 'diffuse' and could have been improved had he 'driven for greater unity', while he also thought that he had let down Tennessee Williams by not being stronger in planning the 1953 play *Camino Real*. It was May before a 'final' screenplay had been completed, and Osborn later explained that 'I wrote it – Gadge and I rewrote it and I think all parties were pleased'.[7]

Osborn set to work to dramatise a story set in the northern California of 1917, in the agricultural town of Salinas, Steinbeck's birthplace, and in the fishing port of Monterey some 15 miles away. The key characters are Adam Trask, his estranged and separated wife Kate, their two sons Cal and Aron, and Abra, a young woman who is at first pledged to Aron. Two key strands of the screenplay are Cal's resentment at his father's preference for his brother Aron, and his discovery of his mother running a brothel and gaming house in Monterey. Following the failure of his father's entrepreneurial plan to freeze lettuce Cal goes into business with Will Hamilton, using money borrowed from his mother to invest in the ascending First World War market in beans. The film's central emotional moment becomes Adam's rejection of Cal's birthday gift to him of the money gained from this enterprise, a crisis that sets in train a more melodramatic series of events, including Cal confronting his brother with the truth about their mother, Aron's traumatised response, and their father's subsequent stroke. The film concludes with Cal winning Abra's love and ultimately gaining the blessing of his stricken father. Kazan and Osborn made significant changes from the novel, where it is Adam's Chinese manservant Lee who lends Cal the money to speculate on beans and later asks Adam, on his deathbed, to forgive his son. Steinbeck also has Kate committing suicide and Adam suffering his stroke when he hears news of Aron's death in the war, whereas Osborn dispensed with the Lee character and kept Kate and Aron alive.

By the time Kazan arrived in Los Angeles in April 1954 he had already cast several of the key roles. He often decided that a particular actor had the part within him or her, that their personality and behaviour chimed so closely with those of the character that they had a clear claim on the part, whatever their formal inexperience. To Kazan this was the case with James Dean's suitability for the central role of Cal Trask. He reported to Warner that the 23-year-old, who Osborn had spotted in a New York play and who had experience in New York television and had attended a few Actors Studio sessions, was an 'odd kid', but was 'o.k.' for the role. This 'oddness' was part of the attraction: to Kazan the young man was a 'genuine Bohemian in the best sense of that word'. Warner was happy to go along, although he was worried about the capacity of 'odd people' to throw a smooth machine out of gear. In his television work Dean had begun to specialise in sensitive adolescents who were deprived of love and understanding and often in conflict with authority, and his screen performance seemed to relate to the experiences of fifties' adolescents who found their fathers emotionally scarred by war. The director felt, as filming commenced in the summer of 1954, that 'Certainly there was never such a hero before'. In terms of Dean's pairing with Julie Harris as Abra, Kazan was concerned that the 29-year-old actress, one of the earliest members of the Actors Studio, might seem 'too old' in the relationship. He had a friend take photographs of Dean and Julie Harris together before he was convinced of her casting. [8]

The casting was completed with Jo Van Fleet in the role of the brothel-madam mother, New York actors Lois Smith and Albert Dekker, the folk singer and Broadway actor Burl Ives as the sheriff, and Richard Davalos as Aron Trask. Van Fleet was also in the Actors Studio and had extensive Broadway experience but this was to be her first Hollywood role, while Ives, a benign if sentimental presence in the memory of many whose childhood was in the fifties, became a natural surrogate father for Cal, tolerant of Kate's profession (to the disapproval of the Production Code office) but firm in calming the crowd who harass a German in the fairground scene. 59-year-old Raymond Massey, who had been particularly identified with the role of Abraham Lincoln in stage and film versions of Robert Sherwood's *Abe Lincoln in Illinois*, was the only member of the cast to have extensive Hollywood experience. For the role of Adam Trask, Kazan had first thought of Gary Cooper and Freddie March, preferring the former as more of an 'outdoor type'. He had also considered Spencer Tracy for a role that he saw as the 'heavy' in terms of the structure of the piece. Quite apart from the high cost of securing Tracy, however, and the likelihood that the actor might well be insulted by being offered the fourth part in a film, Kazan also wondered 'How is an audience going to "understand" a boy that can't get along with the genial Spencer Tracy?'[9] Ultimately he preferred Massey, feeling that the actor's essential stiffness and his traditional approach to acting was likely to feed the emotional tension that he wanted evident between him and Dean.

Cinematographer Ted McCord had photographed one of the director's favourite films, *The Treasure of the Sierra Madra* (1948), as well as *Johnny Belinda* (1948), but had never worked with CinemaScope before, having a lack of preconceived notions about the process that Kazan welcomed. The film was shot on locations in Mendocino, in Northern California, and in Salinas, as well as on the Warner back lot – with much attention being given to the 50ft. camera crane used to capture Cal and Abra in a carriage on top of a Ferris Wheel, in the scene at the fair. Approaching his first colour film, Kazan was keen to ensure that the scheme, with its emphasis on green and brown earth colours, was not 'prettified' by studio processing. The young characters are associated with these colours, while the director wanted a sombre and shadowy green for the final reconciliation between Cal and his dying father, suggesting both death and growth. He was worried that the Warners laboratory would fuss with the film and that the colours would come out, as he put it, like the illustrations on candy boxes. To prevent this he worked closely with a colour consultant, John Hambleton, who represented the director with the Warners colour technicians, and who he felt 'carried out my instructions and gave me just what I wanted'.[10]

In his book *The Composer in Hollywood*, Christopher Palmer argues that a case could be made for Elia Kazan being the 'main architect of musical reform in Hollywood'. Alex North had been the director's first choice to write the music, but given that they were no longer in contact after Kazan's testimony the director turned to the 28-year-old pianist and composer Leonard Rosenman, who was a New York friend of James Dean. His score for *East of Eden* (he also wrote the music for Nicholas Ray's *Rebel without a Cause*, a year later) has what Palmer sees as a 'thematic and contrapuntal complexity' that cut across the standard, romantic temper of Hollywood film music. Kazan remembered his experience at MGM and was suspicious of the power of the highly organised studio departments. Although he felt that the studio got 'Lennie damn cheap', there was friction with the Warners Music Department, and its head Ray Heindorf, over Kazan's man being put on salary. Rosenman, who was unusually present throughout shooting, was interested in creating a condition 'wherein the elements of literary naturalism are perceptually altered', creating a kind of 'super-reality', a sense that connected to Kazan's own interest in this film in a heightened or mythic sense of reality. The composer's dissonant motifs underscore Cal's loneliness and disturbed state of mind in the opening, 'silent' scene where he follows Kate to her 'house' in Monterey, while a lyrical theme marks the emerging love story. The repeating of the love theme over the last scene, the mythic resolution at Adam Trask's deathbed, reflects Kazan's key notion that the real love story in the film was that between Cal and his father.[11]

A key element of Kazan's responsibility to the studio was in securing a Production Code seal. When Fox had shown early interest in Steinbeck's novel Breen had felt that the material was 'unacceptable', drawing particular attention to the fact that the Kate character was a practising prostitute, yet 'escapes punishment'. In late 1953 Breen was telling Warner that he was still concerned with the brothel scenes and the sheriff's apparent condoning of Kate's house of ill-repute. Kazan, however, found the censors to be cooperative and tried to persuade them that he had no interest in depicting a 'whore-house' in detail, but that 'who their mother was' was crucial to the novel and screenplay.[12] In particular, as these issues remained unresolved, Kazan argued that it was morally better to present 'Kate's place' realistically as a grim and unattractive place ('I know whereof I speak') rather than as a more attractive 'social club', as in Fred Zinnemann's *From Here to Eternity* (1953). Breen's colleague Jack Vizzard was unconvinced, arguing that Kate should appear as the owner of a 'cleaned up' saloon, and that the director's protests would be more persuasive for a stage performance, rather than for the 'family audiences' that they were catering for. In fact the film presents a bar and gambling joint, although reference is made in the opening to an adjoining house that Kate also owns. Everything indicates the nature of Kate's 'business', and Cal later tells his father that he knows where she is and 'what she is'. Further, Breen wrote to Warner in June 1954, after the Code seal had been issued, insisting that Kate's reference to having the 'finest clientele' be omitted, but in fact the line appears in the released film. It was at this time that Kazan also made inquiries about the Code prospects for a film of Robert Anderson's play, *Tea and Sympathy*, which he had directed on Broadway in 1953. He told Warner that he had two offers to make the play into an '"art" movie for the art houses – no seal, no Legion approval', in the manner in which Otto Preminger's *The Moon is Blue* had been released without a Production Code seal in 1953.[13] The homosexual theme made any adaptation of the property problematic, although the film was eventually made by Vincente Minnelli at MGM in 1956, with changes made to satisfy first the Code office and then the Legion of Decency.

The opening images of the film, of the ocean waves breaking against the Monterey rocks, suggest an American duality between traditional morality, stern and biblical, and currents of thought and feeling that are more experimental and open. Kazan, looking for personal meaning in the text, responded to those parts of Steinbeck's novel that recalled for him his own fearful relationship with a father steeped in patriarchal, Anatolian ways. The young Kazan had resisted his father's injunction that he should join him in the family rug business, conspiring with his mother to discover other options for his life by going to college instead.[14] In the film it is the Julie Harris character, Abra, who acts as a surrogate mother in pointing the way forward for Cal. Although Kazan came to be unsympathetic to Dean – he felt he was quickly spoiled by success – and to the cult that developed around him, his sympathy in the film is with the misunderstood and unloved son, and the style of the film directly reflects the son's torment. The choice of Raymond Massey accentuates the father as unbending, unable to recognise and discuss his own pain at his separation from his wife, while Dean's awkward, Bohemian qualities made him perfect for Kazan's understanding of the spine of the film. When Adam rejects his son's gift of the money he had previously lost on his failed business venture, Kazan is happy to let Dean, apparently to Massey's surprise, improvise an anguished embrace of his father.

In *East of Eden* and *Rebel Without a Cause* the James Dean character played against equally problematic fifties fathers, both perceived (in different ways) as 'weak'. Adam Trask refers to a wound he has as a legacy of the Indian wars, and the resonance of Kazan's film, at the time and later, owed something to the experiences of children and adolescents who found their fathers to be emotionally remote following their war service. The director's enthusiasm for questioning puritan notions of morality, and absolute notions of good and bad, may also have related to his understanding of his own recent political experiences. As he later explained to Michel Ciment:

> I was trying to show that right and wrong get mixed up, and that there are values that have to be looked at more deeply than in that absolute approval-or-disapproval syndrome of my Left friends.[15]

Abra's line, 'It's awful not to be loved', could stand as an emblem of the feelings of the children of seemingly cold or absent fathers, the men in grey suits, in the business-oriented family structure of the mid-fifties. The sentiment also links *East of Eden* with the more explicitly contemporary and sociological context for *Rebel Without a Cause*, and with Nick Ray's more personal and persistent romanticism of the world of the young. Kazan was more sceptical of Dean's talents – seeing him as good only in a narrow type of role – but he certainly favoured the young actor in his direction and associated Cal with the good earth, particularly when he lies flat by the rows of beans that he sees as restoring his father's love. Kazan and Osborn also strengthened the women's roles, giving Kate – a woman who has rejected her sons – a self-respect and bitterness that is absent in the source novel. It is Julie Harris as Abra, however, who comes nearest to being the fulcrum of the piece, pointing the way towards personal renewal and emotional warmth and awareness. Her character rejects the unrealistic ideals of womanhood that Aron and his father share, and looks forward to the earth mothers of the sixties' counter-culture, like the emotionally open, generous and not always well used Alice in *Alice's Restaurant* (1969).

Abra tells Aron that his brother scares her and is 'like an animal'. Kazan exploits Dean's strangeness and insecurity right from the beginning, when he is shown *stalking* his mother in Monterey. The image fits in with Kazan's recurring interest in the primitive and animal instincts of his characters, evidenced in his writings and production notes, and in his emphasis on the primary expressive role of behaviour. (The director also observed wildlife in Africa, and later wrote about it in his novel *The Understudy*, while television scenes of animal behaviour are used in *The Arrangement*.) This interest was reflected in his long-term friendship with the playwright, screenwriter and anthropologist (and future student of the relationship between animal and human behaviours), Robert Ardrey. The sheriff (Ives) asks Cal if his father knows that he *'roams around at night'*, while later Cal climbs up on to a roof to talk through a bedroom window to Abra, and ascends and jumps down from the funfair Ferris Wheel. Cal is also seen retreating to and springing from groves and sheltering under the leaves of a willow tree, while at the fair he steps in with a flying leap to defend the German against locals stirred up by wartime jingoism. Kazan's notion is that animal behaviour is instinctive and true, and can enrich a performance and root it in reality.

Early work in this widescreen process tended to lead to longer takes, as the form was considered to be less suitable for the traditional montage filmmaking of classical Hollywood, and this is evident in much of the film. The format also tended to be seen as favouring the spectacle of the Western, musical or historical pageant, and Kazan's use of the medium for a more intimate, family drama was an innovation.[16] He often softens or obscures the edges of the screen and uses lighting to break up the frame, particularly in the high proportion of night or low light interior scenes. In the first of the four scenes in Kate's place, when Cal meets Anne (waif meets waif, said Kazan), a third of the horizontal image is taken up with the shadow of Dean's head. A limited range of generally sombre shades and colours is used, with particular reference to earth colours – dark browns and greens. This scheme is used in particular in the last scene of the film, at Adam Trask's bedside, where the old man makes peace with his son and life passes to a new generation. Elsewhere Kazan uses objects in the immediate foreground to create depth, as with the early scene in the ice-house – another notion (together with the breaking up of the frame) that he had noted in the John Ford films he ran at Twentieth Century-Fox. Depth of field, considered difficult given the lenses available in the early widescreen process, is used most effectively when Adam, with Cal behind him, watches the train set off for Chicago carrying all his hopes. The black smoke bodes rather ominously

Period pastoral: Julie Harris and James Dean, *East of Eden* (1955). Courtesy of BFI.

for the plan, and for the relationship of father and son. The tilting of the camera during the early Bible reading and at the climactic birthday party further suggests the unbalanced and artificial nature of this relationship, while the sense of equilibrium is restored in the elevated view of Adam's bedroom as father is reconciled with son and the young couple become the hope for the future.

Writing for the new mid-fifties magazine *Film Culture*, Andrew Sarris saw Kazan as mastering the widescreen process and as stripping away the social context of the story to 'concentrate on the feelings of the characters' and the Cain and Abel parable. It was perhaps strange for Kazan to be criticised for an 'elliptical style that never fully explains or resolves any situation with language'. Instead Kazan creates for the first but not the last time a strong sense of the pastoral – particularly in the first extended conversation between Cal and Abra in the field of wild mustard, with the mountains far off in the distance. As Leo Braudy has argued, Dean, like Brando, represented and articulated 'feelings of insecurity and impotent rage' that were outside the formal concerns of the story but which had resonance in the society of the time; these feelings opened the film to a rising generation who were uninterested in biblical fables. Michael Butler, son of the blacklisted writer Hugo Butler, remembers seeing the film in a theatre in Mexico and being profoundly affected. He notes Dean's 'palpable access to emotion and his pitch-perfect rendering of what he felt' and sees Kazan as the 'alchemist who had legitimised my generation's pain'.[17]

One critic at the time, however, found that 'Dean tries so hard to find the part in himself that he often forgets to put himself in the part'. There are those who have seen Cal Trask/James Dean as 'taking over' in *East of Eden* rather as Brando dominated, at the expense of broader social analysis, in *On the Waterfront*. To the *Time* reviewer Kazan's concern with Cal's 'father problem' over-dominates the film, while Jonathan Miller argued that 'Steinbeck's tendentious story, with its heavy, uninformative symbolism, is only rescued from complete absurdity by Dean's piracy and Kazan's bravura direction'. At one level the film is over-expository, with too much emphasis in the script on goodness and badness. Yet Kazan was aware of John Howard Lawson's notion of unity in drama in terms of climax and felt that the climax should be a 'concrete realisation of the theme in terms of an event'. The key scene in terms of Lawson's schema is that of Cal's birthday gift to his father, an event that leads directly to the story's resolution and new equilibrium. While presenting a contemporarily resonant story Kazan serves the original parable with an at times baroque visual style that was unusual in his directing career, but the film does achieve a pared down essentialism in its treatment of the need for love.[18] Cal cannot buy it, and nor can customers at his mother's establishment.

East of Eden was released in April 1955 and Kazan declined to go to the Cannes Film Festival in 1955 in support of the film, fearing the kind of 'pushing around' that he had experienced the year before. Despite the entreaties of the Festival, James Dean did not go either as he was already at work with Nicolas Ray on *Rebel Without a Cause*. Joseph Hummel, the Warner Bros. man in Paris, was disappointed that the film missed out on the first prize, which 'we thought was "in the bag"!' Instead *East of Eden* was awarded a separate prize for 'best dramatic picture'. To Hummel the studio's 'enthusiasm and manoeuvres were no match for the severe pressure exercised by the Communists against Kazan', a pressure manifested by booing from the 'Communist front' when the award was announced. He quoted the verdict of *Le Figaro* that the jury had, in awarding the top prize to *Marty* (1955), 'placed the "small masters" above the "GREAT" masters'. On 30 September, having just completed the film *Giant*, for George Stevens, James Dean died in a car crash. Kazan wrote to Jack Warner: 'Wasn't that terrible about Dean? Everyone's reaction here is in two words: it figured. I know it must be a blow to you all out there because he had the makings of a big star. Just a waste.'[19]

The origins of *Baby Doll* (1956), Kazan's first film for his independent company, Newtown Productions, lay in discussions between director and playwright in late 1951, when Tennessee Williams drove down to the Mississippi Delta with Kazan and his wife to collect background material. Jack Warner was keen to follow up the success of *A Streetcar Named Desire* and the studio purchased the rights to six of the playwright's one act plays, although Kazan was to use only two of them, *Twenty-Seven Wagons Full of Cotton* and the shorter work, *The Long Stay Cut Short* or *The Unsatisfactory Supper*. For much of 1952 Jack Warner was impatient for Kazan to sign a contract for the proposed film, although Joseph Breen had reacted with 'deep concern' to a loose, initial script, disliking its 'low and sordid tone'. Writing from Germany, Kazan told Warner that he was 'trying to get Williams to sit down one of these months and really complete his job on the script', but despite these problems, he signed a contract with the studio in May 1953. Kazan was to be paid $50,000 – half the fee agreed for the partly 'pre-sold' *East of Eden* – together with 25 per cent of the net receipts, while casting was to be by mutual agreement between Kazan and Warner.[20] Scripting and Code problems, together with the other commitments of playwright and director, meant that the screenplay was still incomplete in mid-1955, when Kazan, enthused by his success at the Academy Awards and with the release of *East of Eden*, made a final effort to make the film as his first for his own production company.

The script that slowly emerged in the first half of the fifties was a chamber piece for three major characters, set in rural and small town Mississippi over two days. The story concerns a 19-year-old child bride, Baby Doll Meighan, who lives in a dilapidated mansion with a husband, Archie Lee, of twice her age. In an opening, definitive assessment, Baby Doll describes her husband as 'a mess'. We learn that there is an agreement that their marriage not be consummated until Baby Doll's twentieth birthday, two days hence. The only other inhabitant of the once grand building is the sister of Baby Doll's dead father, an ancient and rather addled visitor and sometime cook, Aunt Rose Comfort. Archie's Lee's livelihood, such as it is, is based on the operation of a run down cotton gin, employing a number of local black workers. An outsider, Silva Vacarro, a Sicilian immigrant who operates a neighbouring cotton gin, becomes the catalyst for the drama. When his cotton gin is burnt down, Vacarro rightly suspects that Archie Lee is responsible and he engages with Baby Doll, apparently with the objective of collecting evidence on the crime. The published script is imprecise about the precise extent of Vaccaro's 'seduction' of Baby Doll, but the Sicilian is happy for Archie Lee to be so frustrated by his suspicion that he finally goes wild with a rifle and is taken away by the local marshal. In the published script Vaccaro stays with Baby Doll, but in the film he leaves, promising to return. In a closing line supplied by Williams only in January 1956, with location filming half completed, Baby Doll tells Aunt Rose that 'We got nothing to do but wait for tomorrow, and see if we're remembered, or forgotten'.[21]

There were frictions between Kazan and Williams over the script. Williams objected to some of Kazan's suggestions concerning the ending (at one point Archie Lee was to kill the Sicilian, while at another one of the black characters was the victim of a stray bullet), while he also disliked changes that his friend had pressured him to make to the third act of *Cat on a Hot Tin Roof*, which Kazan had directed on Broadway in March 1955. The playwright constantly returned to Kazan as his director and collaborator of choice, yet complained at times both of his undue influence and tendency to 'excess'. In July 1955 Williams even talked of the director being given a writing or 'adaptation' credit, although his agent Audrey Wood advised him to leave such 'business' negotiations to her.[22]

The other problem related to the need for a Production Code seal. There were extensive discussions in the summer of 1955, when Geoffrey Shurlock, who had replaced the ailing Joseph Breen, still saw 'serious Code violations' in the script. The office objected to the use by Vacarro of adultery as a means of achieving revenge against Archie Lee, although Williams wanted the issue of whether the seduction is completed to be left to the audience. Shurlock also urged the removal of a series of elements in the screenplay that underlined Archie Lee's 'sex frustration'. The bulk of these issues were unresolved when the company gathered in Mississippi for rehearsals and to absorb the local atmosphere. Kazan reported to Warner in November that he had no problems with the concern of Shurlock with adultery, because to him 'there is going to be no adultery in the picture, not even the deferred variety'. In a rather slippery way he told Warner that 'Nothing is going to happen and there is going to be no hint of anything happening'. Yet Kazan flatly refused to make the other changes, feeling that the whole story was based on Archie Lee's 'sex frustration', and that if he tampered with this 'I'd have to throw away the whole picture'. In November Warner advised Kazan to 'go right ahead and make the picture', reassuring him that Shurlock and the 'boys' would 'not stop the wheels of progress'. Despite last minute telegrams and consultations, shooting began with the understanding that the Production Code office would decide on the Code by viewing the completed film.[23]

With cast and crew based in Greenville, Mississippi, Kazan began rehearsals, before filming began in the small town of Benoit, where there was a nearby plantation house which perfectly represented the crumbling edifice of the old white South. The three-storey building had no doubt been imposing, with its pillared frontage, but was now falling to pieces. Built in 1848, it had once been the centre of a plantation where more than 300 slaves engaged in the cultivation of cotton and corn. It was a perfect symbol for the Old South in the mid-fifties, before both the economic boom and the civil rights movement that would lead to radical change. Shooting continued in Mississippi from November until the end of January 1956 and the company then flew to New York, where the bulk of the interiors were filmed at the recently refurbished Warner Bros. studio in Brooklyn.[24]

With production wrapped at the end of February, a rough cut was ready to show Production Code Administration officials in July 1956. Although the basic story was deemed acceptable, there were still objections, and it was not until September that Kazan persuaded the PCA vice president Jack Vizzard to issue a seal. Vizzard was struck by the 'spirit of self-assertion of the new independents' and interestingly saw the film as a 'socioeconomic commentary', emphasising the efforts of the 'trashy whites' to sustain the status quo. Vincent Brook, in his study of the censorship saga relating to the film, concluded that with the issuing of a seal Kazan had 'won on almost all counts'.[25] Epithets such as 'wop' and 'nigger' survive in the film against the express instructions of the Production Code, while the doctor scene (discussed later) remains, with its implication of Archie Lee's impotence. In short, Lee's 'sex frustration' remains central to the story. Arthur Knight's comment, in reviewing the film, that it 'makes no effort to reward the good and punish the wicked', can be taken as a broader reflection on the now weakened enforcement of the Production Code on American cinema, as well as a comment on the way the film differed from mainstream Hollywood practice.[26]

Yet, as with *A Streetcar Named Desire*, the Production Code judgement cut no ice with the Legion of Decency, which felt that the Production Code office was falling down in enforcing the Code. Given wartime and post-war social changes the Code was becoming less relevant to fifties America, while the Paramount anti-trust decision, forcing the studios to divest themselves of their control over theatres, had lessened the impact of the Code by weakening the power of the major studios. The Code still presumed a Hollywood product designed for a mass, family audience, while many filmmakers and producers now looked to adult themes to stem the post-war decline in audiences. Kazan argued, in a letter to Jack Warner from Greenville: 'We've got to break down our taboos and strike out for interestingly unusual and daring material. Either that or just quit and sign up with the TV guys.' On 27 November 1956, a month before the film's New York opening, the Legion of Decency gave the film a 'C' (Condemned) classification. The Legion found the film to be 'morally repellent both in theme and treatment' and declared that its 'subject matter' indicated 'an open disregard of the Code by its administrators'. The *Motion Picture Herald* characterised the film less as 'entertainment' than as part of a 'school of picture-making' associated with foreign producers.[27] Martin Quigley, who had co-written the Production Code back in 1930 and who had acted for Warners during the additional censorship of A *Streetcar Named Desire*, now persuaded Francis Cardinal Spellman of New York, just back from Korea, to denounce *Baby Doll* publicly – sight unseen, from the pulpit of St. Patrick's Cathedral – as unpatriotic and immoral. On Sunday 16 December 1956 he exhorted Catholics not to see the film 'under pain of sin'. Spellman's involvement gave the film publicity, while undoubtedly reducing the number of the film's bookings throughout the country. The *Time* notice did not help: the reviewer called the film 'possibly the dirtiest American made motion picture', a 'sullen drama of degeneracy in the South'. Kazan felt that the Church campaign had hurt the picture, although Brook concludes that 'Spellman's condemnation not only failed to kill the film at the box office but may have helped it turn a slight profit'.[28]

The film's box office prospects were also hurt by the absence of Hollywood stars. Kazan had considered using Marilyn Monroe as Baby Doll but instead decided on Carroll Baker after Tennessee Williams had seen her play the role at the Actors Studio. Baker had appeared in the yet unreleased *Giant* (1956), and Kazan talked about her to that film's director, George Stevens. *Baby Doll* was to be Eli Wallach's first film role as Silva Vacarro, while Karl Malden (Archie Lee) was making his fourth film appearance for the director, and Mildred Dunnock (Aunt Rose) was reunited with Kazan having been in the Broadway cast of *Death of a Salesman*. All these principals, together with Lonny Chapman and the uncredited Rip Torn and Madeleine Sherwood, were Actors Studio alumni, while the other 'bits' are taken by locals. To Leo Braudy the so-called Method actors were naturals for the film medium, where 'sound engineers could pick up the most inaudible anguish or cameraman focus on the most fleeting gesture'. Kazan always had a more catholic approach to Method acting than Lee Strasberg, installed as Artistic Director of the Actors Studio in 1951, and was quite happy to use what worked. Baker recalls Kazan taking each actor aside and delving 'deeply into the analogy between the character's traits and your own', while Wallach remembers the director inviting and then accepting his suggestion that the Vaccaro character would not push his seduction of Baby Doll to its ultimate sexual conclusion. Kazan also remembers encouraging Wallach to act like Vittorio De Sica and 'not be afraid of gestures', while the actor recalls the director warning that he would cut away from him if he did not make the lemonade sufficiently interestingly. Karl Malden recalls discussion of the stock characters of the Italian theatrical tradition of commedia dell'arte, and of his own character's resemblance to Pantalone, or a buffoon. A French critic at the time of the film's release saw Varacco, whip in hand, as

'An unhealthy relationship': Carroll Baker and Karl Malden in *Baby Doll* (1956). Courtesy of BFI.

a sort of Mississippi Petrucio, and Archie Lee as stupid to the point of being touching, with Malden's 'remarkable' performance recalling that of Emil Jannings, most memorably perhaps in *Der Blaue Engel* (*The Blue Angel*) (Josef von Sternberg, 1930).[29]

Writing at the time in his production notebook for the film, the director felt that the 'nearest thing to it is Pagnol, who also mixes comedy and tragedy!' *Cesar* (1936), directed by the French playwright and filmmaker Marcel Pagnol from a screenplay based on his own play, was shot in Marseilles and used local sound and accents that captured the texture of regional French life. Characters reveal themselves by extended conversation and sexual issues are to the fore. There are no really base or vile characters in Pagnol's films, and both Kazan and Williams came to see something similar in the relationships in their own creation. Although Archie Lee is pathetic rather than tragic, there is certainly some attempt to encourage sympathy for his desperation, as he shares a bottle with one of the mansion's black retainers and is genuinely desperate and distraught at the prospect of losing his wife. Kazan felt that the situation in the Williams script was essentially comic – 'I don't mean farcical, or even "funny" – but by nature, comic'. He mentioned Pagnol to Williams, and although the playwright was not sure that he had ever seen a Pagnol film, he immediately saw the implication in terms of a lightness and a playfulness of tone.[30] In an early scene in which Lee enters Baby Doll's bathroom, provoking first laughter and then screams, the frustrated and 'wet' suitor is left alone with the camera, rather like Oliver Hardy contemplating 'another fine mess' with his audience.

Kazan noted that he made *Baby Doll* 'as I saw it': 'I did the best I could to get on film what I felt in the South. Not the way things should be. Not the way they will some day be. But the way they appeared to me there and then.' He is in part describing an elaboration of the semi-documentary method used first in a studio context with *Boomerang!* and *Panic in the Streets*. He worked to implant his script with the life and character of the locality, and for him this meant not just the racial iniquities of the Deep South, but also the sense of generosity that he found there. A poster for the film captures something of this goal: '*Baby Doll* is real. All its people are wrong and right, magnificent and foolish, violent and weak – the way all people are. It is not meant to be moral or unmoral, only truthful. It is bold. But it is real.' The most noticeable addition to the script is the 20 or more roles for local black people. There are only three references to black characters in the published Williams script. Five local residents were also flown to New York for the scenes in the Café, including the real Sheriff of Benoit and his Deputy and a black waitress who sings the 'negro spiritual', 'I shall not be moved'.[31] Her appeal to scripture foreshadows the political resistance to come in the South. As well as the recurring role of African Americans in observing and commenting on the action, two local Chinese Americans also get to use laughter to 'place' the supposedly dominant white man.

A particularly effective example of both directing actors and staging comes with Archie Lee's early trip down town to consult his doctor. While Baby Doll spars with a young dentist (played by Rip Torn, his first screen role), Archie Lee suffers the double embarrassment of making a public spectacle of the distance between his desire – for a woman 20 years his junior – and his capacity. It is suggested that Lee is impotent and also possibly a cuckold; the black 'workers' have already suggested, before Vacarro's arrival, that there have been other gentleman callers. In the doctor's office a nurse (Madeleine Sherwood) watches Archie Lee's humiliation. When the doctor (played by Kazan's friend, the Actors Studio lawyer John S. Dudley) prescribes a minor sedative she tells Lee that 'it's not going to help what's wrong with you one bit'. All the while, on the doctor's desk, a small skull casts a beady eye on proceedings. Generally seen through the related perspectives of sex and sordidness, *Baby Doll* in fact works well in its own comic terms as a black comedy about small town life and sex, and about a social realm still waiting to catch up with the ideals of the New Deal.

Kazan says that he tried to capture 'the South in microcosm' in the film, while later he added that it was a 'black comedy' that was 'not intended as a criticism of the soul of the South'. A number of subsequent commentators have discussed in some detail a political sub-text of the film that was largely Kazan's creation and which was neglected in interpretations of the time. Michael Stragow, for example, has argued that 'Almost accidentally, the movie captures the historical moment just before the Old South finally gave way to the New'.[32] The story is set in the early fifties, at a time when Baby Doll is awaiting her twentieth birthday (she tells Vaccaro that she was born on the day that Franklin Delano Roosevelt was first elected as President). Even when viewed in 1956 the film preceded the main momentum of the civil rights movement. The black characters are outside the main drama, but collectively they play an important and privileged role in defining the overall tone of the film. They are half 'waiting for Godot' and half waiting for history to give them the chance to step out of the narrative sidelines. They help define the main characters, particularly the two male protagonists and their 'comic' concern with their masculine power – limited as this may be in Lee's case.

Philip C. Kolin, appropriately of the University of Southern Mississippi, has most strongly articulated the view that *Baby Doll*, far from lacking an overall perspective, was an 'attack on racism at a crucial junction in American social history'. Certainly this was an important time, with the first shoots of the civil rights movement beginning to show. It was in 1954 that the Supreme Court had issued its dramatic ruling on school segregation, following it the next year with the injunction on the authorities to desegregate with 'all deliberate speed'. In reaction to what was seen as unjustified federal meddling the white Citizens' Councils were mobilising in the State to resist the Court and restrict any shift towards greater integration. To V.O. Key, writing in 1949, the state of Mississippi 'manifests in accentuated form the darker political stains that run throughout the South'. The race issue became more important on the national agenda in December 1955, when, as *Baby Doll* was being shot, Rosa Parks refused to give up her seat to a white man on a bus in Montgomery, in the neighbouring state of Alabama, leading to a year long city wide boycott of buses that led eventually to their desegregation and to the emergence of Martin Luther King to national prominence. In addition, it was in the Mississippi Delta in August 1955 that a black teenager from Chicago, Emmett Till, was murdered, his body thrown into the Tallahatchie River with a cotton gin fan tied to his neck with barbed wire; in what was to become a notorious case, the white suspects were acquitted, although they subsequently admitted the crime.[33]

On location, *Baby Doll* (1956): Eli Wallach and Carroll Baker on the right. Courtesy of
Wesleyan Cinema Archives.

The appearances of black characters, singing, watching, laughing or making
pointed comments, are a planned and persistent element in the structure of the
film, from the opening scene in which Archie Lee tries ineffectually to give
instructions to a black man on the roof of his house. The respective position of
the two characters in relation to this dilapidated old plantation house immediately undercuts the dominant local status – by nature of race – of the white
man. The fact that Archie Lee is not ginning cotton may explain their inactiv-
ity, but collectively they represent an active chorus. To underline the local segregation there are signs in the café, and when Baby Doll accompanies her
husband to see the doctor they pass water coolers, one for 'Coloureds' and one
for 'Whites'. The blacks, disenfranchised in the real world of Southern politics
and largely invisible to the whites (so that Archie does not mind playing the fool
to them, secure in his sense of racial superiority), do make their point. It soon
becomes clear that the black characters who watch and comment on the action
at regular intervals – lurking like plantation ghosts – find Archie Lee to be a
man completely without status, racial or otherwise, and to be deserving only of

laughter and derision. At the conclusion of the story there is little expectation that Archie Lee will face 'justice', as he appeals to the marshal as 'white man to white man'.

Kazan enjoyed the community of the New York-based crew on location, holding parties for the locals and also celebrating Thanksgiving and Christmas. He used Boris Kaufman again as his cinematographer, and later reflected that he made great use of 'white on white to help describe the washed out Southern whites'. Baby Doll has bleached blonde hair, the mansion is white, or off-white, and the land around seems parched also, with winter trees. (Set in late fall, the film was shot in December and January.) Kaufman was aware that the film did not 'fit into the conventional forms of comedy or melodrama', while Kazan was happy at Kaufman's ability to transform a 'beyond-repair Mississippi mansion into a symbol of a civilisation long gone by'.[34] Anna Hill Johnstone dressed actors with clothes bought locally, while the young art director Richard Sylbert, assisted by his brother Paul, assembled the objects given expressive use in the film, from the antique car, a Pierce-Arrow, to the elaborate swing that is the centrepiece of the long 'seduction' scene. Kazan introduced another composer to post-studio American filmmaking, in Kenyon Hopkins, and his score, directed by Warners' head of music Ray Heindorf, combines pop, jazz, blues and rock and roll influences, and lightly suggests the story's mix of innocent and erotic possibilities. Kazan seemed to welcome a return to the 1.33: 1 aspect ratio (*On the Waterfront* had been released in 1.85:1), using long and medium shots while also using a tight two shot to show Baby Doll's 'seduction' during their near 'real time' afternoon encounter. Working for the first time for his own production company, Kazan reluctantly entrusted the processing to the Warner Bros. laboratory, although he insisted on supervising closely to ensure that it is not 'prettified or velvet-ized, or Leon Shamroy-ized'. He also threw himself with gusto into issues of advertising and showmanship, suggesting for example that a 60-foot billboard be used to promote the film in New York.[35]

Contemporary reviewers were uncertain about the content of the film, while they generally admired Kazan's direction and the performances. Bosley Crowther wrote of Kazan's 'superb direction', yet referred to all the roles as 'without character, content or consequence', with Baby Doll in particular being 'White trash' to Blanche DuBois's 'woman of a certain culture'. To Arthur Knight *Baby Doll* was 'Kazan's most skilful film to date' as well as being 'one of the most unhealthy and amoral pictures ever made in this country'. Crowther also compared *Baby Doll* unfavourably with Federico Fellini's *La Strada* (1954). Performances in that film were also both broad and affecting, although arguably Zampano (Anthony Quinn) is more authentically tragic, as he, too late, pines for his lost partner. Kazan and Williams – born in Mississippi – stand back, but the film is never a cosmopolitan or patrician view of the local culture. This is more the tone of several reviews, such as Crowther, in his 'Streetcar on Tobacco Road' column. However, Max Lerner in the *New York Post* was more sympathetic to Kazan's own semi-documentary method, writing of the film's feeling for local faces and its 'portrayal of how the Southern tradition of gentility (the Chivalry, as it used to be called) has come to a tattered and degenerate end'. Into this decaying world comes the 'outsider', a Sicilian from Corpus Christi – 'How unusual', comments Baby Doll on hearing of his origins. There is an element here of Kazan the Anatolian outsider, a primitive cutting through the gentility and hypocrisy of local manners. Tennessee Williams was not consistent in his views on the completed film. He first saw it as primarily Kazan's creation, but in 1965 he noted that *Baby Doll* pleased him very much. He was less enthusiastic in his 1977 memoirs, where he expressed the view that the 'wanton hilarity' of his work had not been 'rightly used'.[36]

Williams ends his Chaucerian story, his 'Mississippi Delta Comedy', with Archie Lee clearly getting his comeuppance, as he finds that membership of all the organisations in the Delta is insufficient to prevent him being thrown in jail like a black man. Although the ending of the film is open, with both Vacarro and Archie Lee leaving and the two women waiting in the house, it is the outsider who is vindicated. A synopsis issued at the time by Warners ends with the statement that 'Vacarro has promised to return the next day, and it seems likely that he will'.[37] Kazan's feeling for Vacarro as an immigrant, a fellow citizen of an ancient race, is obvious. If he does return, or even if he does not, there is a strong sense that Baby Doll has grown up and become a woman because of the experience. She wears light, girlish clothes in the early scenes and a dark, more formal outfit at the supper at the end.

François Truffaut, in his 1957 review, saw the film as daring in its treatment of sex, although he felt that Kazan was a director of scenes rather than of either shots or films. The film 'plays' at times rather like the Actors Studio exercise that it once was, as an exercise in the games and glances of sexual game playing. The question of whether the seduction actually occurs – the director leaves the issue unclear despite his assurances to Warner and the Production Code office – is less important than the game itself. Kazan, having fought to retain the clarity of the key rape scene in *A Streetcar Named Desire*, seems to delight in creating ambiguity about the 'climax', or anti-climax, of the dalliance between Vacarro and Baby Doll. Those used to reading the standard Hollywood means of circumventing the Breen office are certainly given some 'evidence', although as the French critic and director argued the gestures and glances, the animal behaviour, is more important than any overall thesis or resolution.[38]

In no other film does Kazan make better use of what seem to be found objects – the mansion left empty for 30 years and the junk surrounding it. When Vacarro and Baby Doll climb into the wreck of a car the action is in part motivated, if motivation is needed, by the lack of furniture in the house. Kazan might here have had his own sense memory of 'driving' a similar rubbish tip wreck of a vehicle, in the making of the experimental mid-thirties short, *Pie in the Sky*. The film also demonstrates the achievements of the director's documentary technique, using non-professional actors and the local environment as an element of the story. The humour is now more evident than the sexual excess that was seen in 1956. As for the characters, Baby Doll defends herself with some spirit, grows at the story's end, and has a last word of some awareness. Even Archie Lee and Vacarro come near to engaging our understanding, particularly as they sit silently on the bottom step of the staircase, all passion spent after their respective afternoon exertions. Elsewhere the lack of a clear resolution and the moral ambivalence, together with the game playing, the 'hide and seek', suggest something of the feel of the emerging worlds of 'art' theatre and film. A parallel might be made with Joseph Losey, who had worked briefly with Kazan (and Nicholas Ray) in the short-lived Dollar Theatre project in 1940 and had moved to Britain in the early fifties to avoid the blacklist. Losey's own, distinctive use of space to denote struggles for dominance – and the role of an outsider as a catalyst – is seen most clearly in his 1963 collaboration with Harold Pinter in *The Servant*. The social aspects of Kazan's film – capturing something of the benighted American South of its time – have been neglected, yet it is also a much riskier, genuinely independent project, a chamber piece of convincingly human and semi-comic struggles for respect and survival.

6

Journeys in the American South

It was in the mid-fifties that Kazan made or planned three films that explored the problematic American culture of the South. After *Baby Doll* (1956), set in the Mississippi Delta, came *A Face in the Crowd* (1957), a film which charted the rise of an Arkansas 'country boy' entertainer to the new and powerful New York world of television and public relations. Intended as a warning about the potential of television to provide a platform for right wing politics, Kazan's renewed collaboration with Budd Schulberg was, under an agreement of January 1955, to be his second film for Newtown Productions. It was also in the mid-fifties that he had the idea of developing a script from a novel about the Tennessee Valley Authority in the thirties by Southern writer and investigative journalist William Bradford Huie. The result of a protracted period of work was *Wild River* (1960), a film that was shot entirely on location in Tennessee, in CinemaScope. *Baby Doll* had dealt with the impact of an immigrant outsider on the Old South, while an early idea for *Wild River*, from Molly, was that it would chart a 'clash of two civilisations', represented by a Jewish New Deal intellectual on the one hand and on the other by a Southern matriarch who wants to resist change and the federal imposition of 'progress'.[1]

One of Kazan's friends, the playwright and screenwriter Robert Ardrey, paid tribute in the mid-fifties to what he saw as the director's desire to 'make available to the screen the writing of first class people', although he also pointed out that it was not an easy matter to combine 'the creative freedom that a director must have with the creative freedom that an author must have'.[2] Schulberg and Kazan felt that they had solved the problem with their agreement, made before *On the Waterfront*, that the director would respect Schulberg's screenplay as he would a play by Tennessee Williams or Arthur Miller in the theatre. Yet some tensions were created by Kazan's new role as producer and by his increasing involvement in setting the main story line and themes of his film projects. With the huge success of their first collaboration, recognised at the box office and at the 1955 Academy Awards ceremony, both of them cast around for a follow up project. They discussed the theme of Puerto Rican immigration to New York, and would return to this as a notion in the late sixties, but as an immediate project Kazan suggested that Schulberg work on 'Your Arkansas Traveller', one of the short stories published in his 1954 book, *Some Faces in the Crowd*. The story dealt with a morally bankrupt country boy (from Arkansas) who, with the help of an educated woman, a radio producer, becomes a national media figure in Chicago and then New York. He dies accidentally and huge crowds attend his funeral, while the woman contemplates her role in shaping his career and legend. Lonesome Rhodes is a monster, while the woman looks down her nose both at him and at the television audience that he comes to enslave.[3]

Kazan and Schulberg were engaged by the growing impact of television in politics. They discussed how the new medium might have enhanced the impact of thirties figures such as Huey Long, while they also talked about Richard Nixon's 'Chequers' television broadcast during the 1952 campaign, and the apparent role of the new medium in the dissemination of the anti-Communist agenda and subsequently in the downfall of Senator Joseph McCarthy at the televised 1954 Army–McCarthy hearings. In his original story Schulberg had mentioned the celebrated Oklahoma cowboy turned columnist, broadcaster and movie star Will Rogers, a figure described by historian Peter Rollins as 'one of the most important moulders of opinion in America from 1922 until his untimely death in 1935'. Kazan and Schulberg were also concerned at the commercialisation of television in the second half of the fifties, a period in which serious journalists such as Ed Murrow felt that the public service role in broadcasting was being marginalised by an increasing emphasis on celebrity and entertainment. A figure mentioned a number of times in Kazan's notes is the radio and early television star Arthur Godfrey. With his Southern folksiness and apparent spontaneity on live television, Godfrey generated millions of advertising dollars for the CBS network, and was described in Vance Packard's classic study of the 'American Advertising Machine', *The Hidden Persuaders* (1957), as 'the most powerful salesman of our times'. In the ending used in the film Schulberg and Kazan also refer to the apocryphal story of children's broadcaster Don Carney, who, as 'Uncle Don', was supposed to have lost his position following an unguarded remark on a radio show. (In the film a mock *Variety* headline announces 'LR'S BLOOPER TOPS UNK DON'S. 50 MILLION FANS SHOCKED'.) Kazan felt that power was flowing to newly wealthy figures 'whose only culture is Las Vagas and the *Saturday Evening Post* and the *Readers Digest*', together with people like Godfrey who 'think they know something because they can entertain people'.[4]

Schulberg remembers that he and Kazan saw eye to eye on most issues. In the summer of 1955 the two of them prepared for their new project by researching the world of Madison Avenue advertising and also the emerging role of television in political campaigns. It was in the 1956 Presidential race that, for the first time, more campaign money was spent on television than on radio. Dwight D. Eisenhower had been the first candidate to use television advertisements in 1952 – crude efforts showing the General's supposed responses to the queries of ordinary citizens – and in 1956, campaigning for re-election, he was advised on the new medium by actor Robert Montgomery. In their efforts to research the new significance of the media for politics, Kazan and Schulberg talked to Senators Al Gore Sr. and Stuart Symington, and also Senate Majority Leader Lyndon Johnson. Johnson was certain that television was giving people a chance to look close into the eyes of politicians and that this was changing the nature of politics. Politicians, he argued, had not been seen that close before, and he felt aware of the need to keep his own eyes steady when looking at the camera.[5] The film also makes other references to the media of the time, with appearances from legendary columnist Walter Winchell and news anchors John Cameron Swayze and Mike Wallace, while the choice of Memphis as a setting points to the disc jockey Dewey Philips, who dominated mid-South airwaves in the early fifties and was first to play rhythm and blues music by black artists. It was also in 1956 that the Memphis-based Elvis Presley first appeared on television and became a national phenomenon.

On *A Face in the Crowd*, despite their closeness, there is some evidence that Kazan sometimes found it difficult to reconcile his pact with Budd Schulberg with his new role as producer. Kazan wrote about his understanding of this role to Ardrey, arguing that although he did not want to 'write a line of dialogue', he did want 'to be creatively involved in the choice, shape, and telling of any stories I do from now on'. Certainly *A Face in the Crowd* was to present Kazan with new responsibilities, given the high budget, of $1,600,000 and the extensive use of the newly opened Gold Medal Studios in the Bronx. The bulk of the film was shot there, with additional location work in Memphis, Tennessee and Piggott, Arkansas. The refurbished studio, which was the largest outside of Hollywood and which was to aid the fifties revival of New York filmmaking, had started out as the Biograph Studios (1913–28), where D.W. Griffith and others had launched their careers. Kazan certainly saw his production company as an opportunity to avoid a number of the constraints of the past. As he told Schulberg before starting out on *Baby Doll*, 'I didn't start this fucking company to hurry or be hurried'.[6]

Following the joint work on research and scouting locations Schulberg worked on the script with the goal of completing it in April 1956. Yet Kazan became anxious about the screenplay, and particularly the ending, which at that time involved the suicide of the central protagonist, Lonesome Rhodes. While Kazan liked the ending he expressed doubts to his partner, worrying that the 'high, old fashioned theatrics' had to be believable to the audience and that if they were not it could 'all suddenly ring hollow as hell'. Molly also advised that 'This guy is not a suicidal type', a line that was included in the final script. Paul Osborn was also consulted, and as well as questioning the suicide he asked a broader and pertinent question: 'Is point of this: power corrupts, or is he a louse from start?' Following this, in late May, there was a slightly uncomfortable script discussion between Kazan, Osborn and Schulberg which also involved Sam Spiegel. It was Spiegel who had called for seemingly endless script revisions to *On the Waterfront*, to the writer's frustration, and here the producer felt that the ending was 'terribly theatrical', that the Lonesome Rhodes character had insufficient stature, and that the script needed 'another couple of months of hard work'. Schulberg generally defended his script, although he did agree to look again at the ending.[7]

In the first part of the film we see Marcia Jeffreys, an Arkansas woman in her late twenties who has returned South after graduating at Sarah Lawrence College, 'discover' 'Lonesome' Rhodes. Lonesome is introduced as a heavy drinking country boy with an eye for the main chance but also a gift for powerful, blues based songs about his experience. Working for her uncle's small town radio station, Marcia sees that Lonesome has a gift for the medium, while also falling for his mix of crude energy and charm. He sings and tells folksy stories, projecting a populist stance that causes a stir and soon attracts interest from agents and television stations in Memphis. There his television career takes off, despite his lack of interest at this stage in pleasing his commercial sponsors. The central section of the film works as a satire on New York PR and advertising, represented by Lonesome's rising star agent Joey De Palma and the 'organisation men' of Browning, Schlagel and McNally, the company that hires Lonesome for its sponsored TV show, the 'Vitajex Hour'. Thereafter, script and film deal alternately with the personal and public roles and relationships of Lonesome Rhodes. In public terms, the wealthy owner of Vitajex sees Lonesome as a potential 'wielder of opinion' on behalf of a right-wing political agenda associated with his friend and would be President, Senator Worthington Fuller. The increasingly powerful figure of Lonesome Rhodes loses much nuance, while he betrays Marcia personally: a previous marriage is revealed, while he marries and then 'fires' a 19-year-old girl from Pickett, Arkansas. Finally Marcia, who uses New York writer Mel Miller as adviser and sounding board, exposes her 'Frankenstein' to the people by turning up the sound during one of his television shows, so broadcasting to the nation his unguarded ad break remarks, contemptuous of his public. Lonesome Rhodes suddenly loses the popular appeal that makes him a political asset, although we see others being primed to replace him.

Another of Kazan's key responsibilities was to deliver a film to the studio with a Production Code Administration seal. As with *Baby Doll*, this was not achieved at the script stage, but only following a viewing of the completed film. In a letter of 10 July 1956, with filming due to begin in August, Geoffrey Shurlock found the script to be unacceptable under the provisions of the Code. He objected to the emphasis in the leading man's character on his 'illicit sex relations' and to the absence of any balancing sense of sin or 'feeling of moral wrong-doing'. In detailed complaints he referred to frequent references to Lonesome's promiscuity and to the 'intimacies' between him and Marcia, and pointed the filmmakers to the clause that stated 'Pictures shall not infer that low forms of sex relationship are the accepted or common thing'. Yet the film was issued with a Code certificate in April 1957, with Kazan thanking Jack Warner for his help, and in May, a few weeks before release, Kazan informed Shurlock that they had 'cut about 8 more minutes out of the picture', although comparison with the published script indicates that most of the cuts were designed to reduce dialogue and plot that was tangential to the main narrative line.[8] *A Face in the Crowd* was shot on location and in a leased New York studio from August to November 1956, with three days of additional work the following January. Kazan's production notes again reveal some tension with Budd Schulberg. Despite his rationale for forming his own company he complained, during the Memphis shooting, that he was being rushed too much, was not rehearsing enough, and that as a result 'you are not getting the benefit of your directing ability'. He also recorded that 'BS swayed you last night and you were swayable because you had not found your construction'. Frustrated, he urged himself not to 'satisfy Budd or Harry (Stradling, the cinematographer), or the Schedule; Satisfy yourself'. In his autobiography Kazan reflected that sometimes Schulberg, who had moved to a house near him on location and who was on set throughout, was 'too close and I caught myself trying to please him'.[9]

As with his previous film, Kazan did not use stars, or even, for the most part, established Hollywood character actors. He originally thought of Jackie Gleason for the Rhodes character, but eventually decided on a sometime stand-up comic, Andy Griffith, who had no film experience but who had played for two years in the Broadway play *No Time for Sergeants*. Kazan's choice for Marcia Jeffries, Patricia Neal, had followed Barbara Bel Geddes in the director's recent theatre production of *Cat on a Hot Tin Roof*. Elsewhere he used mainly New York theatre actors, including 75-year-old Percy Waram as General

Hainesworth and Anthony Franciosa as Rhodes's self-appointed New York
agent, Joey De Palma. As it was for Griffith, this was Franciosa's first film performance, in a role that recalls Schulberg's Sammy Glick in *What Makes Sammy
Run* and is full of drive, excitement and sexual energy. Kazan noted that De
Palma was not to be a 'heavy' but someone who believed totally in the system.
When he fixes up Lonesome's New York deal, and tracks him down in his
Memphis hotel room, he does an impromptu dance, a characteristic Kazan
piece of physicality, in celebration and excitement. Later he ditches Rhodes and
lines up a successor 'country' star (a brief appearance by Rip Torn). The choice
of Marshall Neilan as Senator Fuller was Schulberg's suggestion. He had
worked with his father as a director and actor in the silent days, directing Mary
Pickford, and had not been in a film for over 20 years. Despite his training from
Lonesome Rhodes he seems, even for the Eisenhower era, a less than credible
presidential candidate. Mel Miller is a rather dry and typical fifties intellectual
commentator, a 'voice of morality' of sorts, redeemed by Walter Matthau's distinctive style (this was only his third film) and his sense of self-disgust as a
writer forced to serve the new cultural forces. Charles Irving, who played
Lonesome's Memphis sponsor, a mattress king, doubled as an adviser on television and advertising, while Kay Medford (as the first Mrs Rhodes) came from
cabaret and musicals, P. Jay Sidney (the black prisoner) from Broadway, and
Rod Brasfield (Lonesome's hobo sidekick and adviser) was a comedian at the
Grand Ole Opry.

From the beginning there is a tension between the topical references, the
rootedness of the work in contemporary liberal concerns, and the broad satire,
particularly in the advertising agency episode and the montage of scenes in
which Lonesome is supposedly made into a national figure and a potential political force. In his notebooks Kazan referred to the paintings and lithographs of
the French painter and caricaturist Honore Daumier and contemplated an
angry, unsentimental perspective on the material. Yet Kazan as director is also
interested in capturing human behaviour that is more nuanced. The account
executive Macey, for example, who finally has a heart attack when he loses the
Rhodes account, is briefly sketched by Paul McGrath as a sympathetic and
tragic figure. Lonesome Rhodes himself however is too one dimensional in the
later scenes for his failure, at the climax of the film, to move an audience. Early
on Kazan wanted the Rhodes character to have moments of 'bewilderment and
humanity', but after his apparent corruption by 'the system', in New York, only
one short scene, in which he confesses to Marcia that he is lost in 'tall grass',
suggests any sense of self-awareness.[10] As Lonesome becomes a monster, personally and publicly, the forbearance and masochism of Marcia becomes more
difficult to understand.

In one of the most effectively human moments, before Lonesome's career takes off in New York, he loses his television sponsor in Memphis and is about to return to his old life. We see him knock on the door of Marcia's hotel room to say goodbye, and Kazan plays the scene from one end of the corridor, catching the characters on the cusp of changing or staying as they are. Just as the Lee Remick character in *Wild River* leaps on the ferry, seizes the moment, so Marcia reveals her feelings for Rhodes and ushers him back towards her and inside her room. Neal, both here and in the New York scenes, suggests a complex and believable mix of emotions, including an attraction for Lonesome's charm and energy, a disgust of the same, and a producer's eye for him as a valuable commercial asset. There is something true and adult in Lonesome's roving eye, particularly as, in big close-up, he irises in on drum majorette and baton twirler Betty Lou Fleckum (Lee Remick), a face in the crowd on the Pickket football field.[11] The woman's role is written and performed with a much greater subtlety than Griffith can achieve with his character, even with Kazan's help. Director and screenwriter also drew on their own relationships for the Marcia role. Kazan later described Molly as his 'talisman of success and my measure of merit', while Lonesome (in a rare moment of reflection) sees Marcia as his 'lifeline to reality'. In his autobiography the director goes as far as to say about Molly Kazan that 'I was her creation – as Lonesome Rhodes was the creation of Marcia in our film'.

In a reference to the nativist, anti-immigrant tradition of the 1850s, Kazan also noted that there was great health in the American 'grass roots tradition' but also a great danger of 'Know-nothingness'. Both writer and director were in part reflecting a contemporary liberal concern that mass political movements were a potential threat to the pluralist political fabric. For many this was a conclusion drawn from reflection on McCarthy's impact in the early fifties, despite the fact that he quickly declined as a public figure following criticism by his fellow Senators in 1954. The director also drew on his own recent experience, writing about the 'fascist' potential of the James Dean fan clubs and of the way that Dean himself became corrupted by his increasing power and adulation.[12] Yet the film shows some sympathy towards the populism of the Lonesome Rhodes character at the beginning – the grass roots tradition – and only later, when he becomes a vehicle for big business and right wing politicians, is he presented as a political threat. In this sense Schulberg and Kazan are closer in their outlook to the 'culture industry' position, with its analysis of corporate and media power, than a 'mass culture' view that feared popular movements as inevitably nativist and right wing. In support of this the General Hainesworth character, a central figure in terms of the political analysis of the latter part of the film, advises Lonesome Rhodes that 'in every strong and healthy society from the Egyptians to our own, the mass had to be guided with a strong hand by a responsible elite'. It is at this point that Marcia Jeffreys, as Rhodes' 'business associate', and also the film's chief source of identification, begins to have doubts as to what she has created.

The principle characters, and particularly Mel Miller, provide a steady dose of cynicism about the fifties American dream that runs counter to the popular sentiment of the day. Rhodes returns from Pickket with his new wife in tow and is greeted at the airport like an early pop star, while the marriage is acted out on TV, with baton twirling routines played to the sound of Beethoven's Seventh Symphony. Seeing this, Marcia Jeffreys is thoroughly compromised, and tells Mel that the whole idea of Lonesome Rhodes had been hers and that now she was 'going to be an equal partner'. Later, recalling the contemporary *Sweet Smell of Success* (1957), she says that there is 'an awful lot of money at stake'. This sense of Marcia Jeffreys as Rhodes's 'business associate', owning him 'for better or worse', harks back (with a twist of gender relations) to the old Popular Front writing in which relationships and marriages were essentially issues of ownership and control. All the rest, as the blacklisted writer and director Abraham Polonsky wrote in the script of *Body and Soul* (1947), is 'conversation'. The music for Kazan and Schulberg's film, which the Communist Party's West Coast *People's World* saw as 'one of the finest progressive films we have seen in years', was composed by the Popular Front folk singer Tom Glazer, who had written the anthem 'Because All Men Are Brothers', as performed by Pete Seeger in the late forties. The title song, as well as the guitar solos by Lonesome Rhodes in the jail, were played without credit by the country blues singer and guitarist Brownie McGhee, who also has a bit part in the film. However, as Michael Denning points out in his study of the politics of what he calls the 'Cultural Front', the musical side of Lonesome, crucial to his early credibility, disappears in the latter half, and the film, having referred to the grass roots rise of country music, thereafter reduces the 'culture of Elvis Presley to an advertisers plot'.[13]

There are also references to the terminology of David Riesman, whose book, *The Lonely Crowd* (1950), had charted what he saw as the apparent shift in American society from inner-directed to other-directed behaviour. Kazan wrote of Schulberg seeing Lonesome Rhodes as starting out with his own values, but as becoming dependent on popular adulation and his ability to maintain it. To Kazan, Rhodes loses his sense of being himself, although his sense of his own identity is never clearly established in the film.[14] Implicit also in the film's treatment of the television-based culture industries of the time is a sense of the way that advertising was increasingly exploring the underlying emotional needs of consumers rather than their rational preferences, both in terms of commercial

Andy Griffith as Lonesome Rhodes and the fifties media event, in *A Face in the Crowd* (1957). Courtesy of BFI.

products and political candidates. Lonesome dismisses Macey's market research, but nevertheless emphasises emotional values in the process of selling, acting out the sexual effects of Vitajex, while coaching Senator Fuller to reveal a personality that the people can love. Kazan shows his contempt for the overstaffed placemen of the agency and indicates more sympathy for self-promoters such as Lonesome Rhodes and De Palma.

What the film does have in abundance is the energy of Rhodes himself, as his ambition carries him upward and onward. Crowds send him off from Pickket railway station like the hero of Preston Sturges' *Hail the Conquering Hero* (1944), but even then, as the shot of him is held after the crowds are left behind, the audience is alerted to his basic cynicism. In Pickket and then in Memphis his radio and TV populism does for a time kick against the traces, as he encourages kids to swim in the station owner's swimming pool, appeals to bored and overworked housewives, and, most importantly, champions the cause of a black woman with seven kids whose house has been burnt down. Mel Miller remarks, watching from the gallery: 'Hey, a coloured woman! In

Memphis that takes nerve.' There is also a point made about race in Arkansas in the opening scene, in which Marcia Jeffreys pokes a microphone through the bars of a (segregated) cell in the local jail, hoping to get a black prisoner to perform on radio. The man answers ('quietly', the script notes): 'Just because I got a black skin ... I'm no minstrel man.' Yet as the film progresses it tracks a shift from a genuine local populism, pitched against the local (male) white powers that be, to a populist veneer for the interests of the New York and Washington corporate-media-military complex.

A *Face in the Crowd* was certainly sharp in charting the changing culture of the fifties, from the TV ads to the mix of charity and self-promotion known as the telethon and the baton-twirling media event from Pickett. After the preponderance of smoke-filled rooms and medium shots, Kazan blew scarce money on building a large platform so that the baton-twirling spectacle could be covered in depth. Following this there is the re-enacted wedding between Lonesome and his new bride, although here the broadness of the satire chips away at the believability of the central character, and the sense that Marcia means something to him. At the end, with Rhodes's true nature 'revealed' to his public – mainly working class in this instance – he is promptly deserted by the 'fighters for Fuller' that constitute a rather sketchy political threat. Alone and railing at the world from his New York apartment balcony, the final image of Lonesome is hardly tragic, but is a sharp image of yesterday's celebrity, his words lost in the traffic noise in a city of eternally new sensations. Lonesome Rhodes is now the 'heavy' that, certainly since *East of Eden*, Kazan had warned himself against constructing. Mel's line, 'We'll get wise to him – that's our strength', is a vote of confidence in the public that the film has done little to support beyond Marcia's turning against the man and institution of Lonesome Rhodes. A far more complex character throughout, she has beaten Mel Miller's proposed book to the punch and is at the end a chastened figure.

In Robert Rossen's *All the King's Men* (1949) the Willie Stark (Broderick Crawford) character became a believable hero to the working classes in a poor state, but Rhodes's folksy populism is perhaps less credible in the context of 1957. The filmmakers are more prophetic in their exploration of trends in Cold War domestic politics and in their realisation of emerging power elite interests in the characters of General Haynesworth (Waram) and his political ally, Senator Fuller (Neilan). From his early support for housewives and black Americans, Rhodes's later agenda embraces a mix of elements from the evolving Republican 'Southern strategy', including traditional isolationism, family values ('a family that prays together stays together') and an antipathy to federal welfare schemes. In fact the latter scenes of the film look forward to John Frankenheimer's 'power elite' and conspiracy films of the early sixties, notably

The Manchurian Candidate and *Seven Days in May*, and suggest something of the 'power elite' notion coined by maverick political scientist C. Wright Mills in his 1956 book on the collaboration between political, military and corporate elites.[15] In practice, in the immediate future, it was the liberal John F. Kennedy who would make most effective use of the newly powerful national and global media. Yet the theme of *A Face in the Crowd* sets out a powerful template for the mixing of politics, charisma and entertainment values both in film, for example in *The Candidate* (Michael Ritchie, 1972) and *Primary Colors* (Mike Nichols, 1998), and also in real politics, from the emotional power and vulnerability of Bill Clinton and his relationship with his wife Hillary, to the role of corporate interests and real or constructed Southern charm in the campaigns of George W. Bush and his father.

Kazan was badly hit by the film's poor commercial performance. He wrote to Budd Schulberg, telling him 'in five days, in two theatres in Boston, we did $8,700. This is, as you realise, disastrously bad.' Reflecting on the experience six months later, in early 1958, he felt that the didactic purpose of the film, its intended role as a warning to the American public, was its weakness. He added that 'our fellow was a puppet designed to show what a son of a bitch he was'.[16] Reviews were mixed. The *Time* notice, in what would be a staple motif in critical writing on the director's film work, sees 'rage as Kazan's undoing'. Bosley Crowther saw the early scenes as entertaining and enlightening, but finally became bored with Lonesome Rhodes, and suggested that the public also would have done. Arthur Knight rightly praised Patricia Neal for bringing warmth to the movie and being convincing in the unlikely role of a woman who 'has succumbed to the same animal magnetism that attracts the crowds'. To Andrew Sarris, in *Film Culture*, the film is 'preposterous liberal propaganda' with a central protagonist who, as a result of over-direction, is wearyingly loud and intense, yet he finds that the intimate scenes help cancel the bombast, making it 'the most interesting film from Hollywood this year'. Perhaps this mixture of reactions was a characteristic of the reception. While some pointed to the power and coherence of *On the Waterfront* by comparison, François Truffaut was as impressed by the new film as he had been unimpressed by Kazan's earlier film with Schulberg. To Truffaut:

> There's no denying that the film lacks consistency, but to hell with consistency! What's important is not its structure but its unassailable spirit, its power, and what I dare call its necessity.[17]

First published in 1942, William Bradford Huie's semi-autobiographical novel, *Mud on the Stars*, came out in paperback in early 1955. The book discusses aspects of Roosevelt's New Deal from the point of view of an educated Southerner who is sympathetic both with Roosevelt and with those in the Tennessee Valley and elsewhere, who resisted what they saw as changes imposed on them by Washington carpetbaggers. The first part of Huie's novel includes a section dealing with the last days of a very old woman who resists any adaptation to the changes to the Southern way of life imposed by the federal government through the Tennessee Valley Authority (TVA). It was in December 1954 that Kazan read the book and sent a copy to his *East of Eden* screenwriter Paul Osborn, suggesting that he pay particular attention to the parts dealing with the submerged island and the 'power house'.[18] Osborn did not work on the screenplay until much later, however, and after Kazan's completion of *Baby Doll* and *A Face in the Crowd*, but Kazan did consult Huie, who felt that it was an appropriate time to deal with the issues of the 'Roosevelt revolution'.[19]

It was in 1957, while he prepared to direct William Inge's play, *The Dark at the Top of the Stairs* (which opened on Broadway in December), that Kazan asked Ben Maddow to write first an outline and then a screenplay, and discussed possibilities with the new head of production at Twentieth Century-Fox, Buddy Adler. Kazan owed Fox a final picture under his original seven picture deal with the studio, but under Adler's 'gentler regime' (Kazan's phrase) he had been allowed to delay this project until after the completion of *A Face in the Crowd*. Maddow had written socially engaged short stories and poetry in the thirties under the name of David Wolff, and was also associated with the documentary films made by Frontier Films, writing for *People of the Cumberland* (1937) and the key drama-documentary, *Native Land* (1942). After prominent writing credits including *Intruder in the Dust* (1949) and *The Asphalt Jungle* (1950) he was blacklisted, but began working again after signing a cooperative statement before Representative Donald Jackson, a member of the House Committee on Un-American Activities. Maddow researched the project, and his screenplay introduced a central protagonist, a New York intellectual from the Tennessee Valley Authority. At this early stage Kazan seemed to contemplate a 'big, lusty, physical comedy' and was interested in the notion of a man who is 'sent to kill an old woman for the good of the country', and who 'falls in love with the enemy'. (This last notion chimes to a degree with what Marcia, the educated Sarah Lawrence girl, does in *A Face in the Crowd*.) Yet Kazan was also concerned from an early stage about the commercial prospects of such a film, particularly one in which the central character is an 80-year-old woman.[20]

Kazan felt that the planned film would not just be about 1935, but would also address the South, and the 'federal interference' of 1957. Southern resistance to such 'interference' emerged strongly that year, with Democratic Senator (and former Dixiecrat Presidential candidate of 1948) Strom Thurmond of South Carolina making a record, 24-hour filibuster effort to defeat the new Civil Rights Act. The same year President Eisenhower sent federal troops to Little Rock, Arkansas when the local Governor sought to forestall a local school board plan to desegregate its schools in accordance with the decisions of the Supreme Court. Little Rock became a national and global news event as the federal troops stood on the high school steps to ensure that nine black children were admitted.[21] As a liberal Kazan supported these changes, yet some of his energy for the new project came from his own sense of distance from the political certainties of the thirties. It was at the end of the fifties and in the early sixties that the national Democratic Party moved towards a civil rights agenda that would ultimately drive Southern Democrats, at ideological odds with their Washington leaders, away from the Party. There is perhaps a degree of parallel between the New Deal mission in Tennessee in the thirties and Washington's later desire to dictate the civil rights and other social policies of the Southern states. Again, as in *Baby Doll*, there is a dying part of Southern culture, but here the concern is less to celebrate this demise but to sympathise with those who have to change, or cannot change.

The American South had long held a fascination for Kazan. The iniquities of the American South were central to the Communist agenda and Kazan used to hitch-hike down South after he left college, becoming friendly with the head of a Communist unit living in Chattanooga, Tennessee. He also worked in Tennessee as an assistant to director Ralph Steiner on the Frontier Films documentary *People of the Cumberland*, while in 1941 he worked closely with Department of Agriculture officials on a sponsored stage production, with some filmed inserts, called *It's Up to You*. Another thirties documentary, Pare Lorentz's *The River* (1937), had explored the problems of impoverished farmers on the banks of the Mississippi and concluded by celebrating the TVA and the construction of new dams. The TVA Act had been enacted in 1933, in President Roosevelt's first year of office, with the object of building a system of dams and reservoirs on the Tennessee River to control flood waters and provide for the generation of electric energy. The TVA, and particularly its huge dams, became central and iconic symbols of New Deal progress and change, while its motto of 'Build for the People' also stood for the principle of equal treatment of the races, at a time of strict segregation and racism in the Southern states.[22]

At the end of 1957 and in the first four months of the next year Kazan engaged in furious work on the project, embarking for the first time in his career on writing a complete script himself. He had felt that the New Dealer, Dave Lantz, was 'too much of a shit' in the Maddow draft and between January and April 1958 he wrote or rewrote three versions of the screenplay, the last one

being called 'The Coming of Spring'. Kazan used the Huie background – of the
TVA, the island and the old lady – but also developed a parallel love story
between the New Dealer, sent from Washington to Tennessee to supervise the
flooding of an island, and the old lady's granddaughter. For Kazan, now in his
late forties, this was now a labour of love, and his research, consultation and
writing on the subject reveal the ways in which the project allowed him to
reflect personally on his political development since the thirties. As well as
meeting with Huie, Kazan went to see Democratic Senator Estes Kefauver, a
key figure in Tennessee politics in the fifties and a man who stood up to Joseph
McCarthy in Washington, fought to protect the Tennessee Valley Authority and
took liberal positions on race.[23] The interview indicated his attempt to
strengthen the social and political underpinning of the story, the conflict
between state and individual, between collective benefits and individual
rights. In his notes he urged himself – as he had with the Terry Malloy character in *On the Waterfront* – to identify with the Dave Lantz character, a young,
Jewish, Harvard educated TVA lawyer and evangelical New Dealer. Before
Kazan began his own third draft he wrote the following, under the heading
'I AM DAVE':

> Actually I was Dave once. I remember when I taught a class in
> Directing down at the New Theatre League. I was about 25, and Jack
> Garfein at his most cocky was nothing to me. I was the hero of the
> young insurgent working class movement. I knew about direction and
> could teach anybody. But I simply did not suffer from self doubt. The
> world was like a huge red carpet out ahead of me to be walked on.[24]

Kazan also mentioned in his notes his own certainty and power as the taxi
driver in *Waiting for Lefty*, and reflected on American communism in the
thirties, and beyond that the heroic stance and image of the Soviet leaders. In
the completed film something of this questioning of the certainty of thirties
progressivism is implicit, although in the final script and film the New Dealer
is given little to say explicitly about politics.

Kazan's third script version begins with Lantz in 1959, telling the story of his
encounter with Ella Garth to a foreign dignitary. Although Kazan later wrote
that only a few scenes he had written remained in the final script, examination
of the script indicates that this slightly understates Kazan's writing role. Some
of the key dialogue between the New Dealer (Chuck Glover in the film) and
Carol Garth (Ella Garth's widowed granddaughter) is present in Kazan's work.
The Chuck character is less insecure than in the final script, and in the film,
but nevertheless it is Carol who takes the initiative in this version. There is also

a scene, realised in the film, in which the inhabitants of the island, in a 'pitiful little procession of patched up cars, wagons and barrows', cross by the ferry on to the mainland.[25] The scene seems to suggest another form of 'crossing' that Kazan was beginning to think about in this period, that of his own family from Europe to America at the turn of the century. The black folk of Garth's island are making the shift from the feudalism of the old South – again there are connections to *Baby Doll* here – to the new values of the modern America being created – as liberals saw it – by the New Deal. It is reminiscent, as are the graveyard scenes, of John Ford's work – in particular the West bound settlers of *Wagonmaster* (1950).

Also more or less as in the completed film is the scene in which Chuck returns to his hotel room, accompanied by Carol's local boyfriend (called T.C. Maynard in this script, Walter in the film). In his room he finds Bailey, proprietor of a local gas station and local cotton farmer, waiting for him. As Bailey confronts the man who seems to threaten his livelihood, we see something of the racism and thuggishness that is an element, for all Kazan's keenness to see both sides, of the local culture. Bailey recounts how he brutally beat a 'nigger' who deserted him and started working for the new TVA gang. He also uses violence to force Chuck to recompense him for his lost earnings, although the script cuts away at this point to a scene in the hotel's lobby, where a group of mostly elderly residents are listening to the radio. The complex relationship between Carol and the man from Washington is more problematic, with the later casting of Montgomery Clift providing for the director's playing of dialogue with and against the more powerful sub-text of gesture, behaviour and emotional need.

In early 1958 Kazan also discussed the project with a series of friends and associates. Among those who offered Kazan comments on his efforts were Paul Osborn, who wanted a broader, 'documentary scale' to the project, Bill Huie, who called for more of a sense of TVA politics in Washington and Knoxville, and crucially Molly Kazan, who argued for a stronger rationale for the New Deal and a sense that 'Values of the old are lost when change comes'. John Steinbeck and 'Joe' Mankiewicz also provided enthusiastic comments in early 1958, while Kazan's old boss and fellow Greek Spyros Skouras, in another apparently influential intervention, urged that the central character not be Jewish, feeling that it was unfortunate to 'associate New Deal and Jews'. In another response to Kazan's April screenplay, Twentieth Century-Fox production head Buddy Adler enquired sceptically about 'the selling feature of this story?' He felt that the script attacked too many problems and became over emotional about the 'negro problem in the south', while he also objected to treatment of the 'Jewish problem' and to 'cracks' about glib intellectual liberals and 'fascists'.[26]

In early 1959 the novelist and screenwriter Calder Willingham produced a further screenplay, but Kazan was disappointed by the last quarter of it and returned to Paul Osborn, who had remained interested in the project. Osborn completed three further versions of the screenplay, including the final one, between July and October 1959. As producer Kazan again had problems obtaining a seal from the PCA. Shurlock felt that there was no proper voice for morality, and that the September version was unacceptable 'by reason of improper treatment of illicit sex relations between Chuck and Carol'. Shurlock continued to call for the idea of an affair between the two to be dropped, and a seal was only granted after the reviewers saw the completed film in March 1960.[27]

In terms of casting Kazan wrote to Marlon Brando, asking him to play the central character. Brando replied affably – 'God knows you certainly put a lot of work into it' – but did not reply when Kazan sent a script to him in LA. Kazan also sent a script to Frank Sinatra but received no reply from the star, who will have remembered how he had been summarily replaced as Terry Malloy. Instead Kazan turned to Montgomery Clift, an actor who had performed on Broadway since 1935, and who was part of Kazan's 1942 production of Thornton Wilder's The Skin of Our Teeth. Clift had been one of the original members of the Actors Studio, although to his biographer Patricia Bosworth he was 'never truly a Method actor in the sense often associated with that term'. His performances in A Place in the Sun (1951) and From Here to Eternity (1953) won critical praise, but a car accident in 1956 had changed his looks and adversely affected his confidence.[28] He had begun drinking heavily and Kazan insisted that he did not drink during the ten weeks of location shooting, from mid-October 1959 to early January 1960. The other key cast members were Lee Remick and Jo Van Fleet, who had made their screen debuts in, respectively, A Face in the Crowd and East of Eden. The 44-year-old Van Fleet arrived early for each day's shooting to be disguised – by veteran Fox make-up artist Ben Nye – as the 80-year-old matriarch Ella Garth. (Buddy Adler had earlier proposed that Marilyn Monroe play the part of Carol, a suggestion described by Kazan as ridiculous.)

Kazan later described the decision to shoot in colour as one taken 'thanks to a sudden impulse on my part'. A late change in the script resulted in the use at the beginning of the film of black and white newsreel footage, with a narration voiced by Pat Hingle. Kazan used this shocking material, of a man telling of how his wife and children died in a flood, to immediately establish the film's rationale for the TVA and the flooding of Garth Island. In the newsreel the man talks to camera about the way the river in flood carried them away, while other scenes are used from Pare Lorentz's The River, making a personal connection for the director to his own documentary work of the thirties. Even during filming Kazan was writing to Osborn asking for small script additions, and in one letter he argued that 'I still want very much to get that little scene in which an old negro works an electric light for the first time', a scene that was written and does appear in the film. Kazan hated 'not to show the positive side of the TVA'.[29] The case for collective action is made throughout, while Kazan also salutes the dignity of the old woman, who finally leaves her home, but dies on her own terms. Yet this story of individual and collective purpose is most powerfully projected on to the lives of the two younger protagonists, Chuck Glover and Carol Garth.

For all the opening narration, explaining the TVA as necessary in order to 'stop the devastation, the waste, the loss of life caused by the Tennessee river in flood', the TVA representative as played by Clift seems from the beginning a problematic 'leading man', insecurely personifying the collective purpose of the federal government. He has no sooner occupied his seat in the TVA office, grandly expounding on the 'American way', when he overbalances on his chair. Although the script tells nothing of his life in the national capital, in Tennessee he is out of his depth, particularly when picked up and thrown into the river by Joe John (Big Jeff Bess), one of Ella Garth's sons. Glover's first visit establishes the circumstances of the island, with the black workers doing the work for indolent sons of the white family of landowners. Writing to Osborn from the Hotel Cherokee in Cleveland, Tennessee, where the whole cast lived and ate together, Kazan reported that 'Monty is excellent and more upright and leading man-ish and fine and sensitive every day'.[30] Nonetheless the casting of Clift changed the relationship between Glover and Carol, making him personally more passive, relative to his role in representing the authority and narrative drive of progressive government.

Chuck's second visit to the island begins a long sequence of scenes that appear to take place, like the long afternoon sequence in *Baby Doll*, in near real time. Kazan establishes in long shot the crucial geography of the river, the track beside it, the simple ferry and the island. We see the local economy of the island, Ella Garth's feudal sense of ownership, and the slow emergence from under her grandma's authority of Carol Garth. To Chuck, Ella Garth loves *her* land, and not *the* land, while the old woman likes things 'running wild', and is 'agin dams – of any kind'. Carol is pictured by the gravestone of her husband as her grandmother recounts her own dead husband's pioneering role in settling the island. As Chuck and Carol talk Kazan breaks up the CinemaScope frame with trees that are entwined, almost strangled, by roots. When he asks her if she has a boyfriend, she replies with 'Oh yeah, that answers everything if you've got a fella!' We see Carol in thought, as she walks Chuck to the ferry; upward shots of the trees against the sky are perhaps little more than cutaways to facilitate the editing, but they do signal the more lyrical tone of the scenes to come and the sense of the man from Washington's new (and for him disorienting) environment. At the river bank she watches silently by the 'TVA KEEP OFF' sign (again, dividing the frame), as he patiently explains the mysteries of electricity to Sam Johnson (Robert Earl Jones), the most loyal of Ella Garth's retinue of black workers. The camera on her simulates the ferry, drifting slowly away, until she suddenly asks if she can come with him and leaps on board.

Lee Remick at the doorway of her house by the river; Montgomery Clift in the background, in *Wild River* (1960). Courtesy of BFI.

Returning to the island: Lee Remick in *Wild River* (1960). Courtesy of BFI.

Carol's decision acts as a catalyst for the personal drama, as she takes Chuck to the house that she shared with her husband and opens it up for the first time since his death. As a black man sings 'See What Tomorrow Brings' outside (also an echo of *Baby Doll*), Carol explores the inside, and emotions long dormant. She brushes leaves off the marital bed and lies briefly on it, lost in memory. In his script Kazan had written 'Surround Remick w. props redolent of memories'. In a long take Carol talks aloud of her relationship with local man Walter Clark and asks if she would get to love him if they were married for a while, to which Chuck, looking awkward throughout, answers 'No'. As the small house is bathed in evening light, Carol sits in a chair, imaging her grandma in her place. 'Don't go', she says unexpectedly, several times, and there follows a slow dissolve to a wide shot of the river bank early the next morning, with Chuck leaving in his government car and Carol crossing back on the ferry alone, in the mist. We see Chuck, still with some uncertainty about what has happened, blow a kiss. Here Kazan delivers on his notion that the art of motion pictures is chiefly one of 'photographing looks', and stretches these looks till a point of crisis or decision occurs.[31] The whole set of scenes, minimally but aptly punctuated by Kenyon Hopkins's score, balances memory, emotion and behaviour, together with the given circumstances of economics and history, in a way that Kazan has rarely bettered.

In the town scenes Kazan, city man turned pastoralist, reveals the nature of the town economy and its racially divided wage structure. Three 'responsible' figures of the town – an undertaker, a businessman and a Bank President – visit Chuck in his office, a picture of President Roosevelt behind them, and try and warn the TVA man away from a course that they see threatening their economic interests. Chuck is prepared to use segregated gangs, but not to alter the policy of paying the races equally. The rather sinister trio of notables make a veiled threat, referring to 'other elements' who may act if their advice is ignored. Kazan again uses a series of close-ups to check reactions, including that of the watching secretary Betty, played by Barbara Loden. The scene has all the elements of the liberal Hollywood tradition of dealing with the South, from *They Won't Forget* (1937) to a similar scene (using depth of field rather than montage) in Otto Preminger's *The Cardinal* (1963). A short scene that follows shows Chuck showing the blessings of civilisation (and in particular of electricity) to many of the black inhabitants of Garth Island, convincing them to leave the island the next day. Without its racially defined proletariat the Garth family's presence on the island is untenable.

We return to Carol's house by the river and here Kazan again captures Carol's sense of limited time, as the sun of summer gives way to the rains of autumn. Chuck hesitates on the doorstep, as Carol seems to do the thinking for them both. Carol tells him that she does not want to tie him down, and does not want him to marry her, yet in terms of behaviour and looks Kazan presents a tension, a state of flux. The past exercises its pull through the dead husband's boots and his gun, but the director plays action, or inaction, against the spare dialogue. We watch from the open doorway as Chuck announces he is going to leave and buttons his raincoat, and Carol responds by closing the door. After a brief series of shots of Walter Clark, arriving and then retreating when he sees the two of them inside, Kazan cuts again to the following morning, and to a single shot, panning from right to left, revealing the people of the island making the river crossing and moving in a procession of wagons into the future, a vision of collective change and growth.

Chuck continues to respond passively to Carol, even as he represents public action and change. But as elsewhere with Kazan, violence or conflict precipitates a resolution, as Bailey and the locals come round – in part in apparent support of Walter, and in part to intimidate the government man to pull back on his radical hiring plans. A mob lays siege to the house, jumping on the roof and ramming the wall with a truck, and it is Walter and Carol who physically respond. Perhaps aware of earlier criticisms of his work, Kazan had fretted over this fight scene. He had written to Osborn that 'I don't know what the hell I'm going to do with the fight. Leave it till the last moment and depend on my hic! genius. Wish me luck with that one, I'll need it.'[32] In fact it works quite well, more braggadocio than real violence, as 'good old boy' Bailey knocks everybody flat, including Chuck (the first to go), Walter and Carol. There is a bit of jocular commentary from a black character before the sheriff decides that, with a woman on the floor, it's time to do something. But what happens, unexpectedly, with Carol and Chuck lying in the dirt alone, everyone else having departed, is Chuck's proposal of marriage. We cut to a local marriage parlour, and he makes it legitimate by handing over a muddy $5 bill.

Usual sexual role-playing is here subverted. While Carol seizes the moment, Chuck is passive and tentative, more so as the story progresses. In a conversation with Kazan about film in 1980 the writer and filmmaker Marguerite Duras referred to the Clift character as 'l'homme tremblant'. But as Donald Chase has argued, *Wild River* 'never makes Carol out to be a domineering lust-pot and never condescends to Chuck's passivity or suggests he's sexually dysfunctional'. The extended encounter between Chuck and Carol is, as Chase suggests, both comic and poignant.[33] In this sense there are similarities in tone with the scenes between Baby Doll and Vacarro in *Baby Doll*, but here there is a stronger social dimension to the story, and a stronger sense of personal change. Kazan comes nearer to his often-repeated wish to attain what he saw as Jean Renoir's ability to suggest that all his characters have their own reasons. Here also Kazan makes most explicit reference to John Ford and also to another filmmaker who Kazan revered, Alexander Dovzhenko. There is a closeness to nature here, and to the seasons, and a willingness, in tension with the director's nervous, New Yorker's sensibility, to stretch time. We get to see the bank and river at different times and seasons; there is a strong sense of place, beyond Kazan's usual – in this phase of his career – 'documentary' work, drawing on the reality and specificity of the location, and using around 30 locals in speaking parts. *Wild River* is not a hymn to nature – although several hymns are sung – but the feel for place and season is an element of the central strain between change and what it puts at risk. In Dovzhenko's *Earth* (1930) modernity is in one sense an enemy of backwardness, but is also seen as consistent with the cycles of rural life, of death and rebirth. A death, Ella Garth's, is also central to *Wild River*, to its tensions between outsiders and locals, technology and nature, change and stasis. Dams also suggest the great Soviet experiment – as in *Dr Zhivago* – and Kazan, in his notebooks if not in the film, refers not only to the thirties tradition of political change and commitment that he was once a part of, but also to the even more titanic struggles in the Soviet Union and to the lost hope that this represented the building of, in the famous phrase used by Sidney and Beatrice Webb, a new civilisation.

The film moves to its end in a series of short scenes, as history takes its course. Chuck – back in his three-piece suit – arrives on the island with the Marshal in a flotilla of barges and canoes. The men go to work in chopping down the trees outside the old lady's house. Sam Johnson, the most independent of the black characters, is paradoxically the most loyal to his mistress. Earlier he had refused to sell his dog to her and now he refuses to leave the island. Only just before the island is flooded, and after Ella Garth has left, does he row himself (and his cow) across to the mainland. The old woman's final scenes are played without sentimentality. She is taken to her new home, on a newly constructed and tarred street. She ignores the rocking chair provided for her and tells her granddaughter to pay a 15c debt, all she owes to anyone. In the next scene Carol tells her husband in a matter of fact way that 'grandma just died' and that he could not have done anything different. The homestead becomes a blazing pyre and after the flooding there is a funeral, and the old woman is laid to rest near her husband on the small patch of land left above water. Finally we see the flooded valley from the air, as a small plane takes Chuck, Carol and her children away. As they fly over the huge white dam the CinemaScope screen irises down, so that it is the last image of the film – a cathedral of modernity but also a shrine.

The film was unsuccessful at the box office, despite Twentieth Century-Fox changing the name to *The Woman and the Wild River* in an effort to play up the love story. Kazan later recalled having to put pressure on Skouras to open the film in Paris, something that reflected his increasing sense of a broader European appreciation of his work. In time *Wild River* came to be one of the most critically praised of Kazan's films, with Robin Wood, for example, seeing it as avoiding the problems of tone that he found elsewhere in the director's work. French critical circles have continued to discuss and celebrate the film's visual strength, elegiac feel and sense of the play of place and memory on character.[34]

7

William Inge was born (in 1913) and brought up in Independence, Kansas, and his most successful plays deal with attitudes and behaviour in small town Mid-Western America. Personally inspired by the example of Tennessee Williams, Inge was most successful with his theatre work of the fifties, including *Picnic* (1952) and *Bus Stop* (1955). While co-producing and directing Inge's play *The Dark at the Top of the Stairs*, in 1957, Kazan suggested that he and the play-wright might at some point collaborate on a film project. Kazan recalled that as a result Inge sent him a 'dramatic narrative with dialogue' and that he turned it into a draft script to which the playwright made a few 'adjustments'.[1] To Inge the script dealt with 'the pain my generation expressed in coming to maturity, and with the conflicts we fought to find our personal standards when society demanded we accept only her own'. Later, after the film was released in October 1961, Inge complained to Kazan about the inadequacy of both his recompense and his Associate Producer credit, but Kazan responded robustly, pointing out that he had cut and rearranged Inge's narrative and given it 'form and shape'; many respected directors, he added, would have 'demanded co-authorship of the screen play for what I did'.[2]

In contrast to the personal involvement in the gestation of *Wild River* at the end of the fifties, Kazan saw his work with Inge as one of serving the author's design, albeit by structuring and visualising it for the cinema. Writing in 1958 Kazan was clear about the source of the ideas: 'This is Inge; not you or TW or Odets, Miller etc. It is Inge.'[3] Yet there were certainly elements of the story that resonated with Kazan's own experiences, notably the effect of the Wall Street Crash and the power of parents, and particularly fathers, to obstruct and distort the efforts of their children to develop their own lives and identities. Kazan had already used his own problems with his father in his work on *East of Eden*, and *Splendour in the Grass* would not be the first or last Kazan film in which the father is portrayed as the 'heavy'. The director's script annotations of May 1960 also indicate his feeling for the work's hostility towards the rising middle classes of pre-Crash America. In his notes on the New Year country club party scene Kazan refers to George Grosz's satirical drawings of twenties Berlin, a classic view of the decadence of middle-class life in that period, as a key inspiration.[4]

In addition Kazan also had a personal interest and involvement in another key theme of the film, that of psychiatry and psychoanalysis. He had consulted the Hungarian born Dr Bela Mittelmann, originally his wife's analyst, from 1945, when Molly had made the sessions a condition for the restoration of their marriage after his affair with Constance Dowling. Mittelmann died in 1959 and thereafter Kazan began a more intense and in his view more productive relationship with another distinguished psychoanalyst, Dr Harold Kelman, tracing his greater confidence in writing his own family's story for the screen to these sessions. Robert Ardrey, in a letter to the director at the time, took a 'dim view' of hearing from Kazan's wife about 'you and analysis'. A central spine of *Splendour in the Grass* concerns a case history of the breakdown of Wilma Dean (Deanie) Loomis (Natalie Wood) and of her return to society after two and a half years of therapy in a mental institution. In preparing the film Kazan had sent the script to a psychiatrist, seeking an analysis of the characters, while he also visited the renowned Menninger Clinic, the pioneering psychiatric institution that had been founded in Tepeka, Kansas, in the mid-twenties, and which specialised in the problems of young people.[5]

Kazan was keenly aware that he needed to make a film that was commercially successful. In terms of Newtown's producing and releasing arrangement with Warner Bros., *Baby Doll* had yet to go into profit, while *A Face in the Crowd* had lost $1,500,000 and had still to make back its print and advertising costs.[6] In addition his commercial hopes for *Wild River*, the filming of which was completed in early 1960, were also limited, in part because of the lack of interest in the film shown by its distributor, Twentieth Century-Fox. (The film was the picture that he owed Fox under his original contract with the studio; the studio production head who had been most involved in the production, Buddy Adler, died of lung cancer as the film was released.) *Splendour in the Grass* was again to be financed and distributed by Warner Bros. and produced by Newtown Productions, although the studio's agreement of January 1960 was formally with a new company, NBI, which reflected the additional involvement of William Inge – thus his latterly contentious Associate Producer credit. Kazan complained at the time, before shooting began in May 1960, that 'the pressures on me from Warner Bros. have been onerous and constant'. The studio wanted him both to use studio facilities and to make the picture in Kansas with a Hollywood crew, while he felt, having visited Kansas, that he could find more authentic looking locations in New York State.[7]

Filming *Splendour in the Grass* (1961). Courtesy of BFI.

Kazan made other 'research' trips to look for 'business': he observed behaviour in a high school for a couple of days and also visited an oil pumping depot in Tulsa. As production designer Kazan again used Richard Sylbert, who had worked with a number of New York directors and with Kazan on both *Baby Doll* and *A Face in the Crowd*. Sylbert had learnt much from William Cameron Menzies, who as a director had worked from storyboards, but saw his East Coast directors, including Kazan and Lumet, as having little interest in this approach. He recalled that Kazan fitted the model of 'Homer – the blind storyteller' and that his 'overriding concern was with the emotional dynamics of the narrative'. He remembers Kazan talking in metaphors, seeking out 'what was beyond the text, around the text, behind the text', but felt that it was remarkable to have produced 'a huge colour movie for $1,800,000, including the cast!'[8] For music for the film Kazan turned to a composer and soloist who had worked with him on his last ever Broadway production, of the Archibald MacLeish play, *J.B.*, in 1959. David Amram combined jazz and numerous other musical forms and styles, and particularly favoured the French horn.

As cinematographer Kazan had wanted Ellsworth Fredericks, who had been part of his Hollywood crew on *Wild River*, and he made an unsuccessful appeal to the cinematographers' union to obtain permission to use him as part of an East Coast crew on *Splendour in the Grass*. Kazan wanted to keep what he called his 'tiny office' in New York open, and pitched strongly to the Union Local, arguing that he had 'brought about a revival of big picture making in the East'. Yet the Board of Local 644 insisted on a full East Coast crew for East Coast productions, and so Kazan returned instead to Boris Kaufman for the colour and widescreen production.[9] The exteriors were filmed on Staten Island, Long Island and in upstate New York, while the bulk of the film was shot at the Bronx's Filmways Studios on 46 sets, during a generous 63-day schedule that began in early May and concluded in August of 1960. In terms of casting, Warren Beatty had been recommended to Kazan by Willliam Inge, and had appeared in the playwright's unsuccessful production of *A Loss of Roses*. The 23-year-old Beatty, new to filmmaking, convinced Kazan following a screen test, while Natalie Wood, the same age, was under contract with Warners and had been a child actor in Hollywood. Apart from these two leads Kazan used East Coast, Broadway actors, many of them from the Actors Studio. Pat Hingle, for example, had contributed a cameo in *On the Waterfront* and the opening narration for *Wild River*, as well as appearing in the Kazan production of *The Dark at the Top of the Stairs*.

Censorship problems seemed to track Kazan's steps. Geoffrey Shurlock had signposted the Production Code Administration's concerns with the story at an early stage and objected in April 1960 to 'the type of excessively blunt language by young people which is proving extremely offensive to our audience'. No seal was issued before filming, and on viewing an initial version of the film, in February 1961, the PCA argued that the film could not be approved under the Code because of its 'overly vivid portrayal of sex in a number of sequences'. 69-year-old Jack Warner wanted the picture re-edited to 'eliminate' a number of scenes seen as sexually explicit, having been urged on this course by Ben Kalmenson, the studio's New York-based head of distribution. Kalmenson felt that the film lacked any 'pre-sold' quality that would help it at the box office, and was also aware of Kazan's previous problems with both the Code office and the Legion of Decency. Kazan argued with Shurlock and Vizzard, made some concessions, and threatened to appeal to the Board of the Motion Picture Association of America (MPAA) in New York.[10] He felt his film was wholesome and innocent and that he was being discriminated against compared to the makers of other contemporary films, particularly Daniel Mann's *Butterfield 8* (MGM, 1960), which he had just seen and which he saw as 'a picture that sells sensationalism for its own sake and with an eye towards the box office'. He also mentioned *The World of Suzie Wong*, released the same year; how, he argued, 'Geoffrey Shurlock could pass it and make any objections to *Splendour in the Grass* I do not and never will understand'.[11]

The film finally secured a Production Code seal in March 1961, but as with *A Streetcar Named Desire* and *Baby Doll*, the Legion of Decency then intervened, threatening to give the film a 'C' Classification. In May, Kazan wrote to Warner and Ben Kalmenson: 'I want to go on record that I have heard that you may wish to have the picture cut further to meet the demands of a private group.' He warned the studio not to further tamper with the film contrary to their contract and threatened that if they did so he would go to the courts and to the public and 'sue for millions of dollars'. Throughout the negotiations Kazan argued that he could have made more money doing other film work: 'I probably could have earned a million dollars in salary in that time, instead of $125,000. But I preferred $125,000 in order to make a fine work independently and without interference.'[12] In a later letter to William Inge the director argued that his work on the picture included dubbing, cutting, recutting, scoring, fighting with Warners and 'fighting with the Legion of Decency'.[13]

Whether because of Kazan's threats or not the studio did not make any significant additional cuts in the 124-minute print, although Inge wrote some additional lines of dialogue, and the Production Code Administration, in their account of the discussions with the Legion, referred to adjustments in the scene in the parking lot at the New Year's party, to ensure that there was no implication that Ginny Stamper had actually been raped. These 'protracted negotiations', as Kazan called them in a contemporary letter to Clifford Odets, may even have helped in promoting and marketing a film which lacked 'pre-sold' elements. The controversy and 'adultness' of the production was made a selling point and the film was rolled out gradually, beginning with carefully arranged single performances that were seen in the trades as demonstrating the film's entertainment values and spreading word of mouth in advance of the official opening. A full page ad in the *New York Times*, referring to these pre-release showings, proclaimed: 'A Controversial New Motion Picture has caused an Event Unparalleled in Theatre History.' Kazan felt that the 'audience caught on to it' at the showings and told the Warners New York office, including the sceptical Kalmenson and publicity chief Richard Lederer, that he had 'enjoyed, more than ever before, being close to the exhibition of this film of mine'. The Legion gave the film a B rating and *Splendour in the Grass* was released in October 1961. To Odets, however, Kazan felt that the studio was 'low on it', were not backing the picture with any real effort and that they 'would have cut a couple of hundred feet if I hadn't been there, teeth bared'.[14]

The theme of the early part of the story, dealing with two Kansas families in late twenties Kansas, is the impact of a puritan society in inhibiting the lives of two young lovers (Beatty and Wood). First it is Bud Stamper who is frustrated by Deanie's resistance to his advances, a reflection of her mother's notion that sex is something that 'nice girls' don't do, and only married women engage in to please their husbands. Together or with others the young couple return throughout the film to the waterfall that is used throughout as a symbol of their natural passions. Later, when Bud finally consents to his father's insistence that he go to Yale for four years rather than marrying Deanie and taking her with him to agricultural college, it is she who has a breakdown and is propelled into mental illness. A dutiful boy, Bud also seems to be influenced, in breaking off with Deanie, by his sense of the wildness and self-destructiveness of his older, flapper sister Ginny, who openly confronts both their father and the prevailing hypocrisy of society. Following the Great Crash of 1929 Bud's father, Ace Stamper (Hingle), commits suicide and his son meets and marries a waitress, Angelina (Zohra Lampert), and leaves Yale to start up a small farm. Meanwhile the rejected Deanie recovers in a mental institution, where she agrees to marry a fellow patient, before recovering sufficiently to return home to confront the past and her unfulfilled love for Bud.

Kazan later saw Inge as a miniaturist, and the film's visual strength similarly relies in particular on careful period detail in the interior scenes. After an opening which introduces high school seniors Bud Stamper and Deanie Loomis, we follow both of them back to their respective homes and parents. Bud is the son of Ace Stamper, a wealthy oil man with an obsessive desire to live vicariously through his son, on and off the sports field. In contrast the Loomis family lives modestly, with the father running a grocery store and both parents most enthused by the rising fortunes, in 1928 Kansas, of their stock market investments. Mrs Loomis in particular seems to sublimate her sexual inhibition, not only in her constant eating, but also in a desire to see her daughter make the 'catch of a lifetime' by marrying Bud. The names, Stamper and Loomis, suggest the different balance between male and female in the two families. The director suggested to art director Richard Sylbert that the Loomis house 'should be like a homey stew', neat, comfortable and frugal, while the mock baronial Stamper home was to be a 'man dominated home', full of panelled walls, hunting trophies, candelabra and coats of arms. Miniature oil derricks throughout the Stamper mansion and estate call attention to the source of the money and also to the accident – he fell from the top of an oil derrick – that limited Ace's own sporting and social advancement (he clearly sees himself as marrying beneath him). Both sets of parents are preoccupied with money and class, and the filmmakers give these concerns a Freudian emphasis. In a 1958 note Kazan wrote of the proposed film being a 'Romantic tragedy', the story of 'Romeo and Juliet in the age of Business'.[15]

Whereas Chuck and Carol in *Wild River* play out their relationship in complex and adult relation to the conflicting social forces of thirties America, the two young protagonists of *Splendour in the Grass* have less autonomy and are nearer to being blank canvasses, 'victims' of the wider society. They are icons of youth confusion rather than revolt, and Kazan noted that in his view the couple were far too attached to their parents.[16] Kazan and Inge both emphasise the tragedy of Deanie's experience and the director suggests her point of view in several close-ups and in the last scenes. Only the Ginny Stamper character, played by Barbara Loden, with whom Kazan was involved at the time and who later became his second wife, is shown in open rebellion against family and social norms, and her stance, which contrasts with Bud's acquiescence in his father's demands, leads to her sexual humiliation in the parking lot outside Ace Stamper's New Year's Eve party and to her early (off-screen) death. The scenes of Deanie in the mental hospital, and of her slow recovery, seem to prefigure the more autobiographical treatment of mental disturbance, linked to a rejection of contemporary social norms, in Kazan's later novel and film, *The Arrangement*.

While the film may have been too early to catch the zeitgeist of the sixties, it does chime with the shifting of identities of the time it was made and released. Its social resonance owes something to the passage towards maturity of the baby boom generation and the 'generation gap' that was becoming apparent between the views and experiences of contemporary adolescents and traditional fifties' notions of the family. At the same time the cinema was also in transition from a medium directed at an adult or broad family audience to one in which the young and their concerns were central. For teenagers in the early sixties, and indeed for their parents, issues of youth identity were of growing significance as alternative 'youth cultures' and lifestyles emerged as options. In a marginal note opposite a scene in which Ace Stamper complains to Bud about his 'late hours'. Kazan writes, as a prompt for his direction of Beatty in the scene: 'Bud stiffens up visibly into the identity his father has for him.' Elsewhere Kazan writes of Deanie straightening her skirt in the presence of her mother, 'pulling herself back into a nice girl position'.[17] In the opening scenes of Deanie and Bud returning to their parents' houses Kazan uses the body language of the two protagonists to quickly sketch the film's premise. Alone, Deanie flexes her body, straining against the 'little girl', 'nice girl' role that her mother encourages. Lying full length on her bed, when her mother leaves her room she discards the teddy bear as a symbol of her childhood, while in a parallel scene in the much grander Stamper mansion Bud, in his room, throws a basketball at the framed crest above his bed, in confused and mute protest against his father's social ambitions and plans for his future at Yale and in an eastern oil business.

On the ending Kazan wrote at the time of how all three characters (including Angelina) attain adulthood and 'become themselves!'. Tom Hayden expressed something of a new generation's values when he wrote the so-called Port Huron Statement, for Students for a Democratic Society, in 1962. The statement discussed the aspiration of young people to find 'a meaning in life that is personally authentic' and argued that 'the object is not to have one's way so much as it is to have a way that is one's own'.[18] In retrospect some of the themes and motifs of the film do anticipate trends of the sixties, from the 'dropping out' of rich kids, the adoption of simpler, often rurally-based livelihoods, as suggested by the final scene of the film, to the notion – which Kazan himself was to popularise – that 'madness' was in part a normal response to corrupt and hypocritical social relations. Kazan himself drew attention to the way Inge paralleled the collapse of twenties puritanism to the economic crisis, as the 1929 Crash led to both Depression and New Deal. He felt that the theme of Inge's work was that 'You should accept your own nature and shape your life from it'. In a conclusion in which the central characters show a greater complexity of emotion associated with their new adultness, Deanie's reaction to meeting Bud and his wife and child is ambiguous. Yet she seems strong enough to come to terms with her encounter with Bud and recites the Wordsworth quotation – previously a mere schoolroom incantation – with new self-knowledge. Beatty as Bud is also able to suggest both his sense of the loss of Deanie and also his satisfaction with his lot. Both recognise, in Kazan's script annotation, 'the mentality of limited objectives, limited happiness'.[19] Kazan wrote in his autobiography of wanting both a bourgeois family life built around his wife and a more independent and risky emotional relationship, at that time with Barbara Loden. The director also took from Inge, and later developed in his own writing, a related opposition between what Odets called the 'general fraud' and the notion of a simpler, more frugal and less compromised life.

From the parallel scenes in the Loomis and Stamper houses, establishing the central characters and themes, to the extended conclusion, the narrative is played at a pace that contrasts with the deliberation of *Wild River*. Neither Bud nor Deanie have the experience to reflect on their lives and not for the first time in Kazan's work there is occasional tension between a richly textured social detail, both in the period design and in the performances, and a broader sense of exaggeration or satire. To Michael Walker the unremitting intensity of Pat Hingle's performance, certainly till his later scenes, 'constantly threatens to overbalance the film'.[20] Unlike Douglas Sirk, for example in *Written on the Wind* (1956), a film that also draws on the imagery of new wealth and the oil business, but in a contemporary setting, Kazan rarely plays ironically with Hollywood stylistic excesses, but instead encourages an intensity in key performances that is in uneasy tension with his dominant social realist form. The effectiveness of the later scenes in *Splendour in the Grass* derives in particular from a stylistic shift in which the older characters emerge from their carica-tures and are allowed to reveal a broader sense of their humanity. Even Mrs Loomis (Audrey Christie), earlier something of a parody of herself with her Red Indian war whoops at the rising stock market, is given the space, and a greater emotional depth, to make her case. In fact Kazan comes nearest in the last scenes to a broad sympathy with everyone's struggles, from major to minor characters.

The Wall Street Crash seems to have the effect of slowing down the pace of the narrative, but throughout Kazan uses several short scenes effectively, as when Bud and Deanie contemplate Ace Stamper's oil wells as a none too attrac-tive inheritance, and later when several hobos watch as, after Ace Stamper has thrown himself from his hotel room, Bud identifies his father's body. Elsewhere Kazan is particularly adept at revealing the thin line between 'normal' and 'hysterical' emotions, as when Deanie, in a bath of apparently scalding water, suddenly turns on her mother: 'Spoiled! No I'm not spoiled.' As Arthur Knight noted, 'the sudden eruption of the girl's madness as she thrashes about in the bathtub strikes a note of pure terror that few directors would even attempt'.[21] Elsewhere Kazan plays on Romeo and Juliet misunderstandings. When Deanie is in hospital and Bud tries in vain (and off camera) to visit her, Kazan cuts to her waking up, insisting to a nurse that 'somebody was there'. The director first slows the pace, re-engaging the story with psychological nuance, with the scene in which Bud meets his future wife, Angelina, a waitress. She smiles a toothy smile, lures him into the kitchen and gives him pizza, apparently then unknown in Kansas. Rather as with Abra in *East of Eden*, Angelina points the way for-ward for the confused male protagonist, while also acting entirely convincingly as a character.

Before the Wall Street Crash capitalism runs wild and alcohol and sex are presented as related taboos. After the Crash there is a change of tone and the last few scenes are in a different, more reflective key. After two years Deanie is ready to leave the hospital and she tells her doctor that a fellow patient, now a doctor in Cincinnati, wants to marry her. At home Deanie unpacks with the help of her mother, who for the first time shows something of her own doubts, as she talks of how she has done her best in bringing up her daughter. Deanie looks at the white marks on the wallpaper, where the pictures of Bud used to be, and we learn that Ginny has died in a car crash and that the old Stamper home has been turned into a funeral parlour since Ace Stamper's suicide. The mother is still anxious that Deanie will want to see Bud again and when two school friends, Hazel and June, come to see their friend, she asks them to keep her daughter away from him. But Deanie is now more assured and when she comes downstairs, resplendent in a white dress, she calmly announces that she now wants to see Bud. We see Hazel, June and Mrs Loomis on the settee, eating fudge, with Mr Loomis (played by Actors Studio stalwart Fred Stewart) to the left in the background, playing patience at the table. We see a closer shot of Mr Loomis, listening, letting his wife hold court. In the wide shot the two girls look embarrassed, unsure if they should reveal Bud's whereabouts, and it is Deanie's father who breaks the spell by telling everyone, without moving from his seat by the window, that Bud is staying at 'his father's old ranch'. Deanie rewards her father's unexpected defiance by giving him a kiss, a gesture pointed up by music.

The coda is played out at the Stamper ranch, where Bud has 40 head of cattle and is fulfilling his earlier wish to go into agriculture. Deanie arrives with her friends and first sees Bud, in a typical Kazan setting, at opposite ends of a country track between two high, untended hedges. The banks of foliage, one in shade, the other in sun, block off the wide screen, concentrating attention on Deanie in the distance and Bud, in blue overalls, in the foreground. Deanie runs some of the way towards him and when they greet each other there is a long silence, a coming to terms. Bud invites her to meet his wife, and Angelina, who is cooking a pork chop in the kitchen in their modest home, walks awkwardly forward. Everyone's humanity is respected. Angelina underscores her rather uncertain invitation to come further into the house by instinctively beckoning to Deanie with a fork, a typical Kazan piece of naturalistic business. Deanie bears up under this succession of shocks, including the revealing of the couple's baby boy, sitting on the floor next to a live chicken. Even the baby has a prop and a bit of business as he taps the bird with a wooden spoon.

There is an understandable stiffness here, undercut only partly by glances and gestures. Wordlessly, Deanie asks and receives Angelina's permission to pick up Bud Junior. Husband and wife exchange side glances, she looking for reassurance and he betraying for a moment a regret at losing Deanie. The awkward but necessary visit is over and Deanie, followed by Bud, passes the camera, leaving us looking at Angelina, slightly embarrassed, but also in some sense perhaps excited to glimpse her husband's past, now that it is firmly in the past. Deanie touches her white dress, able to laugh a little at it, and walking to the car, she announces, perhaps also to herself, that she is getting married the next month, and the two of them make reference to the relation between happiness and taking 'what comes'. After the formal goodbye, with the car in the background, Bud gestures to ask Deanie for one further, private moment, recalling an earlier, silent encounter in the school corridor. They stay back a little from the car and the silence ends with Bud providing closure, telling Deanie, to her evident pleasure, that he is 'awfully glad to see you again'. Bud talks to Hazel and June, promising to invite them out to the ranch for a beer party, while we see Angelina at the door, in a moment that is entirely natural but also suggests her awareness of the significance of the moment. Returning to her, Bud sees that she is tense and moves to kiss her, before we cut to the back seat of the car. Hazel asks Deanie if she still loves him, and we hear her response, over a shot of her in the car, in a narration of her reading of lines (used earlier in the school scene) from Wordsworth's *Ode on Intimations of Immortality*. The last shot is of the car moving away from us, and from the imperfect pastoral idyll. This was clearly a final goodbye; Kazan wrote on the script that, 'like Tennessee Williams and you – you can't go from real closeness just to a "relationship"'.[22]

The film divided critics. Despite detecting 'a certain strained emotionalism' that was not in keeping with the supposed period and place, Paul V. Beckley also found truth and restraint and saw it as 'one of the strongest American films of the year'. The *Newsweek* review saw it as a 'sympathetic satire' that was 'funny, moving and finally beautiful'. To Arthur Knight the combination of detached writing and impassioned direction made the film 'fascinating to watch'. He felt that the issues were honestly presented and that Kazan brilliantly handled key scenes of Inge's 'case history'. Some of the writing mirrored the hysteria that some critics detected in the film. Dwight Macdonald liked the restraint of the ending, but that alone. Otherwise he found Kazan entirely lacking in cinematic savvy and ambition at a time when Antonioni, Renais, Godard and Cassavetes were showing the way forward. Macdonald attacked the film on all fronts, seeing dated technique and clichés (waterfalls as background), vulgarity ('prurient interest') and lack of authenticity ('Kazanistan' and 'Ingeland'). An unnamed *Time* critic found the 'show' to be 'slick, exciting, professional in every detail', but also saw it as obvious and didactic, 'an angry psycho-sociological monograph describing the sexual mores of the heartless heartland'. Kazan was particularly riled by this notice, seeing it as 'invective passing for review'.[23]

French critics have been particularly supportive of the film, from filmmaker Jacques Rivette to critic Roger Tailleur. Robin Wood found a flair for decor and detailed characterisations, but a stridency of tone, playing the 'laboured explicitness' of the script for more than its worth. He cites the prudish old nurse in the scene when Bud seeks guidance from the doctor. Yet some of this stridency reflects the nature of the Stamper family, its neuroses and tensions. Others saw the film as unduly partisan in the generation war, or reacted against what they saw as scenes of emotional excess. Perhaps predictably, a British (and English) critic Penelope Houston, editor of the British Film Institute's *Sight & Sound* magazine, referred to the 'kind of hysterical thrashing of emotions found in Kazan's *Splendour in the Grass*'. Although the film was not commercially successful in France on its release it has since become a strong favourite of French critics. As well as Rivette and Tailleur the critic and publicist turned filmmaker

Bertrand Tavernier, together with a number of *Positif* critics – not just the magazine's editor and Kazan's friend Michel Ciment – have given the film a high placing in their canons of American film.[24]

Kazan was sensitive not only to the pressures for commercial success, but he was also at this time becoming more explicit about his approach to directing. Haskell Wexler, who was the cinematographer on Kazan's next film, was to accuse him of 'lacking an eye'. But as part of Kazan's much more determined effort to sell this film, including to film magazines and critics, he defended the cinematic qualities of his work in bringing the work of good writers to the screen. To a British magazine he argued:

> I am trying in all the films I do to either eliminate as much dialogue as I can or to make it an embroidery on the outskirts of action. Part of the behaviour *is* what they say, but not the essential part of it and in that sense I think my work is getting more cinematic.[25]

> My name is Elia Kazan. I am a Greek by blood, a Turk by birth, and an American because my uncle made a journey.[26]

In his mid and late fifties films Kazan sympathetically explored America's distinct ethnic and racial makeup. *East of Eden* makes fleeting reference to the hostility exhibited towards German immigrants in America during the First World War, while in *Baby Doll* it is the Sicilian who is the catalyst for change in Mississippi and the white man who is the laughing stock, tied to the racist and reactionary Old South. While the character representing the old order is given great respect in *Wild River* (1960), the forces of change are seen as inevitable, and the most sympathetic character is Carol Garth, who embraces change in her own life. The procession of black folks from their feudalism on Garth Island to the mainland of New Deal America, complete with electric light and the presumption of race equality – however compromised in practice, particularly in Tennessee – seems to reflect Kazan's renewed interest in immigration as a social and a personal theme.

Kazan had briefly considered making a film with John Steinbeck on a Greek theme, following a trip he made to Greece with Spyros Skouras in 1951. But the director's first return to his Anatolian homeland since a family holiday in the early twenties was a 1955 trip to Greece and then Turkey, initially with Molly. Kazan had always remembered his grandmother's stories of the old country, but it was during this visit to the town where his father had lived that he discovered a 'calling' to speak both for his father, and for his uncle who had brought the whole family to America.[27] During his work on *Baby Doll* Kazan went on record as wanting to 'do a picture about immigration', a picture 'on my people, the Greeks'.[28] Later he tape recorded his father's memories of the old days, and when his father died in September 1960 he began turning this family history into a first draft screenplay.[29] A script was ready a year later and filming took place in Turkey (four days work, brought to a halt by the censors) and overwhelmingly in Greece, in the latter half of 1962. The independent production was originally to be financed by Ray Stark and Elliot Hyman, but when they withdrew, with the crew preparing to shoot in Istanbul, Warner Bros. was prevailed upon to back the production, despite earlier having turned it down.

Novel, script and film follow the relentless drive of 20-year-old Stavros Topouzoglou to reach America from his home on the Anatolian plains. He is, as Kazan's opening narration explains, a Greek in a land where both Greeks and Armenians are subject to the rule of the Turks. In fact Stavros' Anatolian Greek dream of a better life in America is closely associated with that of two Armenians: one, Vartan, is killed early by the Turkish authorities, while the other, Hohanness Gardashian, makes his own journey. In part out of shame Stavros's father decides to send his eldest son to Constantinople with the plan that he will obtain work with a cousin of the family and eventually send for his brothers and sisters, and parents. Yet on the road Stavros is beaten and robbed and when he finally reaches Constantinople he has also lost some of his innocence. He works as a beast of burden, a 'hamal', to try and raise the 110 Turkish pounds needed for third-class passage to America, but finally agrees to his cousin's plan that he court one of the daughters of a well-off rug merchant, Aleko Sinyosoglou. Stavros is attracted to the prospect of life with Thomna that her father offers him, but remains conscious of his larger mission.

Guilty about the effect of his duplicity on Thomna, he finally reveals to her his plan to go to the United States and declines to accept the dowry. Instead he is reunited with Hohannes, who is one of a group of eight young men who are going to New York to work (for two years without pay) as shoeshine boys. Unable to join this group, Stavros meets the wife of a rich American rug dealer, who pays for his passage to America in return for his services as a gigolo. Yet the husband discovers his liaison with his wife and decides to have him sent back to Constantinople on arrival in New York. A desperate Stavros is briefly tempted to betray Hohannes, who has a consumptive condition, but when his friend jumps to his death from the ship, unable to face being returned to Constantinople, he assumes his identity. Stavros feels that he will finally be 'washed clean' in America and we see him adjusting quickly to American life as a shoeshine boy and preparing, in time, to bring his family, the 'people waiting', to join him.

America America deals centrally with immigration, and is an epic in terms of its treatment of a perilous, uncertain journey. In March 1962 in Paris, where he began casting, Kazan wrote in a notebook of his preparations for the film, including his desire to give the story 'poetry and size', so that stylistically it became a 'moral legend'. He made explicit reference to John Bunyan's *Pilgrim's Progress* and to 'a *Candide* with Hope'.[30] In Bunyan's seventeenth-century allegory (its full title was *Pilgrim's Progress from This World to That Which is to Come*) the protagonist makes a journey from the City of Destruction to the Celestial City, while Voltaire's picaresque novel recounts its hero's adventures, including in the mythical city of El Dorado. Something of this is suggested by the episodic form of Kazan's work, in which Stavros encounters a series of characters who aid, try or tempt him along the way. Also central to Kazan's thematic plan was the hunger for dignity and the terrible things people will do to get it, although he warned himself about making Stavros seem aware of this theme and of reducing his protagonist's experience to a simple lesson. The director wanted people to interpret the central experience differently. Rather as in his thinking about the myth and legend of Emiliano Zapata, Kazan saw Stavros's dream of America, a country of which he had no knowledge, as a product of his desperate need for a romantic, utopian vision that is the opposite of his existing experience. The director wrote in Capri that 'the wonder and the romance of the boy's total EXPERIENCE is the source of the real richness of this legend'.[31]

Another focus of the film was to be Stavros himself and the battle within him between the dutiful son and someone who would do whatever it took to achieve his goal. The second draft of Kazan's script was titled 'The Anatolian Smile', which was also the release title of the film in Britain. Here the reference was to the way minority peoples ingratiate themselves with their masters and cover their shame or hostility. Kazan wrote of Stavros's smile in the face of the insults of the Turkish officer, in the opening scene:

> It is so often the unhappy brand of the minority person – whether Negro, Jew or yellow man – the only way he has to face his oppressor, a mask to conceal the hostility he does not show, and at the same time escape the shame as he violates his true feelings.[32]

Yet he was also aware at the time of preparing the film that he was also thinking of his own life. Kazan had turned 50 in 1959 and he was conscious of his reputation for ruthlessness, not least in terms of his volte-face before the House

Committee. And while the contexts of the fictional and real cases are different there seems to be some emotional parallel between Stavros's leaving (perhaps betrayal) of Thomna in the film, to fulfil his broader mission, and Kazan's own sense of guilt, discussed in his autobiography, about leaving his mistress Constance Dowling in 1945 to return to his wife, after a passionate affair lasting six years. The temptation of a comfortable life as a contract Hollywood direc- tor is associated in this sense with the appeal for Stavros of a life with Thomna and her extended family in Constantinople, while Molly Kazan is identified, as before in Kazan's thinking, with America, and in particular with New York and his ultimate goal to achieve success there. Before filming Kazan drew a paral- lel between Stavros and himself: 'Stavros (you) goes to America, as you went into the world of ART.'[33] In discussing the 'hamal' phase of Stavros's life in Constantinople, where he carries huge loads in order to try and earn his fare to America, Kazan mentioned his own experience at 'taking punishment', taking on multiple jobs to pay his way at Yale and in the early Group Theatre days. The middle-aged Kazan is interested in the 'Man who'll do anything' and in the 'violation of SELF' that this entails. Writing towards the end of the filming, Kazan wrote: 'I started to tell a story about someone else, and gradually tried to turn it into a story about myself.'[34] It is true that during the later stages of Stavros's journey there is a more intense psychological focus on his struggle, on the pressures on him and the conflicts within him. Kazan also contemplated the actual life in America of his uncle, Avraam Elia Kazanjioglou, later 'Joe' Kazan, the man who (like Stavros) brought his family to America. He doubted whether the innocence of that old man, who Kazan had given a bit part in *Boomerang!*, was recoverable. Kazan emphasises what his hero had lost in reaching America, and the scene of his re-baptism by the immigration officer also suggests a merging, at the end, of the qualities of Stavros and those of the much more accepting, more Christian, figure of Hohannes.[35]

The film brings a strong documentary technique to constructing the look (especially the look of faces), as well as the sound and feeling of Anatolian life of the end of the nineteenth century. Haskell Wexler had specialised in making industrial films in Chicago and documentary features and shorts, and *America America* was to be his first major American feature film. Kazan presumably spotted and wanted Wexler's particular expertise in hand held, 'documentary' shooting. Yet while there is much effort, as in *Splendour in the Grass*, on attain- ing maximum cultural authenticity in the use of dress and decor, this goes hand in hand with a consciousness of the events of the drama as 'fable' and myth, in the tradition of the Greek storytellers. The dancing, for example, invokes local traditions and identities, but also transcends the dominant style of documentary realism, reflecting, in the early scene in the Turkish raki house, and later on board ship, the director's notion of the intensity and the 'madness' of the quest.

Kazan uses music as part of his effort to represent Anatolian life, the life given up, as well as to unify and structure the two hours and 45 minutes. At the editing stage he brought in the composer Manos Hadjidakis, a master in both popular music and theatre in Greece and the winner of an Academy Award for his score for Jules Dassin's *Never on Sunday* (1960). Hadjidakis provides different themes for the main episodes of the story, while musicians play a persistent role in the events depicted. For example, after Stavros's mother has chased him home, fearing the consequences of his association with the Armenian Vartan, Stavros is taken in to see his father, who slaps his face before requiring that his son kiss his hand. (Stavros and Vartan have been selling ice, but the early scenes indicate how the Turkish authorities are clamping down on Armenians following the burning of a church in Constantinople.) Reminded of his father's authority, Stavros is sent upstairs to join the other children, but he immediately rejects this status by leaving by the window, and the next change of scene, part of the building of tension towards the moment when Stavros's journey begins, is indicated by a new musical theme. Only when Kazan cuts to the 'Guitars', a Turkish raki house in which musicians play the taut strings of a sanduri, a kind of Greek zither, with drumsticks, is the music revealed as an element of the drama. As Kazan explains, the 'Guitars' is a combination of raki house, coffee house and cabaret, owned and operated by the Turks. Here, in this vignette, is the instability of the opening situation, explained in Kazan's scene setting narration about the inevitability of revolt in circumstances of oppression. A montage of hand held shots, occasionally slightly out of focus, reveal the Turkish customers viewing Stavros, the Greek, and Vartan, the Armenian, with increasing suspicion. Desperate but determined, the two men enact a strange dance, separately and yet in synchronisation. To Kazan the two men were like crusaders taking an oath, while the incantation of the phrase 'America America' suggests the mystical nature of their defiance, and their projection of their hopes for a different life.[36]

Dance also plays a recurring role in the story. Two belly dancers dance for and with Abdul (a thief who attaches himself to Stavros on the road to Ankra), while the dance between two of the Sinnikoglou brothers is a minor but typically textual element of the extended Constantinople sequence, as Stavros is tempted to betray his mission. Mr Kebabian shows what little humanity he has in a night club dance, while at the journey's end, matching the early raki house scene, Stavros becomes a 'whirling dervish' to the amazement and bewilderment of the first-class passengers on board ship. A dance of frustration and anguish, it also seemingly brings about the miracle, for Stavros, of

Hohannes slipping over the side of the ship, in effect bequeathing him a passport to America.

The visual and verbal references to memories and dreams, together with Kazan's introductory and concluding narration, and the role of Stavros's parents as a typical Kazan chorus, all enhance the status of the film story as myth and fable as much as period documentary. A number of scenes, including the first meeting between Stravos and Hohannes and the protagonist's flight from the scene of his murder of Abdul, a speck in a vast expanse of mountainside, suggest the timelessness of Greek mythology. Perhaps most impressive is the pitching of the bodies of the defeated anarchists over a cliff and into the water below. Accompanied by a dirge begun by a woman at the hospital in the previous scene, the episode transcends its narrative purpose and mere decoration and 'business'. Kazan picks out details of the scene at the cliff edge: the horses, the soldiers, and the great expanse of sea below and behind. In simple shots and with no sound except the song and the sound of the waves, we see the women in black dresses and veils, looking on, and the horses, resting. We then see the bodies pitched into the sea, from above, from a remote distance, and then at sea level. The sequence is rare in terms of the absence from it of the film's central character. It marks Stavros's survival and the end of his life as a hamal, but it works separately as a meditation on death, and on the fate of so many would-be rebels and migrants. There is a cut, finally, to the moment of a body's impact, shown from above: a seemingly abstract, circular ripple, a perfect design in an imperfect world. The scene also suggests something of the Aegean legends of Jason and the Golden Fleece.

Cinematographer Haskell Wexler made a strong contribution to the film with extreme long shots and vivid hand held footage. Wexler, who had done second unit work on *Wild River*, was assisted by a camera operator and a first assistant, while a further assistant, Michael Butler, son of the blacklisted writer Hugo Butler, was hired on-site. The production ran on a six-day week, while the camera assistants worked 70-hour weeks, with some working days extending to 14 hours. To Butler, 'Haskell and Kazan worked well with each other', and Haskell 'worked quickly, knowing what the budget restraints and requirements were'. Butler recalls that the director and cinematographer seemed at times to be in a competition as to who was the most proletarian, and who could take the most punishment in temperatures that sometimes topped 100°F. Despite the limited budget and the problems encountered during the truncated Istanbul segment of the shooting schedule, relentless progress was made. Recalling this tough and demanding location schedule, Butler notes that there was 'something sacred attached to the concept of work', while 'the atmospheric machismo' on the set, as Kazan urged his crew and actors to 'Go to work', just before he called 'Action!', was 'thick enough to cut with a knife'.[37]

Kazan relied in his independent films on a number of regular crew members. Michael Butler remembers Kazan's production manager Charles Maguire, who had fulfilled this role on all Kazan's films since *Baby Doll* and been assistant director on *On the Waterfront*, as a 'ruthlessly competent watchdog'. Another team member was Gene Callahan, who won an Academy Award for his production design. Butler remembers Callahan calling additionally on 'someone called Vassili', and this could have been the Greek art director, Vassilis Fotopoulos, who later received an Oscar for *Zorba the Greek* (1964), but who is said to have worked without credit in building and dressing many of *America America*'s sets a day or two ahead of the camera's arrival.[38] Anna Hill Johnston, whose first Kazan film was *On the Waterfront*, created a convincing period flavour in terms of costume design. She and the others were responsible for the striking shots of the waiting immigrants at Ellis Island, a scene filmed in an old Greek customs house using Bulgarian and Romanian refugees, bussed in from camps in Northern Greece. Here and in the scenes on board ship, Kazan and his collaborators create, at low budget, a convincing visual testament to immigrant lives and experiences of the turn of the century.

As usual Kazan made detailed notes in preparation for the filming, on issues of theme as well as character; much space relates to the casting of the role of Stavros. In France he discussed individual actors in terms of whether he saw within them the right mix of traits and in particular the central character's desperation and drive. Kazan also conducted auditions in London and in New York. Steve Paley remembers his own interview for the part, during which he was asked to discuss his own life, interests and motivations. He remembers the director as informal, pleasant and intense. When Paley failed to get the part Karl Malden reassured him by suggesting that Kazan may well have been looking for a shorter man, nearer his own height. After seeing a number of hopefuls Kazan eventually choose the 22-year-old Greek, Stathis Giallelis. For all his deficiencies in acting experience and command of the English language, Giallelis seemed to convince the director on the basis of his need for the part and because the hardships in his own upbringing mirrored those of Kazan's fictional protagonist.[39]

Faced with the length of the film the director attempted to build and release tension and vary the length of scenes and shots. Drawing cautiously on French New Wave practice, he worked with Dede Allen on the editing in such a way as to move the story forward, at times abruptly to later episodes which force the audience to deduce the intervening events. For example, the extended scenes of the Topouzoglou family preparing for Stavros's departure for Constantinople are followed, suddenly, by an extreme long shot of the boy and the heavily laden donkey, setting out down the road. A second shot reveals the rest of the family in the foreground, as they begin to turn away. After this underplaying of the epic moment at which the son leaves his family, a new musical theme and several jump cuts announce the next episode, involving Stravos and Abdul the thief. Hadjidakis's score provides distinct musical themes for the main locations of the story and the effect is to underscore shifts in time and setting, and to emphasise the distinctiveness and 'otherness' of the local culture.[40] For all the talk of a 'fresh start' and of the 'people waiting', there is also something of the idea found later in Kazan's novel, *The Arrangement*:

> They had left that country with its running water, and its orchards of fruit, and all, all that my grandmother never stopped talking about; they had left that to find a better place to live, and all they had found was a better place to make money.[41]

Kazan worked for a short time with the composer and musician Vasilis Tsitanis, while he also commissioned Hadjidakis's collaborator, the poet Nikos Gatzos, to write Greek lyrics for a song that is used over a shot of the procession of the Topouzoglou family, on the brow of a hill, on the way to see their son off on his journey. Kazan wanted the song to capture the feelings of 'people who have to leave some place, a place they love and regret leaving, but one which they must now leave behind them forever'. Much later the director, choosing his 'Desert Island Discs' for a radio show, remembered the music of *America America* as having for him 'the deepest feelings of sentiment, of nostalgia, of love for the background and culture that it represents'.[42]

The film in part reflects the period in which it was made – the Kennedy years of the early 1960s. Change was in the air and there was optimism and idealism about the nation that would fade as the war in Vietnam loomed larger on the domestic agenda. The March on Washington, climax of the civil rights movement led by Martin Luther King, took place in the year of the film's release, while the young President John F. Kennedy's rhetoric about America and its public purpose still had a fresh, revivalist appeal. Molly Kazan reflected something of the feeling about the President by writing a tribute in the form of a poem that was published in the *New York Herald Tribune*, following his assassination. Kazan's film, and the short novel that was published in 1962, for which he secured an endorsement from Attorney General Robert Kennedy, prefigured the assertion of ethnic identity and the 1970s concern with the tracing of cultural 'roots'. Kazan's film was both a tribute to his adopted country and to the myth of America and what it had meant to immigrants. Even before shooting began Kazan, while dissociating his project from what he called 'the Irving Berlin type of patriotism', expressed the hope that his film might revive in Americans the idea that 'our country once meant everything to people in less fortunate lands'.[43] Berlin, the legendary songwriter and composer, had been an immigrant from Russia and was in the early sixties reaching the end of a prolific career in which he was particularly associated with patriotic songs, most notably 'God Bless America'. Just as in *The Grapes of Wrath* the pioneers of Kazan's journey are undaunted by stories that the Promised Land is a fraud. In *America America* a worker who has been disabled in a building accident in America tells Stavros that, without money, he was unwanted there: that 'just like here life is for the rich'. Kazan affirms the myth of America but he asserts ethnic identity as something that is purer and more virtuous. It is for this reason that Stavros dreams on the boat, in New York Harbour, of starting his journey over again, so as to regain the sense of pride and innocence that he once had. The nearest equivalents to Steinbeck and Ford's Joads in Kazan's film are Stavros's long suffering parents, still waiting at the end for their journey to begin. Kazan's sympathies lie not only with the 'people waiting', but with Hohannes, and Vartan and Garabet, whose struggles to change their lives end in failure.

The sweep of the film has three major locales: central Anatolia, the crucial scenes in Constantinople, and the sea voyage to (and arrival in) America. The opening of the film establishes the Topouzoglou family, and the relations of power between the Turkish majority, and in particular the Governor and the Army, and the minority peoples, the Greeks and the Armenians. When Stavros is held because of his association with the Armenian Vartan, we see the shame of his father from Stavros's point of view, as he secures his son's freedom with a tribute. Stavros's encounter with his grandmother is important, although some find the broad American accent of the black actress Estelle Hemsley disconcerting. It is the grandmother who tells the young man that he can only be his father's son, fearful and deferential, and that he should give up his dream of going to America. Kazan, however, has characteristic faith in his protagonist's capacity for change. It is after the failure of Stavros's visit to his grandmother to seek money that his father decides to send him to Constantinople with all the family's possessions. There are nicely judged moments between son and mother, with the son embracing her and she responding by reaching out her hand, but somehow holding back. The mother is perhaps heedful that this is not the moment, as he sets out as the new head of the family, for either of them to play too emotionally the roles of mother and child. The subtlety and restraint of the gesture recalls the last moments of Michelangelo Antonioni's *L'Avventura* (1960), a film that Kazan went out of his way to tell the Italian director that he admired. (The Italian director, in a reply, noted that Kazan had 'always been a master to the men of the Italian cinema'.[44]) In the ambiguous reconciliation at the end of Antonioni's film Claudia's hand reaches out to her unfaithful lover, hovering for a time without touching him. Here the symbolism of European art film and Kazan's more psychologically based sense of gesture and meaning meet and coalesce.

The Constantinople episodes, featuring Stavros, the rich rug merchant Akeko Sinnikoglou, and his supposedly plain daughter Thomna, have a particular depth and emotional delicacy, recording the conflicting pressures on the central character. The sequence has a slower pace, reflecting the family life that Aleko (Paul Mann) and Thomna (Linda Marsh) offer our hero. For a man caught between 'two homesicknesses' (Kazan's phrase), one for the home he has left and one for the home he seeks in America, what Stavros and we see is a vision of belonging (and of wealth). The living room of Aleko is richly decorated, a cluttered Victorian shrine to the family patriarch, separated from a dining room where the women hold court. Stavros's mission is like an 'arrow', to use the key image in Nikos Gatzos's lyrics to Hadjidakis's main theme, aimed at America. Kazan told him that the words should 'express the internal feelings of all the people who swarmed to America at the end of the last century, leaving oppression behind, looking for freedom and the hope of dignity'.[45] But the arrow notion of movement comes up against Aleko's more circular reverie of stasis, of life as given and unchanging. This world provides the main test of and temptation to Stavros and his grand design.

In the world of Aleko – he is played with great warmth by Paul Mann, who as a drama teacher was a key mentor to Barbara Loden – everything is tactile. He manhandles his daughter like a child, calls for food and then complains that there is too much. All sit around, including Stavros as visiting royalty, and Aleko's trio of rotund brothers as another of Kazan's audiences within the drama. The patriarch holds court while exchanging comments about the food and the noise ('muzz muzz') with his wife Anoola. A younger daughter shows Stavros pictures of the island, which prompts Aleko to a revelry, addressed to his would-be son-in-law, concerning the family life that marriage to Thomna would bring. As he talks the young woman stands uncertainly between the two men, with one hand on each, before cautiously perching on the arm of Stavros's chair. The young man remains inscrutable, giving her no encouragement, while Aleko concludes, turning to Stavros: 'And when we die, we will die properly! Surrounded by women looking after us! How does that sound to you?'

Singing and dancing form a bridge to the scene in which Aleko reveals an apartment designed for the anticipated married life of his daughter and her husband. Thomna is at first delighted, but she begins to read Stavros's silence,

Constantinople: Stavros (Stathis Giallelis), with Thomna (Linda Marsh) and Aleko Sinnikoglou (Paul Mann), in *America America* (1963). Courtesy of BFI.

to see that she cannot rely on him playing the appointed role in her father's vision. Stavros remains detached, standing back by the doorway into their bedroom. He tells her that he likes her, but when she asks, from the other side of the bed, if he likes her 'the way a husband should like a wife?', there is no reply. She understands, and framed by the bright white light of the window, tells of a dream in which Stavros appears to her, as a baby with sharp teeth. Stavros now reveals his own dream, his plan, to go to America: 'You have to be what I am to understand', he tells her, declining when she tells him that he can, if he likes, take the dowry and go to America.

The final stage of the journey begins when Stavros, freeing himself of European entanglements, says goodbye to Thomna, telling her that he believes that in America he will be 'washed clean'. Kazan cuts to a heavy wave breaking against the prow of The Kaiser Wilhelm, and then to Stavros and Hohannes on board, scouring the horizon. Unwilling to take Thomna's dowry and unable to become one of Mr Agnostis's group of shoeshine boys, travelling steerage, Stavros has turned to Sophia Kebabian, the dissatisfied wife of a boorish American rug buyer, as the source of his passage to America. On board ship Kazan and Wexler create and observe the class divisions with something of the pictorial care of Alfred Stieglitz, in his renowned 1907 photograph, 'The Steerage'. That picture of the second- and third-class decks, with a man on the upper deck in a straw hat catching the eye, was taken on the trans-Atlantic steamer Kaiser Wilhelm II, although it was travelling from rather than to America, carrying migratory workers. Stavros is now a 'boy-whore', making the down and up journey from steerage to first class, led by the Kebabian's cigar smoking maid, Bertha. She is another observer of Kazan's drama and serves both Mr and Mrs Kebabian, although in the end it is again the money – his money – that counts. As Aratoon Kebabian concludes, after Bertha has reluctantly told him of his wife's liaison, 'when you force a woman to choose she'll choose money'. He reinforces the 'lesson' by at that moment pressing money into the hand of his manservant. When Stavros is marched off by the authorities, without protector or guaranteed employment and therefore destined to be sent back, Aratoon shouts after him: 'This is America, hamal. Do you hear, this is America.'

Kebabian makes explicit the theme of this last episode of the film. He tells Stavros, the 'boy whore', that he has seen hundreds of boys like him, 'boys who leave home to find a clean life and just get dirtier and dirtier'. It is this that Stavros cannot take, and as he languishes in the ship's hospital he dreams of the beginning of his journey. He wakes on remembering his father's slap, which we see again in a darkened memory shot. His final test comes when the consumptive Hohannes faces the inspection of the visiting medical officer, as the ship waits off New York. Not for the first time – one thinks of *East of Eden* and *A Face in the Crowd* – Kazan uses a corridor, with Stavros at one end and Hohannes at the other. Stavros's internal conflict is represented by the way the right side of his face is cast in darkness. Although nothing here is made very explicit, we interpret the action in terms of Stavros, scoured by the memory of his father, and by Aratoon Kebabian's words, resisting the temptation to betray his friend in order to take his place and avoid being sent back. Hohannes foolishly comes down the corridor towards his friend, to celebrate passing the inspection, only to break into an uncontrollable cough; Stavros can only embrace him, muffling some of the noise, but the inspector reopens his door and sees what is going on.

Kazan wants, it seems, an element of doubt as to Stavros's motives, even though in his script notes he writes of Stavros facing this final 'moral crisis' by choosing 'to like himself', and deciding that 'it may not be worth the complete sacrifice of his integrity to get into the USA'.[46] One might ask why he is not at the other end of the corridor, making sure his friend stays in his room. Yet Stavros has not betrayed his friend and this dark, anguished scene is followed by the lyricism of a moment on deck, with a small boat passing and the setting sun playing on the water. All passion spent, seemingly, the two would-be immigrants face starting their journey all over again. Stavros talks of swimming to the shore, cleanly, independently, yet as he enacts his inner despair in a crazed dance in front of the first-class passengers, it is Hohannes, too ill perhaps to contemplate returning, who slips over the side, leaving his shoes, and his papers, for his friend. As Charles Silver has suggested, the central character 'reflects so much of Kazan's own enervating restlessness and what some would call ruthlessness', while Hohannes, whose identity Stavros takes on in his American baptism on Ellis Island, can be seen as representing the director's gentler side.[47]

The immigration official accepts a bribe, but is otherwise cheery, as he renames Stavros as 'Joe Arness'. Kazan thought hard about the significance of this 'baptism scene', although it plays lightly, after all the tension on board. The waiting 'cages' in the immigration hall are vividly presented, and Stavros kisses the ground, in a scene which Kazan claimed that his friends urged him to leave out. As Kazan saw it, Stavros had regained something of his innocence, although the question of whether he would be 'washed clean' in America is inevitably left open. The shoeshine stand scene does show him quickly adapting to American life, as he successfully places pressure on a client to give him a tip. (We also see a black shoeshine boy competing with the parlor's trade being moved on by its owner.) But the remaining emotional punch of the film is with the glimpse of the 'people waiting' in Anatolia, and with Kazan's own closing narration, recounting that all but the father, who died where he was born, were indeed brought to America to make a 'fresh start'.

Kazan certainly adapts his technique in *America America*. He uses the particular expertise of cinematographer Haskell Wexler to capture textual detail, even if Andrew Sarris was distracted by 'nouvelle vague mannerisms' and felt that the 'pointless intimacy of the close-up' obscured the 'contour of a legend'.[48] The occasional use of jump cuts, and the cutting of conventional Hollywood bridging and establishing shots, was designed to vary the pace in a film of such length, as well as to spare the spectator the repetition of verbal explanations. (In an early scene Kazan also cuts, mid-sentence, from a Turkish governor reading a proclamation on the Armenian minority, to a military figure reading the same text – a technique used in Fritz Lang's *M*, in 1930.) In this sense Kazan certainly made use of, for his own quite different stylistic purposes, something of Jean Luc-Godard's editing style in *A Bout de Souffle* (1959), while he also, as before in his work, noted the influence of the episodic form of Rossellini's *Paisà* (1945). He had sampled Godard's method of shooting, sitting in on the filming of his episodic chronicle, *Vivre sa Vie* (1962).[49] Yet Kazan's kind of authorship, his interest in using an epic form to make a personal statement about his family's saga, and about himself, sits uneasily with the New Wave

Stavros's dance on the first-class deck in New York harbour, in *America America* (1963).
Courtesy of BFI.

films, in which he found 'the philosophy of the non-committal'.[50] While Kazan
was constantly warning himself not to make things too clear, too explicit, he is
rarely non-committal and in no sense distanced.

Kazan was aware, in working with Dede Allen on the editing and Hadjidakis
on the musical score, of the personal and emotional nature of his film. Allen
had cut industrial films and had moved to feature films beginning with Robert
Wise's *Odds Against Tomorrow* (1959). Kazan had previously asked her to
respond to the script with her criticisms and reactions and they corresponded
while she alone worked on the dailies when they were sent from Greece and
printed in New York. Allen remembers some differences of emphasis coming
out of the correspondence, in particular one relating to the character of Sophia
Kababian. As a woman, Allen responded to her character and recommended
that the scene between her and Stavros be played off her, with more shots of
her and fewer of Stavros listening. Kazan never gave her 'instructions': when
she phoned him once to ask permission to change something she remembers
that he asked her not to do it again, but to follow her instincts. She found Kazan

to be 'personally gentle and very sentimental but also Machiavellian', someone who would 'do anything to get a scene the way he wants it'. While cutting, editor and director consulted by telephone, before Kazan saw and worked on the shape of the final assembly.[51]

Warners' marketing executive Dick Lederer told the New York office, having seen the film completely edited, unscored and undubbed, that he was amazed at its actual cost of production and would have guessed that it 'cost at least two million dollars more'. Yet Kazan, with an obligation to his own conviction about it, and having worked 'on the fucking thing for two years', realised that, not for the first time, he had not made a film that would be easy to sell.[52] In terms of the different medium of the novel Kazan had been afraid that the 'superintellectuals' would find the book to be naive. Despite the 'faults' of the film, he had 'the most complete respect for it': 'It's what I wanted to do and, as far as my gifts permit, in the form that I wanted to make it.'[53] He took the 'gamble' of showing it to Hollis Alpert of the *Saturday Review* and was rewarded with good reviews from him and several other prominent New York critics, but his most devoted critic, Molly, was disappointed with the film, expressing that view before her shocking and sudden death in December 1963, just before the film's opening in New York.

Other reviewers were more positive. To *Newsweek* it was 'the best American film of the year', while to Stanley Kauffman it was Kazan's 'most vivid work since *On the Waterfront*', but one that was betrayed by a 'basic artistic flabbiness'. Joan Didion called the film 'massively repetitive, insistently obvious, almost interminable and, perhaps in spite of itself, immensely, miraculously moving'.[54] Veteran director King Vidor sent Kazan a telegram, explaining how 'completely involved I was in the conviction of your splendid work'. Haskell Wexler, who Kazan admired but saw as a 'pain in the ass', nonetheless attested to it representing 'the best photography I ever did, mainly because I could see that Kazan was so driven to make as good a film as he could'. He respected Kazan's drive to make a personal film: 'I appreciated it then, and I appreciate it now.'[55] Yet for all this, and its success in 'art houses or theatres that run special attractions', *America America* lost $1.5 million for Warners. Kazan told Jack Warner that he 'wished to God that the picture had come through commercially for you'.[56]

8

Writing in his autobiography on the sudden death of his wife in December 1963, Kazan wrote that 'I knew that something had happened which had completely changed my life, required that I start all over again'.[1] This slow process of starting again was to lead to a six-year hiatus in his filmmaking career, as he recovered from depression, took stock, rearranged his life, and set out on what in time, over the next 30 years of his life, would be a new career as a novelist. The abrupt ending to what he later called 'the strongest tie I've had in my life' brought different emotions, including feelings of shame and guilt, but in time Kazan came to see the subsequent change in his life as a liberation. Part of this change was his farewell to the theatre. From 1962 to 1965, in part in response to his wife's urging, Kazan had worked as co-director with Robert Whitehead of the newly established Repertory Theatre of Lincoln Center. Yet, despite the success of Kazan's production of *After the Fall*, which also marked his reconciliation with Arthur Miller, the overall project was not considered a success, and by 1964 he had taken a back seat, conscious that his days there were numbered. Early in 1965, and following his poorly received production of the Jacobean melodrama *The Changeling*, Kazan resigned as artistic director and announced that he had permanently retired from the theatre.

Kazan saw his psychoanalyst Dr Kelman, and in 1965 the 55-year-old director travelled widely, and began writing a novel in Paris which was completed the next year and published in 1967 as *The Arrangement*. It received mixed reviews but was an unexpected best seller, remaining on the *New York Times* best seller list for 34 weeks continuously. The novel drew on Kazan's relationships with his wife – he records in his autobiography that in the last few years it was more of a 'partnership than a marriage' – and with the actress Barbara Loden. To Kazan in his autobiography, Molly's rigidity had 'began to suffocate me', and his 'infidelities saved my life'. He had first met Loden in 1957 and claims that she helped him find a new perspective and became an ally in his efforts to write about his family history. Loden had been born in 1932, 'on the wrong side of the tracks', and had left her North Carolina home for New York in the late forties, becoming first a 'pin-up girl' and then a Broadway actress. After her appearances in *Wild River* and *Splendour in the Grass* she had won a Tony award for her role – as the character generally seen as based on Marilyn Monroe – in Kazan's Lincoln Center production of Arthur Miller's *After the Fall*. Loden had moved in with Kazan late in 1965 and in 1967 they were married.[2]

Although there are clearly autobiographical elements in the novel, there is much that in no sense derives from his life and experience. The story is of a successful Los Angeles advertising executive who rebels against what he calls 'the arrangement', a term that refers not only to his relationship with his wife, but to the social and business 'civilization' in which he feels trapped. The protagonist of the story, 43-year-old Eddie or Evangelos Anderson, is, like Kazan, of Greek ancestry, while the treatment of Eddie's wife Florence, and his mistress Gwen, allows Kazan to draw on elements of his own life. Yet the advertising man's artistic efforts are restricted to occasional conscience pieces, profiles of public figures for magazines, while Kazan, by the time he met Loden, had a string of impressive credits in theatre and film. The notion of 'selling out' also seems to derive in part from the later experiences in Hollywood of Kazan's old comrade of the thirties, Clifford Odets, who had recently died, and from the old Group Theatre perspective on the movie industry. Kazan's novel explores Eddie's 'madness', as he balances his arrangement with his wife, and her ordered, bourgeois view of life, against the self-disgust that prompts him to renounce his timidity and 'other-directedness' and try to start again, with or without Gwen's company, in a simpler, more honest life. The book ends with the tentative establishment of this new life.

Parallel to the protagonist's uneasy relationship with Gwen is his coming to terms with his own identity as a second generation immigrant. Much of the novel's later action takes place in New York, where his father is dying, and there are constant sequences that record memories of his family upbringing, of the destructive impact of his father's 'merchant blood'. Eddie/Evangelos's actions finally lead him to temporary residency in a mental hospital and there, with other 'drop outs' and 'lost souls', he finally negotiates his independence, his 'fresh start'. Kazan said of his book that he had 'tried to touch the feeling of people who have self-propelled themselves in life and have been successful at attaining something they find they don't really want'.[3] The last 20 pages – rewritten ten times – sketch something of the tentative new life that Eddie, free both of Florence and of his father, and no longer either an advertising big shot or the eldest son of an Anatolian patriarch, contemplates with Gwen. Drawing on some stock notions and characters, and lacking anything very sophisticated in terms of social or political philosophy, the novel does deliver, after 500 pages, a resolution that has some emotional truth and impact. The restrained, 'all passion spent' conclusion shows us a man who, if not sympathetic, has paid a genuine price for his new beginning.

Granville Hicks praised the lively writing but blamed the author for failing to pose the old questions in a 'fresh way that might give us a new insight', while R.V. Cassill made the telling point that there was persistent confusion between Eddie's voice and Kazan's, and that the character of Gwen was sketchily characterised. Yet for all the cliche and 'compromises with showmanship', the reviewer does see something unique and impressive, 'a kind of lyric scream' emerging from the artifice. Kazan's friends were supportive. To Robert Ardrey the novel dealt honestly with a man with an identity crisis 'in a society that's dedicated to anonymity and boredom, who in his search renounces all security, explores all manner of stimulation pleasurable and painful in his search, and finds himself at last'. Novelist and essayist James Baldwin, who Kazan worked with on several projects in the sixties, was also positive, reviewing the book in the *New York Review of Books* and seeing it as an oral account, a tale told with a 'certain raw gracelessness' to fellow members of the 'tribe'. He admired in particular the struggle between son and dying father and also the sympathy accorded Florence, a woman whose limits he sees as a product of her time and place as she fights for a sense of the decency of their life together, as Eddie undergoes a frightening metamorphosis.[4]

Kazan wrote the screenplay himself, but only after first getting the playwright and ex-blacklisted screenwriter Arthur Laurents to write a script from the novel, telling him that he wanted 'another eye'. Yet in the end he preferred to write his own script and remembered struggling with it, feeling that he was 'reducing something that's value was nonplot into nothing but plot'. Looking back on that time Kazan regretted signing a lucrative financial deal with Warners which provided for a $6,600,000 budget. Marlon Brando at one point agreed to rejoin his old partner, but when he pulled out, following the murder of Martin Luther King, Kazan turned to Kirk Douglas. According to Kazan this change of lead actor led him to decide that Barbara Loden, the person in his own life who had inspired the character of Gwen, should not play the role. (Michael Higgins, who played Eddie's brother in *The Arrangement* and who went on to work with Loden, remembered that the studio objected to the Douglas–Loden pairing.) Instead Kazan approached Faye Dunaway, who had joined a Lincoln Center training programme when the Repertory Theatre was being formed there and who had observed Loden's performance in Miller's *After the Fall* at first hand. She was a hot box office star because of the unexpected success of Kazan's fellow Actors Studio teacher Arthur Penn's *Bonnie and Clyde* (1967). Dunaway felt Kazan had given her a start in the business and accepted despite her uneasiness about replacing Loden. Kazan records in his autobiography that his second wife never really forgave him for choosing Dunaway for the part instead of her.[5]

Kazan's screenplay was completed in June 1968 and some additional changes were made in September. The studio, as ever, were attracted by a pre-sold property and looked forward to a profitable outcome of the confluence of Kazan's direction and an adult novel that explored some of the social currents of the day. Yet Kazan's efforts at adaptation led to a film that was a mix of styles and which was fragmented by his efforts both to recount a complex plot and to explore visually the protagonist's own thoughts. The film was not well received by critics and was a failure at the box office. Kazan later argued that he wished that he had made the film in New York as an independent production, in the way that he had made his films of the late fifties and early sixties. But with these films, with the exception of *Splendour in the Grass*, being commercial failures, and in part given the popular appeal of the novel, Kazan decided to accept the studio's largesse.

The opening sequence, which plays without significant dialogue, is effective in establishing a vision of the American 'good life' that Kazan wants to question. To Eddie Anderson, as he wakes up with his wife Florence (Deborah Kerr) that morning, in well-separated beds, all seems well with the world. He is a successful advertising executive with all the accoutrements of the American dream: swimming pool, gardeners, maid and cook and three cars. Nothing needs to be said and any conversation might lead Eddie to miss the reassurance of hearing his latest radio and television cigarette advertisement. Eddie joins the grid of the Los Angeles freeway system, before he takes his hands off the wheel with the car between two trucks; his sudden turn to the right, in front of the truck, is presented as an attempted suicide even though, as we are told later, he protected himself by keeping his head down.

Thereafter the first, Los Angeles half of the film shifts back in time (from Eddie's convalescence), exploring his work and his fascination with a young woman, Gwen, who seems the only person less than impressed by his apparent flair for his job. Although we eventually are told that he did occasional magazine profiles, there is little enough evidence for the 'other self' that Gwen (and later Florence) claim to see. This is where Kazan compromises the undoubted autobiographical element in the film by making his protagonist seem so completely 'in' the advertising world. Gwen is frustrated by Eddie's unwillingness to leave his wife and the lifestyle that goes with her, to make a real commitment. In the present, responding eventually to Florence's plea, he agrees to give the old advertising routine at Williams and MacElroy another go, and a montage – accompanied by martial music – shows the wound up Eddie Anderson, in corporate suit and moustache, doing just that amid obsequious subordinates, sales charts and computer print outs. The music winds down though, and so does Eddie, breaking off from his presentation on the Zephyr cigarette account with one word – 'Bullshit'. Now comes the real 'crack-up', as Anderson 'buzzes' the agency's building in his Cessna plane, before returning to a Florence increasingly sustained by a part comic gang of advisers including the family psychiatrist Dr Leibman and the lawyer Arthur Houghton (Hume Cronyn), both with amorous designs on her.

It is at this lowest point of relations between the 'Golden couple' that Eddie Anderson receives a phone call from his brother Michael in New York, alerting him to the failing health of their father. The second, New York half of the film now charts the efforts of Eddie and his family (including Florence who ultimately also comes East) to deal with the problem of his ailing and paranoid father (played by an actor, Richard Boone, who was disconcertingly the same age as Douglas – a necessary compromise, perhaps, given the need for scenes of him during Eddie's childhood). Amid the explosion of 'youth movies' of the late sixties the treatment of the social issue of old age is certainly unusual, although a further factor in the film's commercial failure. The key focus of the second half of the film, while Eddie and Gwen work out a tentative new relationship, is on father and son, and on the legacy of the first generation of immigrants – of Eddie's father and uncle. Eddie traces much of his obsession with money and materialism to his browbeating father's sense of his own 'merchant blood', while he also does his muddling best to support his father's last wishes against the 'sensible' consensus of the women, notably Florence and Michael's wife Gloria (Carol Rossen). Kazan represents this debate in scenes where Eddie, the salesman, and Evangelos, the more sensitive man in revolt against his past, appear together at his father's dilapidated but once grand place overlooking Long Island Sound. Here Kazan draws directly on his own father's work in the rug business, and his mother's efforts to protect him and encourage his education. The burning down of the house, recalling *Wild River*, leads directly to Eddie's hearing at a mental hospital and the concluding scenes.

There is a degree of plot overload, particularly for those unacquainted with Kazan's book, and in addition there is visual overload. Although the film at heart is a prolonged study of family relations, Kazan shifts styles from realism to satire and introduces a number of more self-consciously stylistic elements. Examples of the latter are slow motion fantasies, fast motion nightmares, moving torn-up photos, mixes from Eddie's POV between Florence and Gwen, and scenes and memory shots of the two Eddie Andersons. In addition there is a throwaway comic strip sequence in which Eddie's fantasies of fighting Gwen's companion Charles are accompanied by exaggerated sound effects and illustrated by cartoon graphics declaiming SOCK!, POW!!, BIFF!!!, ZLONK! and CRASH! The sequence lacks much motivation in Eddie's character as portrayed, except in terms of Eddie's greater sense of humour since his departure from Los Angeles, a change also indicated by his 'funny walk' on returning home after 'buzzing' the office in his plane. Towards the end of the film, in something of the manner of the last scenes of *Splendour in the Grass*, the director reverts to the central human struggle, and to longer takes which refocus attention on his traditional psychological sensitivity for his characters and their dilemmas. Although Florence and Gwen are given their debating points, the emphasis is overwhelmingly on the struggle between Evangelos and Eddie; the women, even Gwen, are not given the same interiority, while the broader politics is unarticulated, restricted solely to points made by Eddie in relation to his own life, about him wanting 'self-respect' and hating his life. Apart from the opening radio broadcast, which refers to the 'enemy war dead' in Vietnam, there is very little that connects Eddie's struggle to the very evident political conflicts of the end of the sixties.

The original script did not end with the funeral of Eddie's father, but instead with a coda – which was apparently filmed – in which the principals explain their new life. While stylistically different – Eddie and Gwen respond to an unseen interviewer – the sequence provided a sense of tentative resolution. Instead Kazan ended with the father's funeral, giving more emphasis to the father–son strand of the drama than to Gwen and Eddie's effort to forge a simpler life. The last 20 pages of the novel were for many the most moving, suggesting that Eddie Anderson, for all his ego and crudeness, had paid a real price for changing his life. The dream of communal living, and of college kids dropping out, in *Alice's Restaurant* and elsewhere was a motif of the time, but Kazan's film was at the very least unusual in its combination of mid-life crisis and a questioning of American business civilisation. The sixties' baby boom generation was the first to be free to opt for post-materialist values over the general materialism, but the struggle of detachment was much harder for those half-way up the ladder, particularly those over assimilated second generation immigrants. Kirk Douglas recounts that Kazan at one point allowed him and editor Stefan Arnstein to reassemble the shot material to revert to the original ending, but that Kazan, fearing a sense of soap opera and wedded to the significance of the funeral scene, kept to his preferred ending.[6]

The coda in the original, June 1968, script was to take place almost a year after the funeral, at the new home of Gwen and Evangelos and the little boy who may or not be his. Evangelos speaks directly to the camera and to an unseen but presumed interviewer; he points to their house, which is still owned by the bank, and suggests his story is one of 'riches to rags?' 'Not for me', says the pregnant Gwen, laughing. Also as if replying to a question she adds that 'I don't entirely trust him'. They are not married, and the effect is of a tentative, equal arrangement between them. The last line of this script, taken from the novel, is that of Evangelos, again to the camera: 'But I do wonder sometimes. Is this what all that drama, that great over-throw was for – this simple living and working, this day to day confluence?' The simplicity of film style implied here – hand held camera and documentary form – is appropriate to the supposed change in their way of living, while this tentative, reflective addition seems clearer in suggesting what Eddie Anderson has gained, and lost.[7] Instead the final cut concludes with the funeral, where the camera picks out the new relationships – Evangelos and Gwen, Florence and Arthur – and ends with an optical zoom into Anderson's eyes.

Kazan later made oblique reference to the success of *Bonnie and Clyde* (1967), and *The Wild Bunch* (1969), in this period, by writing that his film's critique of materialist values – what Kazan calls the 'general fraud' in his novel – 'did not hide behind allegory'.[8] Kazan also blamed his script for the failure, while suggesting that he had been drawn into a big budget Hollywood production that was not his home ground. While Kazan praised Kirk Douglas's intelligence and the drive he brought to the 'salesman' element of the role – it certainly is a demanding and often impressive performance – he also speculated on the impact that a Brando performance might have had. Kazan's golden age had seen him collaborate with actors who were open and to a degree transparent about their own feelings and hurt. To Kazan, Douglas's 'genes didn't permit him to experience – or demonstrate – before the camera the emotional effect I needed'.[9] Douglas was in some sense the same man, in the scenes in which he debates his alter ego in his parents' house, both with and without his moustache and business blazer. To Ciment, the young audience of the time were unable to identify with a 53-year-old actor who they saw in terms of his previous work as an 'obsessive individualist', while Kazan himself felt later that he did not insist enough on the sensitivity of the Eddie Anderson character.[10]

While the satire of the advertising agency seems over broad, that of the 'defence committee' for Florence and the arrangement does work effectively. Hume Cronyn is persuasive as Florence's lawyer and future partner, and as the voice for establishment values. The 'I smell money' scene towards the end, in which lawyer, psychiatrist and other placemen force Eddie to renounce his worldly goods, is an element of the script's close welding of issues of sex and money (Eddie's remark echoes the line from the Phyllis Diller character in *Splendour in the Grass*). Eddie may be exchanging Florence for a younger, if also much more sardonic woman, but he is also saying goodbye to all the material benefits that his salary has brought him. He is giving up a particular notion of the American dream, and in this sense he pays his dues. Gloria, Michael's wife, articulates the case against Eddie – seeing his actions as merely selfish and disruptive. It is she who masterminds the kidnapping of the old man in one of the most visually striking scenes in the film, at Eddie's father's old house on Long Island Sound. Eddie and Gwen are way out on the water in a rowing boat and we see from their viewpoint the silent, ant like figures on the shore, taking Sam Anderson away. Eddie and audience alike can only watch. There are also impressive helicopter sequences of the freeways at the beginning and, wedged in amongst the urban scrawl, the immigrant's funeral plot at the end.

There are also moments of calm in which human relationships are to the fore. At the hospital Eddie sits down briefly and silently with his mother, while at the Mental Hospital to which Eddie has been committed, when Gwen and her baby arrive we see some of the 'middle aged drop-outs', one in a suit and tie, another a rabbi, wandering about on the hospital lawn. The judge refers to them as people who see the hospital as a refuge from the world. These last scenes, including Charles's shooting at Eddie and the burning down of the old house, all told in flashback from the mental hearing, are particularly crowded together, not easy to grasp on first viewing. As to politics, there is little explicit connection to events of the time, beyond the general rhetoric of dropping out and anti-materialism. In flashback we see Eddie reading *Esquire* in bed, though this is no more convincing than the talk of his serious magazine profiles. Later, at the advertising agency, there are prominent framed pictures of boss Finnegan with LBJ, and a signed photo of Richard Nixon. Eddie gives this up for the uncertainty and anguish of New York, and what passes for politics in Eddie's new world is indicated by the 'student' posters on the walls of Gwen's apartment. Kazan asked Faye Dunaway to decorate the set of her apartment and as a result we see the standard icons – pictures of Bob Dylan and of Allen Ginsberg with a pink flower, and various counterculture mottos, including 'Escape while there's still time' and 'Take a Bath Man, Don't Explain'. The year before the film's release Kazan had attended the 1968 Democratic Convention in Chicago, wearing a George McGovern button and writing an article sympathetic to what he saw as the revolution by the children of the middle class against their parents' materialism, dollar orientation and personal hypocrisies. Kazan also attempted other political interventions. He tried and failed to persuade Warner Bros. to re-release *A Face in the Crowd* during the election campaign and joined world filmmakers to protest the (temporary) 1968 dismissal of Henri Langlois from the Cinémathèque Française.[11] Yet *The Arrangement*, perhaps because the events that inspired it date from the late fifties and because the conflicts are inside Eddie's head, fails to engage with, translate to, the wider social mayhem of America at the time.

It was in 1968 that Andrew Sarris had responded to French auteurism with his own critical assessment of film directors, and Kazan had occupied the 'Less than Meets the Eye' section along with Huston, Lean, Mankiewicz, Wilder, Wyler and Zinnemann. The brief piece recognised Kazan's brilliance with actors but found his 'violence' to be 'more excessive than expressive, more mannered than meaningful'. When Sarris wrote specifically on *The Arrangement*, however, he was unexpectedly supportive, perhaps in part because of their shared Greek heritage. He saw the film as 'Kazan's testament to the tenacity of an entire generation of materially successfully pilgrims in search of moral justification'. He felt that the film owed nothing to 'contemporary pain-killing devices such as pop, camp and absurdism', and compared its 'completely absorbing entertainment' to the 'mad mush' of *Medium Cool* (Haskell Wexler, 1969), and its first person honesty to the 'satirical smugness' of Fellini.[12] Yet Sarris was generally the exception among American critics in responding to what Kazan was trying to say. Pauline Kael, who had immediately recognised the virtues of *Bonnie and Clyde* two years earlier, was scathing, finding its anguish over selling out to be 'painfully bad in a way that isn't fun'.[13] She found the performances to be mediocre and lacking spontaneity, and asked: 'How can he talk to us about spiritual renewal and make a film that looks like this – a big, cliché-ridden, false eyelashes-in-bed, star-stoned movie?' She has a point I think, although I also share Sarris's admiration for the ambition and commitment of the project and for its human scale, and feel that the novel's point about re-examining and rejecting the false values of an immigrant's vision of success does come through. Kazan's film is also a kind of men's movement exhibit (if such a phenomenon existed), loudly debating his own and his protagonist's ideas about relations between the sexes based both on class and his immigrant tradition.

It is interesting to compare the much more positive French reception of the film and also the way in which many French critics responded to what they see as its critique of American business culture. Jean-Louis Cosmolli in *Cahiers du Cinéma* referred to the 'repetition within a repetitive movie', feeling that there were too many themes, none treated in depth, and presented in the form of an avalanche, such that for the spectator the result was vertigo. Yet Robert Benayoun wrote of the legal supremacy of women in the Unites States, and of the two forms of such feminine power represented by Florence and her retainers, and by Gwen. He saw the film as baroque and complex, fiercer and more inventive than the novel, and as providing a 'cruel portrait of materialist America' with echoes of the rebirth of the end of *East of Eden*. To Gilles Jacob,

Kazan 'seemed that he wanted, once and for all, to exorcise the evils of his adopted country', yet he felt that the film should have been longer, found the mechanism of flashbacks irritating, and felt that the madness was sanitised, and that Douglas always seemed too much in control.[14]

The commercial failure of *The Arrangement* further undermined Kazan's ability to raise money for film projects. With Budd Schulberg he had been trying to finance a project to make 'In the Streets', based in part on *Down These Mean Streets*, a 1967 novel by the young Puerto Rican writer Piri Thomas; Oscar Lewis's *La Vida*, a 1966 study of a Puerto Rican family in San Juan and New York, was also an influence on Schulberg's script. The story was described as about 'one Puerto Rican family's physical and spiritual journey from the mountains from which they are dispossessed, to the slums of San Juan, to the streets of New York'. Sam Spiegel agreed to finance the project and Schulberg spent three months in Puerto Rico, with Kazan joining him to consult and scout for locations, but when Spiegel withdrew his backing for the project they were never able to raise alternative finance, despite making periodic attempts up until the early eighties. Also at this time Barbara Loden, working with the documentary cameraman and editor Nick Proferes, who had worked with D.A. Pennebaker and others at Drew Associates, directed *Wanda* (1970), with some marginal assistance from Kazan, who had declined to direct. The low budget super 16mm film, which had little impact in America but which received the Critics Prize in Venice, in some ways indicates the gap between Kazan's own work and that of low budget filmmakers such as Loden and John Cassavetes. A study of a drifting, alienated young woman (played by Loden) who attaches herself to an incompetent bank robber, the film avoids conventional attractions – Loden called it an 'anti-*Bonnie and Clyde*' – and any sense that the central character's bitterness and estrangement would or could be easily reformed or redeemed.[15]

Loden's low budget film pointed the way to *The Visitors* (1971), on which Kazan also worked with Proferes. The idea came from Kazan's suggestion to his son Chris that he explore a contemporary article about a veteran who, while in Vietnam, had reported a fellow soldier to the authorities for raping and murdering a local girl. Kazan's 33-year-old son had graduated from Harvard in 1960 and worked on an Arkansas newspaper, before writing two novels in the late sixties. Daniel Lang's *New Yorker* essay had told a true story of a G.I. who had been a member of a reconnaissance patrol in Vietnam with a sergeant and three other soldiers. The sergeant set out to capture a young Vietnamese girl and take her on the mission for the sexual enjoyment of the men, and when she was raped and murdered, the G.I. prompted an investigation. There was military resistance, with arguments raised about the bravery of the men in other contexts and the similar abuses conducted by the Viet Cong, but courts martial were finally held and the men were sentenced to various terms in military prisons. After the ordeal of giving testimony the 'informer' was discharged from the army and re-entered civilian life with his young wife. The other men had their sentences reduced and all were eventually (by 1969) released. Although the article took the story no further, Lang reported that the man and his wife were not without fear that two of the members of the patrol might possibly try to track them down and seek revenge.[16] It is this last scenario that became the basis for the Kazans' film.

Chris Kazan wrote the screenplay and his father, unable to raise conventional financing, borrowed money himself and made the film with Proferes, a non-union crew of four, and actors who would work without contracts. The bank loan was eventually paid by the distributor, United Artists. The film was made for less than $170,000, with shooting over seven weeks in January to March 1971, using super-16mm stock, in and around the adjoining homes of Kazan and his son in the Connecticut countryside. (Proferes used a 16mm camera that had been converted to Super 16, which had 60 per cent more usable negative when blown up to 35mm. By shooting in 16mm film and processing costs were cut by three-quarters.)[17] None of the cast, with the exception of Actors Studio veteran Patrick McVey, had previously appeared in a feature film. The film became a 'non-union pick up' for United Artists, a not uncommon arrangement at the time, despite union-studio agreements to the contrary. Kazan, who originally claimed that he did not direct *Wanda* because it had a non-union crew, later amicably paid a Screen Directors Guild fine for working on *The Visitors* without an SDG contract. James Woods, who had appeared in the successful Broadway production of *The Trial of the Catonsville 9,* made his screen debut as the ex-soldier who had informed the authorities of the rape, while Chico Martinez and Steve Railsback came from the Actors Studio, and Patricia Joyce (as Bill's partner Martha Wayne) was a senior drama student at Yale. Woods has since spoken without much enthusiasm of Kazan's efforts to encourage enmities between him – he was staying at a local inn – and the actors playing the visitors, Martinez and Railsback, who were put up in a boarding house in town.[18]

At the time that the film was planned there was much discussion of the March 1968 My Lai case, belatedly broken to the public in November 1969. First Lieutenant William L. Calley Jr. had been charged with the murder of a hundred civilians as part of the mass killing in a South Vietnamese village. The trial began in November 1970 and Calley was convicted in March the next year. The case provoked an angry debate between opponents and supporters about the relative responsibility of Lieutenant Calley and of the politicians who had planned and conducted the overall strategy of the war to defeat the Viet Cong in South Vietnam. There was particular anger in relation to President Nixon's invasion of Cambodia in May 1970 and the shooting of four peacefully protesting students by National Guardsmen at Kent State University in Ohio. Ralph Nelson's 1970 film *Soldier Blue*, detailing the massacre of the Cheyenne by the US Cavalry, was seen by some in terms of the news story about events in My Lai.[19]

From his notes on his son's original screenplay of November 1970 it is clear that Kazan was determined that the soldiers, particularly the two ex-convicts who come looking for the man who turned them in, should not be presented as 'psychos' or obvious villains. In a note he stressed that such young military men were brought up 'with the most terrible weapons of destruction in their hands, yet with the souls of kids', a similar notion to his point about the protestors he observed at the 1968 Democratic Convention in Chicago.[20] He wanted the characters to be ambivalent and bewildered – a recurring Kazan term in his notes. Sergeant Nickerson in particular – the leader of the patrol – is seen as a soldier who had learnt to follow orders and who was only now, having been released from jail, beginning to act more independently. Kazan seemed to want neither a polemical film about the war nor a genre piece about revenge. What happens is instead traced both to the brutalising experiences of the young soldiers in Vietnam and to the events, interactions and confusions that play out in front of us in what is in effect a theatre piece. Yet some audiences were made uneasy by what they saw as the too great a role played by the 'victims', Bill and Martha, in provoking or triggering a revenge that, as Kazan saw it, had its roots in the brutalising of 'kids' by their military and Vietnam experience. At the time he made an explicit comparison with a film by a 'very intelligent communist', Elio Petri's *Investigation of a Citizen Above Suspicion* (1970), which he had just seen. To Kazan the problem with films such as this one was that they 'set out to prove something and they prove it'. This predictability, in which 'in the end nothing is human', was, he felt, 'a danger in Chris's script'. To avoid this he wanted a moment in the film when viewers would feel confident that the revenge, suggested as a denouement when the two soldiers arrive at the farmhouse, would not occur. He also wanted the revenge, when it did happen, to seem to flow from the interaction of the characters of the drama, although the danger here is of muddying the moral waters. He argued in his script notes that when the revenge is effected 'it is not for a reasoned and "deep" reason, but because of Bill's character and an erratic reaction to it on Nickerson's part'.[21]

The film, which United Artists opened at a single cinema in New York in February 1972 (and never released nationally), begins by establishing the place of the drama, before the arrival of the 'visitors'. It is a cold and sunny Saturday morning, with snow covering the houses and surrounding countryside. In his plans Kazan had written of people lost in a white and cold landscape, and of a Japanese style of 'small figures in a landscape', 'locked in their own silences'.[22] A baby cries and lights are switched on in a house bordered by a busy road. The coldness contrasts to the veterans' memories of their war experience and to the view of those at home who were watching the newly coloured pictures of the first television war. The brief Vietnam flashback, later in the film, is a visual shock for this reason. Successive shots observe the young couple, whose relationship seems at the beginning to be both affectionate and strained. The camera then reveals a nearby building, through the window of which we see a middle-aged man typing vigorously on a typewriter. This is Martha's father, Harry Wayne (Patrick McVey), a Second World War veteran and writer of Westerns. The surname rather obviously suggests John Wayne, director of the first and most reactionary of the Vietnam films, *The Green Berets* (1966). Harry owns the estate and lives in one house, while his daughter and her boyfriend Bill, recently returned from Vietnam, are 'caretakers' of the other house.

The two Vietnam veterans, a Puerto Rican, Tony Rodriguez, and Sergeant Mike Nickerson, have come east to look up their wartime 'buddy'. Although the audience are given slightly different accounts of the events that link Bill and the visitors, it emerges that Bill turned in the other two when they raped and then killed a 15- or 16-year-old girl, possibly a Viet Cong, in a Vietnamese village. Bill testified at the resulting court martial and the two soldiers served two years in the army prison at Leavensworth before being released on a technicality. This information immediately suggests the motive for their visitation might well be revenge, although Tony, who seems easy going, tells Bill that, as far as he is concerned there are 'no hard feelings'. To Martha, when Bill tells her the story, it was a 'brave thing to do', although Bill now seems less than sure, telling her that he had not prevented what happened and that in any case 'the VC do exactly the same thing', and the soldiers were his 'friends', his 'buddies'. When Martha, who we are told has been on peace demonstrations, suggests that Bill call the police he replies that he 'can't do it to them again'.

Harry strikes up an immediate rapport with the visitors but is suspicious of Bill and his views on Vietnam. When Harry's dog is attacked by a neighbour's Great Dane, Tony kills the dog with one rifle shot and he and Mike carry the dead dog to the neighbour's door, a shot that seems ominous and suggests images of war. *The Visitors*, years before other film treatments of the war, presents it mainly in terms of its effects on home front issues of gender and masculinity.[23] The film's only woman is critical of the war, while Bill, in part because of his role in the court martial, has his masculinity questioned. When Harry and the two soldiers come to Bill and Martha's house to watch the football game on television it is Bill who seems awkward and out of place. He tends the baby, drinks beer rather than whisky, and later, at dinner, has his meat well done rather than rare. Harry is a burnt out case, tangential to the central drama and seeing Martha's partner as a 'weirdo' and Mike as a surrogate son. When Mike later tries to justify the murder, arguing that the Vietnamese girl would have turned them in, he reveals that all but Bill 'had a little fun with her first'. Harry's comment, about Bill, is that 'I always thought he was half queer'. Kazan indicates the gap in understanding when Harry points to the mounted head of a buffalo that he had shot, decorated in sixties' countercultural style with a pair of spectacles. What is machismo to one generation is a joke to another.

The climax of the drama takes place in a series of encounters and conversations before, at and after dinner. Harry staggers drunkenly back to his home and Martha asks the two soldiers to have coffee before they leave. Bill seems preoccupied, playing cards alone. Martha and Mike relax, supplementing their coffee with the whisky that Harry had left behind. Mike tells her that (in relation to the rape) 'everyone was doing it', and he talks of a war in which your friend could get his legs blown off because locals didn't reveal that the Viet Cong were there. Martha tells him: 'You're right you know, I haven't been there and I can't imagine it.' At this point Martha, perhaps confident that the visitors are soon to leave, switches to a radio programme of dance music, and then lies down on the couch, the lighting drawing attention to her mini-skirted legs. Touching Mike's coat, she seems suddenly drawn to him, in part because he seems convincing, in part because of Bill's withdrawal, his lack of confidence in his own position. In various ways and degrees Kazan seemed interested in women who in some sense fell in love with the enemy. Mike tells her that in Vietnam he used to think that the people who went on anti-war demonstrations were 'long haired freaks, with clothes like Indians'. Vulnerable, she reveals something of her frustration with Bill, telling of his offer to 'do me a big favour' by marrying her before the baby was born. She responds, if passively, to Mike's invitation that they dance.

At this point Tony notices the dancing, with Martha with her face on Mike's shoulder, her arms around his neck, and he signals wordlessly to Bill (in the kitchen) that he should check on his girlfriend. Bill looks, and then moves to push the two apart; when he slaps her, she tells Mike that he'd 'better go now'. But Bill provokes a fight by hitting Mike, and the two men go outside to continue their struggle, hidden from view in typical Kazan fashion behind the parked car. Mike smiles, as if he welcomes the opportunity for violence, and gives Bill a severe beating, with Martha urging Tony to shoot Mike before Bill is killed. Finished outside, Mike then comes inside and finds Martha upstairs phoning for help, whereupon he slaps her, pushes her over onto the floor and rapes her, ignoring her shout of protest. Downstairs Tony lugs Bill, who is unconscious, inside. As Mike comes downstairs he seems to signal to Tony that it is his turn, in much the same way as he presumably did in Vietnam. Tony goes upstairs and confronts her, but there is no clear evidence as to whether a double rape takes place.

Downstairs, Mike walks outside and urinates into the snow by the car. He lies back on the bonnet of the car and we get a shot of him in repose, from above. We see what he sees, the branches of nearby trees, before the sudden, short sequence of his memory of the chase and rape of the Vietnamese girl, through long grass. Tony joins him, and the two reverse the car down the drive and are gone into the night. A final coda has Bill pulling himself on to a chair in the living room and Martha slowly descending the stairs, sitting down opposite Bill. A wide shot of the two of them is held for some time before Bill asks her 'You all right?', and she seems to nod slightly in reply. In terms of the revenge story one might read the two as moving together as victims of the assault from outside, yet all along the Kazans seem keen to insist on the ordinariness and banality of the outsiders, and on the way in which their violent intrusion in some sense draws on, takes advantage of, exacerbates, the tensions at home.

The film was certainly the first to suggest the impact of the war on the home front. The director described his film as an 'anti-war story', and his contemporary interviews include disparaging remarks on both the war and President Nixon. Yet the Kazans present no clear focus of identification in the film, making Bill a rather weak and passive figure and giving the sergeant a stronger and more vigorous defence of his wartime actions. The 'sides' sometimes seemed unclear in Vietnam, and this perspective also applies to the home front in *The Visitors*. Martha is a pacifist, a demonstrator against the war, but even she comes to accept that she does not really understand the experience of soldiers. Kazan expressed a related perspective of the war and the home front in his novel *The Assassins*, which was published only a few months after the release of *The Visitors*. One critic called the novel 'yet another masochistic pot shot at liberals and liberalism from an essentially liberal sensibility and conscience', while another found that the author, although clearly 'antimilitarist and anti-establishment', was 'equally disenchanted with the drug culture and revolutionaries'. For whatever reason, dramatic or otherwise, Kazan seems similarly reluctant to point any overall moral lesson in his film. Whether influenced by his own traumatic testimony or not, Kazan as director seems in this film to distrust his own liberalism. In his film it is Bill, the informer, who most would see as doing the right thing, yet script and direction cloud this essential issue.[24]

Kazan's rationale for bringing out the ordinariness of the violent intruders was that the 'whole point of brutality in war is that the nicest people do it'.[25] His position, closely allied to that of his son, seems to be that it was the whole experience of the war which brutalised perfectly ordinary, and often admirable, young men. While the structure of the film, and in particular Steve Railsbeck's playing of Nickerson, suggests revenge as a motive early on, and also perhaps something of the ominous feel of Harold Pinter's The Birthday Party, script and direction suggest how the violence at home feeds as much off latent tensions of generation and gender than the war itself. Kazan certainly resists any notion of a demonic invasion of a rural idyll, or the Manichaean moral polarities of Sam Peckinpah's allegorical Straw Dogs (1971). To Kazan, Straw Dogs 'made it easy for people to reject their own violent natures by saying "Those people on the screen are brutes, but they are not like us!"'. To Kazan '"My Lai" was not done by monsters or psychos, or by any other of those slaughterers out there. They were done by familiar American boy figures.'[26]

Kazan's lack of emotional identification with the victims, with Martha and Bill, seems to have contributed to the uncertain reception of the film in America. Kazan wanted 'to get the audience bewildered', but then wondered why the response was not more positive. The nine-day New York audience, probably weighted with opponents of the war, wanted a more unproblematic message, or found too little visual variation and impact. For others it was too soon and too dangerous for any critical representation of the war on the screen; it would be another seven or eight years, after the American withdrawal and defeat, till the release of Coming Home (1978), The Deer Hunter (1979) and Apocalypse Now (1979). Does Kazan go too far in humanising the sergeant, giving the 'pacifist' couple too little moral power? Or does he test our ability to think about the story of the war's domestic impact without taking our cues from our prior political assumptions or from easy identification with demarcated heroes and villains? The other problem, raised by Jonathan Rosenbaum, relates again to the victims; he asks why this supposedly 'pacifist' man strikes the first blow against Mike, and whether Martha's 'flirtation' with Mike is credible.[27] By making problematic the 'liberal' characters and their position, Kazan may weaken the film's clarity from any stance.

A few critics responded positively to the film during its short, truncated New York run. Vincent Canby found the film to be moving, and liked the assurance of the young actors and the way it was kept 'small scale'. He did feel it credible that Martha allowed 'herself to be sexually drawn to one of the terrifying visitors'. Charles Michener in Newsweek also found the film to be 'a taut, modest psychological thriller that is finally a call to contemplation'. Andrew Sarris referred to the Harry character as a cardboard caricature, but still objected to a cinema distribution system that meant that the film was hardly seen in America. To Hollis Alpert there had been quite enough rape and violence in recent films, and *The Visitors* was 'neither needed nor welcome'. Like others he found particularly unsettling the scene in which Martha, for whatever reason, 'encourages the advances of the creepier of the two visitors'.[28] In May 1972 Kazan took the film to the Cannes Festival, where it was gener ally respectfully received. One critic, Guy Teisseire, found it honest and unsettling, a film that suggested 'an American society in confusion'. To Teisseire the visitors back from hell first try to forget their experience, but revert to the brutality that Vietnam has engendered.[29] Kazan's film had supporters on the prize jury, but the award went (rightly) to Francesco Rosi's *The Mattei Affair*. The chairman of the jury that year was Joseph Losey, who had left America for Britain in the early fifties rather than cooperate with the House Committee. In his jury notes, he expressed admiration for the restrained direction, but he latched onto the 'informing theme' and saw a 'confused metaphor and personal whine'.[30] In any case the commercial failure drove Kazan further away from film, before his old collaborator, Sam Spiegel, the man who had let him and Schulberg down over the Puerto Rican film, invited him back into the limelight.

9

The Last Tycoon (1976): A Coda

With the exception of his 'home movie', *The Visitors*, Elia Kazan had not directed a film for a producer for 20 years, since making *On the Waterfront* with Sam Spiegel. While Spiegel had withdrawn his backing for the director's planned Puerto Rican project in 1973 he had kept Kazan in mind, along with other directors, for his next production, an adaptation of F. Scott Fitzgerald's uncompleted 1941 novel, *The Last Tycoon*. Spiegel had pursued the rights to the novel for some years, and wanted his film to be a 'distinguished' and 'gentle' picture that would contrast with what he saw as the contemporary trend towards violence in film. Spiegel worked closely with director Mike Nichols and then successfully approached the British playwright Harold Pinter to write the screenplay, before turning back to Kazan when Nichols withdrew. Pinter, born in the East End of London in 1930, had made an impact with his early plays *The Birthday Party* (1958) and *The Caretaker* (1960), while his first screenplay was for *The Servant* (1963), directed by Joseph Losey. Although Kazan was now devoting himself to writing, the director quickly accepted, in part because the assignment allowed him to move his seriously ill mother to Los Angeles and to remain close to her. Before Kazan's arrival on the project, Spiegel, Nichols and Pinter had already decided to use only the six chapters of the novel as originally edited by Edmund Wilson and not any of the more melodramatic ideas that the novelist had left on his death for the work's completion.[1]

The renowned Hollywood novel dealt with the 'Love of the Last Tycoon', to use a title that Fitzgerald considered and may have preferred. The tycoon was a studio executive, Monroe Stahr, a character based on Irving Thalberg, the 'boy wonder' MGM production executive who supervised that studio's productions from 1924 until his death at the age of 37 in 1936, and who Fitzgerald had worked with and admired. Spiegel's film was originally to have been made for MGM, which would have facilitated the use of film extracts from the Thalberg era at the studio, but Spiegel shifted the production to Paramount when they offered a better distribution deal, with filming to begin in November 1975. The critic Hollis Alpert, who was given special access to the set, saw the 73-year-old producer as very much in control – 'Auteur theory be damned', Spiegel comments – yet Kazan approached the project with his usual, meticulous concern to explore issues of behaviour, the more so given the typically spare and elliptical nature of Pinter's screenplay. Kazan's ability to distil and define the thematic spines of a dramatic text is evident in the published extract from the production diary written at the time. For Kazan, Stahr was a man with a sense of mission, a 'prince' who has been living a monastic life since the death of his wife, and who is resisting a 'mercenary and reactionary crowd' around him at the studio. Stahr's sudden obsession with a young Irish woman who has a strong likeness to his late wife is an attempt to regain his humanity that instead leads to him to fatally expose his vulnerability, as he is eventually outmanoeuvred at the studio.[2] This is perhaps a characteristic Kazan reading, with its sense of the danger of displaying male weakness, but it goes some way in binding together the work's public and private strands. In June 1975 the director visited Pinter in London to discuss 'last' revisions to the screenplay, but his only major story contribution seems to have related to the film's ending, in which Stahr, having lost both Kathleen and the studio, is seen to walk slowly into the darkness of a sound stage. In retrospect this conclusion gives a further edge of melancholy to the film by signalling Kazan's own farewell to the cinema.

The director's other major intervention was in putting his weight behind the choice of Robert DeNiro, who had just completed *Taxi Driver* (1976), for the central role of the producer. Other cast choices, including the inexperienced actresses Ingrid Boulting, as Kathleen Moore, and Theresa Russell, as Cecilia Brady, came initially from Sam Spiegel. Boulting, whose father was the British director Roy Boulting, had early experience of acting but had turned to a modelling and fashion career at age 21. She later put herself forward to Spiegel for the key role of Kathleen, and was studying with Lee Strasberg in New York when she was awarded the part.[3] Despite Pinter's belief then and later that the choice of Boulting was a mistake, Kazan, who conducted an improvisation with the actress, came to accept that she could be right for what he saw as an 'apparitional' role as the woman whose accidental presence on the studio lot reminds Stahr of his dead wife, the Hollywood actress Mina Davis. Other casting recalled the old studio era, with Robert Mitchum (as rival studio executive Pat Brady), Tony Curtis (as Rodriquez, one of the studio's leading men), Ray Milland (as the lawyer, Fleishacker), Dana Andrews (as a director, Ridingwood), and John Carradine as a studio guide.

In the novel that Edmund Wilson had edited for publication on Fitzgerald's death, Stahr does not meet the mysterious figure of Kathleen Moore until after the half way point. The opening scene on a plane, together with its reflections on the American East and West, is excluded in Pinter's script, as is the narration by Pat Brady's daughter Cecilia. The ailing and lonely executive, a perfectionist who is concerned with quality filmmaking more than the commercial bottom line, is both revived and distracted when he meets Kathleen when she finds herself on the flooded studio lot following an earthquake. The producer pursues the young woman and takes her to his unfinished beach house in Malibu, where they make love. Kathleen breaks off the relationship by letter, explaining that she is to be married, but she then telephones the executive, initiating a final meeting in which he has a last chance to convince her that he is committed to her, an opportunity that he fails to take. This final meeting is absent from script and film, where the last contact between the two lovers, before a fateful telegram from Kathleen informing Stahr of her marriage, is a brief phone conversation. The original novel had ended with Stahr's encounter with the Communist union organiser from New York, Brimmer, and with a note that Stahr is to marry Cecilia. Ignoring this last element, Pinter added a scene in which the Board of Directors of the studio, led by Brady, suspend Stahr from his job as a result of his bruising encounter with Brimmer (Jack Nicholson). Kazan, writing notes on Stahr's character in late 1974, saw Stahr's dialogue line, in novel and screenplay, 'I don't want to lose you', as applying both to his loss of Kathleen and the studio, thus bringing together the love affair, which Fitzgerald had described in 1939 as 'the meat of the book', and the broader Hollywood story.[4]

As Joanna Rapf has pointed out, Pinter's adaptation gives Fitzgerald's story a darker, more elegiac cast and shifts attention from Monroe Stahr to Scott Fitzgerald himself.[5] In this sense the film is reverential to the work of a dying man, the novelist, who was himself writing about a dying man, the tycoon. The critics who disliked *The Last Tycoon* on its release felt that this double sense of reverence deprived the film of impetus and vitality. Others, seeing the glass half full, admired its craftsmanship, its faithfulness to something of the novel, its unforced and contemplative pace, and the absence of either commercialism or easy satire. The slow pace, particularly in the extended scenes at Stahr's beach house, may also reflect Spiegel's notion of 'distinctiveness', but also seems to relate to the welding of narrative cinema and the European art film that was a characteristic strand of seventies American cinema.[6] In planning the beach house episode Kazan warned himself not to 'hop this scene up' and inject conflict that was not properly there. Deferring to Pinter's style he noted, opposite these script pages of the final screenplay, that 'like all Pinter, the important thing is in what is not said'.[7] Kazan does counterbalance the slowness of the two sequences on the beach with the urgency of a short, connecting scene when the couple return to the parking lot. (As Colin McArthur once noted, Kazan often plays scenes of emotion and drama in and around cars.) It is here, in a scene given more weight in film than script, that Stahr for once shows his hunger for Kathleen, kissing her passionately in a way that leads to their return to the beach house for the night.

Despite Kazan's willingness to respect the script, in the manner of his work with Budd Schulberg, the director was unhappy with aspects of the love story. He communicated this view to Pinter, usually via Spiegel, but little was changed. Ingrid Boulting recalls that the director showed her copies of letters he had sent to Pinter about developing the role of Kathleen: 'the letters were sent but Pinter was happy with the character as he wrote her'.[8] Stahr's obsession with and desire for the ghost-like figure of Kathleen fights with a reticence, a reluctance to make the kind of commitment that might capture her and, it is implied, save himself. Boulting had worked mainly as a model with photographers including Richard Avedon and David Bailey; as I write, her website, entitled 'Bringing together art and spirituality', suggests something of the ethereal quality that Spiegel and Kazan saw as fitting the part. In fact Boulting felt frustrated by this apparitional, enigmatic reading of her role, and by being told by such a master of psychologically grounded acting as Elia Kazan that she was 'not to show anything'. She also remembers doing improvisations with Robert DeNiro that were not permitted to reach the screen.[9] While the character certainly appears as otherworldly, as a projection of male longing and search for renewal, she is less convincing as the flesh and blood Irish girl who wants a quiet life, and who ultimately rejects the prospect of competing both with the memory of Mina Davis and with the studio as Stahr's first love.

Indicating the filmmakers' interest in Fitzgerald himself, Kathleen Moore in the film becomes something of a sign or symbol, a kind of green light flashing across the Sound, representing for Stahr an ideal and a past that he can never quite allow himself to reach or recover. In this sense the film does capture an element of Fitzgerald's romantic pessimism, but at the expense – at several points in the scenes between Kathleen and Stahr – of dramatic persuasiveness. In terms of such iconic female images the script makes several references to Greta Garbo, the MGM star who retired from the public gaze around the time that Fitzgerald's book was first published, walking into her own dark sound stage. In the film the Communist writer Brimmer, having dinner with Stahr and Cecilia, looks across the studio commissary, searching in vain for Garbo. Not a man who was inclined to be romantic about Hollywood, Kazan had written to producer Lester Cowan in his first year in the film capital, declaring that she was 'about the best actress pictures ever had' and that he was 'terribly curious to meet her'.[10]

The Last Tycoon gives full weight to the loneliness of power. Scenes of Stahr retiring early to his bed to read scripts are given equal time with those of his professional work, at the studio and particularly in the projection room. He is an old style paternalistic entrepreneur, seeing screenwriters both as 'children' and as little more than 'gag men'. Yet the paternal authority of the Hollywood mogul is seen as being challenged, both by the politicisation of the writers and the emergence of Hollywood as a modern corporate enterprise. As well as the underplayed references to his declining state of health, which is a stronger theme in the novel, we see the increasing concern of the studio's bankers in New York, and their place men in Hollywood, with the arbitrariness of Stahr's decisions. Kazan gives us his usual scepticism of bureaucrats and lawyers – last seen in *The Arrangement* – relative to a more free-willed, central protagonist. Away from the central love story the director brings a good deal of humour to the depictions of Stahr at work. For example, when Rodriguez (Curtis) arrives to see the mogul, complaining of impotence with his wife, the actor shifts nervously in his chair, his lack of confidence unaffected even by reading in the trades of his latest film's success at the box office. In his notes Kazan wanted a sense of the two men as 'Brooklyn boys, buddies', but also of how this kind of crisis was putting a strain on Stahr as the studio father figure.[11] Pinter does not let us hear Stahr's remedy, but Kazan shows us the rejuvenated actor running and jumping into his sports car with all the energy (in a similar scene) of the young protagonist of *Splendour in the Grass*.

While DeNiro was sometimes seen by Spiegel as lacking conviction in his unaccustomed role as an authority figure, he projects a convincing mix of friendliness and distance appropriate to his 'prince of Hollywood' role. Kazan had worked with several of the legendary moguls of the industry and he made reference in his production notes to Darryl F. Zanuck's desire to play the 'regular guy', together with his steely will as the studio's ultimate source of authority.[12] Pinter's script not only changes the nature of the relationship between Stahr and Kathleen by excluding the last meeting of the novel, but it also sets up a play between the love affair and the themes and motifs of the rushes or rough cuts that we see, as Stahr views them in a studio projection room. The first shots of the film are from a gangster picture, with actors very broadly modelled on Greta Garbo and Clark Gable in close shot. The woman seems to say 'you can trust me', but in fact we see her give a signal and then disappear to the ladies room; the floor of the restaurant becomes deserted, and the man is then shot by gangsters who drive up and shoot through the window. The use of such black and white rushes, early in the film, suggests Pinter's notion of the perfidious, betraying woman, while also prefiguring issues of male obsession. A later sequence makes a broad reference to a related theme in the context of

motifs that resemble those from *Casablanca*. These rushes are never a convincing element of the film; their enervating tone seems inappropriate to the
exuberance of thirties film, and neither do they add much comment or contrast
to the central love story in the picture. The suggested gap between reality and
illusion comes instead from our observation of Stahr's inability to move from
the world of stars and spectacle, and of happy endings, to the banal and problematic one of real life relationships, vulnerability and commitment. In this
sense *The Last Tycoon* does provide in darker form some of the elements of
François Truffaut's contemporary story of filmmaking, *La Nuit Américain* (*Day
for Night*) (1973).

Not only are looks and glances important in Kazan's work, but he also uses
framed photographs and portraits as a significant element both of his mise en
scène and his suggestion of his characters' emotional ties and concerns.[13] One
thinks of the framed pictures of Johnny Friendly and of Baby Doll's dead father,
casting their spells. Here Mina Davis, Stahr's first wife, is a constant, staring
presence as a portrait in his office, in the dressing room-cum-shrine that is
shown to visitors, and in his bedroom. Given Dana Andrews' presence, one
thinks also of the portrait in Otto Preminger's 1944 *Laura*. The haunting presence in *The Last Tycoon* is Ingrid Boulting, a ghostly, ever receding image of
romantic fulfilment, both as Kathleen Moore, and as Mina Davis in a short
black and white 'film' scene that is entirely part of Stahr's imagination.
Kathleen's entrances are also spectral. In the flood on the back lot caused by
the earthquake she appears by some miracle clinging to a floating head of the
Goddess Siva, and she later appears unannounced at the Writer's Ball. In this
last scene, as Stahr is drawn to her, the dance band music of the orchestra disappears and we hear instead the melancholic Maurice Jarre score, suggesting
that for him the two of them are now alone, no longer in a crowded ball room.
Once they disengage the orchestra music at the Ball fades back in. In his notes
to the script Kazan anticipated indicating this effect by a shift of lens, but in
fact the same point is made in the movement away from diegetic sound.

Kazan also decorates the picture with smaller scale motifs, as when he suggests the prospects for Stahr and Kathleen by showing the stately dance of their
cars in the deserted car park, as they leave in different directions after their
night together. In addition there is a final reworking by Stahr, straight to camera, of the earlier routine in which he invents a story designed to show the
English novelist Boxley (Donald Pleasance) the secret of making movies.
Except now the story, told directly to the audience, relates directly to his own
recent disappointment. It is Kathleen who 'plays' the woman, and she burns not
her gloves but the letter that Stahr has sent her, as she is watched by a man
who is presumably her new husband, or husband-to-be.

The Writer's Ball: Monroe Stahr (Robert DeNiro) and Kathleen Moore (Ingrid Boulting), *The Last Tycoon* (1976). Courtesy of BFI.

The director remembers someone from Paramount noting that this was not a film for 'the kids'.[14] Critics were divided on a film that failed at the box office, with many deciding that it was an honourable failure and referring to the difficulties of filming an unfinished novel. Others blamed Pinter for underwriting, particularly in relation to the love story, or Spiegel or Kazan, for the casting and performance of Ingrid Boulting. Some critics however liked its restrained tone and elegance, its refusal to satirise Monroe Stahr or the Hollywood of the thirties, and its simplicity compared to the lavish romanticism of Jack Clayton's recent *The Great Gatsby* (1974). The restraint is particularly evident in the scenes of Stahr's loneliness, as he goes to his bed to read scripts. Kazan keeps the pace moving early on, and handles well the scenes played out around the sound stages, with trucks of dancing girls, chats with writers and the encounter with the director Ridingwood. Here is the kind of tireless production head who negotiated with six stars – not to mention the writers and directors – during the making of the Academy Award winner *Grand Hotel* (1932). In terms of its assembly of actors of the classic Hollywood era, *The Last Tycoon* runs the early thirties film close. Andrew Sarris, warming to Kazan since his harsh 1968 verdict, found that the film captured much of the 'irony and subtlety and ambiguity of the book', as well as something of Fitzgerald's 'furtive romanticism'.[15] Pinter's version of the couple's last encounter, a brief exchange on the phone, skews the meaning rather, presenting Kathleen as more coy, quixotic and, like Didi in the 'Casablanca' scene, duplicitous. There is little Kazan could do with this scene, although a younger Kazan, a Kazan who had been on the project at the beginning, might have been bolder, more willing to counter Pinter's English restraint with a more Mediterranean assertiveness. To Pauline Kael the film lacked charge and impetus, and the ending was a 'confession of impotence', but as Richard Corliss suggests the film 'challenges you to accept the tempo', to see why Kazan, following Pinter, is taking his time. Some see it as ponderous, but to me the film has a certain classical grace and assurance.[16]

In the central role Robert DeNiro suggests mastery and control but also a developing uncertainty, what Lloyd Michaels calls entropy. Kazan wanted Stahr to be uncertain sexually.[17] The audience is given Stahr's perspective throughout, and the result for many was a story of frustration, as the dynamic business leader cannot act decisively in his private realm, and nor can he fight back in the board room. The film is ultimately about male frustration and impotence, and at times reaches towards a metaphor about illusion and reality. There are moments when the dreamlike quality of Hitchcock's *Vertigo* (1958) is suggested, not by any visual device but through the acting out of a story of aloofness, obsession and – with regard to Kathleen Moore – ultimate remoteness and reserve. Stahr seems to want to recreate his dead wife just as the James Stewart character did, with similarly frustrating results. He tells the young writer Wylie that he wants the woman in the script he is working on to be 'perfect', and seems to make the same demands on the women in his life, someone who can rescue him from his loneliness.

The film failed commercially but provoked some interesting debates and some respectful writing. The 66-year-old Kazan was not his old self, and in his diary at the time he expressed himself 'worn down to a stub', seeing his work as no better than routine. Yet he displays much of his usual care with his actors. He accepted the two inexperienced actresses and saw his work with them as a challenge. The set design, with the mix between Pat Brady's oak-lined rooms and animal trophies and Monroe Stahr's books and art deco design, has the usual Kazan stamp associated with his long-time production designer/art director Gene Callahan, who the director had recommended to George Stevens a few years earlier as 'the most creative man I've worked with in his field'.[18] *The Last Tycoon* is self-consciously a Hollywood 'art film', a literary adaptation and meditation; instead of a dynamic leading man, the film provides a sense of the inability of remarkable men to achieve or revive their own personal dreams. It was perhaps too late for Kazan too, and Stahr's pause before the empty, cavernous sound stage, and his measured walk into the blackness, is appropriate as the closing image of the director's film career.

The commercial and critical failure of *The Arrangement* (1969) had been a huge blow that all but ended Kazan's film career at the age of 60. The director failed to exhibit the degree of distance from his leading character that he did with *America America*, while his effort to confront a mass audience with debates about American materialism is perhaps inadequately integrated with the parallel theme of the conflict between first and second generation immigrants, a topic hardly likely to appeal to the youth market that was driving the breakaway cinema hits of the late sixties. For a more distanced film which also touches critically on aspects of the American dream one thinks of Nicholas Ray's *Bigger than Life*, in 1956, although that studio film's constantly inventive use of light and colour also suggests some of the limits of Kazan's repertoire. After *The Arrangement*, Kazan's final two films also contained personal elements: *The Visitors* is virtually a 'home movie', while Jean-Pierre Coursoden describes *The Last Tycoon* as 'an elegiac poem about a sad man who retreats from the burden of power into a world of private nostalgia'. Although this parallel with Kazan's life is over simple, there is an element here of the director's own sense of his diminishing opportunities to make the films he wanted to make. Of his film work following *East of Eden* only *Splendour in the Grass* made a significant commercial return, and *The Visitors* (1972) failed even to secure a general release. In the seventies he was involved with Directors Guild of America (DGA) Presidents Robert Wise and Robert Aldrich, and initiated DGA programmes on the art and craft of directing; it has always seemed to me significant that Aldrich, who was close to Abraham Polonsky and other blacklist victims, declared that 'Elia Kazan is a favourite person of mine'. Kazan also supported Emile de Antonio when the documentary maker was harassed by the FBI in making a film about the Weather Underground, and he later publicised the ordeal of the imprisoned Turkish filmmaker Yilmaz Guney. Even Polonsky, whose view on the blacklist was that to 'betray your friends is a moral crime', and who viewed Kazan's autobiography in this regard as 'beneath contempt', saw him as 'extraordinarily talented'.[19]

Kazan worked on his novels and his autobiography (and on an as yet unpublished book on directing), yet as Richard Schickel movingly describes, there was something melancholy about his later professional life, including the

major disappointment of the collapse of financing for his proposed French production of *Beyond the Aegean*. It was in the late eighties (in his late seventies)
that Kazan had worked with European art film producer Anatole Dauman and
others to set up a production based on his son Chris Kazan's adaptation of the
first draft of his novel on the struggles of a 40-year-old Stavros in America and
Anatolia after the First World War. The novel, *Beyond the Aegean*, intended as
the basis for the final part of the family trilogy of films, was finally published
in 1994. Kazan also talked to his old friend Budd Schulberg about reviving
their late sixties' Puerto Rican project, without result, while the director apparently enquired about the rights for a film based on the life of the Japanese
novelist Yokio Mishima. In America, Kazan was no longer bankable for his
personal projects, while he showed little interest in the type of films that were
offered to him; according to producer Robert Evans he was one of several
directors who turned down *The Godfather*, feeling that it romanticised the
mafia. In one of his last published pieces Kazan noted that his 'disappearance'
from the film world had not been intended, and added on the collapse of
Beyond the Aegean: 'I failed myself and I failed my son Chris, that's for sure.'[20]
The sadness is reflected in Kazan's autobiography in the passages dealing with
the deaths of those close to him, including old sparring partners and collaborators. Although Kazan and Barbara Loden had grown apart, a friendship was
re-established, at least in the director's account, during her two-year battle
against cancer before her tragic death in September 1980, at the age of 48.
There are also sensitive accounts, changing the tone of the latter part of
Kazan's memoir, of the deaths, around the same time, of Harold Clurman and
Nicholas Ray. The director's third marriage was with the novelist Frances
Rudge, whom he married in 1982. Chris Kazan, who Kazan had worked with
on *The Visitors*, died of cancer in 1991, during his father's efforts to set up the
Beyond the Aegean film project.

For all the emphasis on the emotional dynamics in Kazan's work, three of his
films, *Baby Doll* (1955), *Wild River* (1960) and *America America* (1963), draw
in particular on the strong documentary strand of his work, integrating his performances with acute and creative use of the cultural specificity of the locations. As discussed earlier, he acknowledged the impact of the neo-realists in
the late forties, while his later reverence for Jean Renoir is dependent, not just
on a fondness for the director's line, as the character Octave in *La Règle du jeu*
(1939), that 'everyone has their reasons', but on the French director's pioneering use of location shooting and non-professionals in his thirties work. Of the
three films noted above, the later two have received most sustained critical
recognition, for example by Robin Wood and by French critics, but in my view
Baby Doll, Kazan's second film adaptation of Tennessee Williams, comes close

to these in its integration of character and location. The use as a chorus of local African-Americans provides a political edge to Williams's human comedy of the old South, placing the pathetic figure of Archie Lee Meighan in a context of ethnic and sexual challenge and black commentary at the moment before the civil rights movement emerged as the first concerted opposition to the structure of post-war American society. As Wood also suggests, Kazan seemed most effective when dealing with ambivalence rather than a clear message, and the long seduction scene in *Baby Doll*, where sex, pride and economics are all elements, slows down the narrative pace and allows the director to create from the location a strange and at times theatrical but socially resonant sense of place.[21] For all Kazan's showmanship, his enthusiasm in correspondence with Jack Warner for 60ft billboard posters of Caroll Baker, the film represents a form of emerging art cinema practice, with no hero, no stars, ambivalent character motivation, and an ambiguous conclusion. Bosley Crowther compared the film unfavourably to Fellini's *La Strada* (1954), but the fact that he made the comparison at all is perhaps most significant. The sense of place is even more noticeable in Kazan's period recreation of thirties Tennessee, in *Wild River*, with seasons passing and the central characters making conscious or sub-conscious personal choices as they act out a drama of national transformation. I think in particular of the passage in that film in which the Montgomery Clift and Lee Remick figures first cross the river together, with Carol Garth reopening the small house where she lived with her late husband. Kazan here achieves near real-time interaction between the characters, and command of the space between them, that is distinctive and unforced, creating a sense of the impact of place and memory: of the track along by the river, viewed in morning and dusk, sun and rain; and of the leaves on the marital bed. Even without its classical associations the ferry plays a role that is both practical and symbolic, ushering people between two worlds and making reference perhaps to the Kazan family's own immigrant odyssey. The moment when the black proletariat of Garth Island makes its 'wagon train' journey across the river, after the two strangers have spent a first night together, links notions of personal and collective growth and change as central Kazan motifs.

America America is Kazan's most personal work given its subject matter and his use of his own script for the first time. He returns to his own American take on the Italian neo-realist tradition, using a non-professional, Stathis Giallelis, for the lead role. Elements of the film recall at least the 'look' of the near contemporary *Salvatore Giuliano* (1962), and that film's director Francesco Rosi remembers that 'Kazan used to tell me that he considered me as his younger brother'.[22] It is also in *America America* that the director combines most effectively the external and internal worlds: the physical movement through space on the road to Ankara and Constantinople and on the ship to New York; and the internal crisis of the soul that the dutiful son undergoes given the weight of family responsibility and of his own burning desire. Drawing on this rhetoric of the Kennedy years Kazan explored a myth of America that drove Stavros and many turn-of-the-century immigrants, while also suggesting that reality – not least in the Uncle Joe character in *The Arrangement* – might fall short. *America America* is much more than a mere film poster for America's redemptive power, and it also most effectively enshrines the autobiographical element in Kazan's cinema. He commented at the time that 'STAVROS (you) goes to America, as you went into the world of ART'.[23]

The director seemed happiest when working – and work was for him a magical word, pushing talents to the limit, including his own – with an alternative family of cast and crew, using generous location schedules and extensive rehearsals, at least in terms of the Hollywood conventions of the day. Patricia Neal remembers Kazan printing more takes than the studios would allow. This approach also included an intense investment of time and energy in preparation, as is clear from the Wesleyan notebooks. Another aspect of his work is evoked by a comment he made on editing in 1974:

> I see the rushes with the cutter and tell her or him what I had in mind, what I hoped to get out of the scene and where in each day's work I think I may have caught what I wanted. I tell him or her how I thought the scene should go and what the mechanical aspects of it are, pace, rhythm and climax. Then I turn away and go about my business, giving the cutter a chance to contribute and again hoping that the artist will perhaps see more in the scene and each day's rushes than I did. You always hope for little miracles.[24]

Collaboration is also implicit in his film work with leading playwrights and novelists, notably Tennessee Williams, John Steinbeck, Budd Schulberg and William Inge, bringing the work without condescension to a wider cinema audience. In terms of music the director, who introduced to film a number of East Coast-based composers, noted that 'like all aspects of film it is collaborative work'.[25] One can also point to his relationships with cinematographers and art directors. In terms of the former, one thinks of Joe MacDonald's deep focus work, Ted McCord and early CinemaScope and colour, the three films – the black and white work in particular – with Boris Kaufman, Ellsworth Fredericks's radiant images of Tennessee, and the difficult but rewarding alliance with Haskell Wexler on *America America*. Other Kazan regulars included Anna Hill Johnstone (eight films as costume designer), Charles Maguire (seven films as assistant director or associate producer), and art directors/production designers Richard Sylbert (three) and Gene Callahan (four).

It is difficult to find actors who do not report that Kazan helped them, and the archives reveal a director who, having put great stress on casting actors with the part 'inside them', worked to provoke and relax them to explore and create sub-textual underpinnings for the story. Marlon Brando felt that Kazan was usually able to respond to the sensitive moment, often around the third take of a scene, when 'you just need a whisper from the director to crystallise it for you', while Eli Wallach talked of how he 'sows the actor's mind', allowing emotion and intent to flow freely, and skilfully 'putting actor against actor within the circumstances of the play'. Lee Remick noted Kazan's ability to prompt an actor with something they had previously told him, and credited him with enabling her to make her performance in *Wild River* 'the truest in my experience'.[26] To Kazan 'the director tells the film, using a vocabulary the lesser part of which is the arrangement of words', while Colin McArthur noted that the director's mise en scène 'works by nuance, subtlety and an extraordinary wide range of gesture and movement from his actors'.[27] Conversation was a large part of his preferred preparation with actors, digging for experience and gesture that he could mine for the part being played, pieces of real behaviour that could make a sequence work and resonate with an audience.

Performance rather than stardom is central to Kazan's best work. Of the male roles one thinks in particular of Brando and Dean in the early to mid-fifties, and of Jack Palance, Anthony Quinn, Karl Malden in particular in *Baby Doll*, Eli Wallach, Montgomery Clift, Warren Beatty, Paul Mann and Robert DeNiro. To Kazan, Marlon Brando was 'fully sexed but uni-sexed', and Dean and Clift also represented masculinity in ways that were discordant in terms of dominant representations of the time, but which captured unacknowledged anxieties and other aspects of the society of the moment.[28] As Steve Cohen has suggested, Brando is often aware of his sexuality in a way that is more associated with female star portraiture, and yet from his entry in his T-shirt in *A Streetcar Named Desire* to his macho pose to Edie ('You want to hear my philosophy of life') and final, masochistic walk in *On the Waterfront*, he also reveals the vulnerabilities and playfulness behind the pose. Mildred Dunnuck, who appeared in Kazan stage productions, notably *Death of a Salesman*, as well as in *Viva Zapata!* and *Baby Doll*, noted that Kazan was 'oriented towards the man's role – his women characters exist in relationship to his men'.[29] As an 'old fashioned man', at least as one of his identities, this seems to me true, although Brando in *On the Waterfront*, and Dean and Clift – Remick called Clift in *Wild River* a 'wounded bird' – were certainly odd and discordant 'authority figures' of their time and possibly of any time. Kazan also presents the hapless masculinity of the Johnny Nolan character in *A Tree*

Grows in Brooklyn, the satiric male leads in *Baby Doll*, and the caricatures of Ace Stamper in *Splendour in the Grass* and Harry Wayne in *The Visitors*.

In terms of women actors, with no great fairness or science (since the judgement relates to the role as much as the individual achievement in it), I would draw particular attention to Dorothy McGuire, Kim Hunter, Vivien Leigh, Julie Harris, Carroll Baker, Patricia Neal, Lee Remick and Jo Van Fleet in *Wild River*, Natalie Wood, Zohra Lampert and Linda Marsh. Kazan's women characters are smart and strong, and often more dynamic presences within the narrative, but as Dunnock suggests, their smartness and assertiveness generally serve their men, and sometimes redeem them. One thinks of Abra in *East of Eden*; of Carol Garth seizing the moment, and the man, in *Wild River*; of Stella's passion for Stanley; and of the sense that Lonesome Rhodes in the emotionally exuberant and politically prescient *A Face in the Crowd* is in part Marcia Jeffries's creation, a relationship that Kazan has compared to his own with Molly Kazan. For all his efforts with the character of Gwen, in *The Arrangement*, inspired we are told by Barbara Loden's challenge to the director and his way of life, neither she nor Florence are given the 'interiority', the sense of struggle and journey, of the central male protagonist.[30]

Many Kazan films feature key identities and family relationships (lovers, parents and children, brothers and sisters) that are compromised or problematic, while the meeting of Stavros and the Sinnikoglou family in the extended Constantinople scene in *America America* represents the strength of the Group Theatre ensemble tradition in his work. The Method, seen at the Actors Studio as a 'pragmatic way of working to create both the interior life and the logical behaviour of a character', was associated as a doctrine more with Lee Strasberg's reign as Artistic Director from 1951–82, rather than with Kazan's use of Studio personnel for his own film work. Kazan was steeped in the technique of Stanislavsky but was eclectic in his work with professional and non-professional actors; as Schulberg notes, he was 'never married to "The Method"'. In the early eighties, when he again became more involved in the Studio, he noted that 'that there seems to us to be an excessive concern now with the techniques of arousing emotion within the actor and that these techniques often result in excessive self-absorption'.[31]

Recurring themes in Kazan's work reflect his choices, and his choice of collaborators, together with the dominant ideas into which he was socialised. His thirties' experience and politics are reflected in his regard for material forces as central to the given circumstances of a story and of each character's objectives and conflicts within it. We see this in the struggle against poverty in *A Tree Grows in Brooklyn*, Father Barry's (and Schulberg's) thoughts on the 'love of a lousy buck', and Stavros's efforts to gather the 110 Turkish pounds necessary for a third-class passage to America from Constantinople. Stavros is told that the only way that men like him can get 'big money' is by stealing it or marrying it, and soon after we see him on parade in church, expensively dressed, and looking 'like money'. In the end Stavros substitutes sex for money to pay for his passage, a not uncommon association. In the puritan pre-Crash Kansas of *Splendour in the Grass* sexual excitement is displaced into playing the stock market, while Bud Stamper defies his father's thinking in choosing the simpler and poorer pastoral life. In *The Arrangement* Sam Anderson, asked how he is by his son, replies that 'I have no money, that's how I feel'. Perhaps most succinctly it is *East of Eden* that turns, as David Thomson has noted, on 'intermingling money and feelings', as Cal tries unsuccessfully to buy his father's love.[32] Certainly with the Dean and Beatty films the issues resonated, beyond the period context of the drama, to contemporary audiences.

When he was working (obsessively) on *Wild River* in February 1958, Kazan reported in his production diary that he had spent a long evening with 'Larry Olivier'. Laurence Olivier was then intending to make a film of *Macbeth* (the film was never made) as a follow up to a recent stage production and to his previous Shakespearian adaptations for the screen. But he was worried about the script, and having just seen Orson Welles's 1948 production he now felt that the film he was planning seemed 'old fashioned' by contrast. Kazan noted Olivier's recollection and added his own comment: 'this got me to thinking – Mine is old fashioned'.[33] Certainly Kazan did not adapt to the looser cinematic styles of the later sixties, or see the opportunities of working through film genre. His mise en scène is not visually original but is most distinctive in terms of its representation of complex human behaviour and at times in realising a strong sense of place. David Bordwell, discussing art cinema practice, has written of 'a cinema of psychological effects in search of their causes', a kind of unspecified and unmotivated unease. Kazan embraces psychological complexity and ambivalence, but never suggests alienation or meaninglessness: his characters generally have a sense of agency, even Eddie Anderson in *The Arrangement*. Commenting on the work of Jean-Luc Godard, Kazan noted that he 'shows people in a static state. I don't see life that way.'[34]

This book observes Kazan's film work as part of American and European cinema practice and reception, in particular his (sometimes contradictory) striving for both collaboration and the development and expression of his own voice. He may have realised this cinematic quest in overly literary terms, yet from *Viva Zapata!* and *On the Waterfront* to *Wild River* and *America America*, the films reveal a striking sense of the interplay of character with landscape and environment. Storyboarding was anathema to him, in part because he wanted to capture and distil his drama from real life. There are suggestions, relating as much to tone as to a consistent visual style, of the influence of European filmmakers (of what he called the 'European masters'), while it was in France that much of the work received its most engaged and sympathetic criticism. He strived as his own producer to construct a film base in New York and to develop a distinctive process of film production – in an at times uneasy alliance with the studios – at a time when notions of the 'art film', in textual terms or in terms of audience or marketing, were undeveloped, particularly in America. Kazan's best work provides characters with both material and psychological contexts that are nuanced, grounded in real life and complex, while, in part by doing that, he helped further the slow demise of censorship and the Legion of Decency. His mature work, particularly in the period 1956–63, the ante-room of the sixties, provides one model (if only one model) of how others of the 'thirties' generation might have fared had they been able to have access to the American industry. For all his outsider's perspective, and his infamous 1952 testimony, Kazan's cinematic project would have been easier had the blacklist not disrupted the potential of others of his generation to join him in welding new cinematic forms and approaches to mainstream American practice.

References

Only the author, main title and date of books listed in the select bibliography are given in the chapter notes; all other titles are given in full. Page numbers of film reviews or newspaper articles are given when available; in most circumstances where they are not given the source is a clipping from an archive or film library or specialist collection.

Introduction

1. Elia Kazan, letter to the author, 20 March 1980.
2. Peter Lev, *The Fifties* (2003), pp. 197–204.
3. On the controversy of the 1999 award see Patricia Bosworth, 'Kazan's Choice', *Vanity Fair*, 469 (September 1999), pp. 166–9, 184, and Richard Schickel, *Elia Kazan* (2005), pp. vii–xxxi.
4. Elia Kazan, *A Life* (1988), pp. 17, 24.
5. Herbert Ratner, interviewed by Robert Hethmon, New York, 21 August 1965.
6. Kazan to Crawford and Strasberg, 1935, *Paradise Lost* materials, Box 3, Folder 7 (B3, F7), Kazan collection, WUCA.
7. Kazan, interviewed by Melvin Bernhardt, 10 June 1983, unidentified periodical, in Kazan clippings file, NYPL/Lincoln Center, p. 29; also see Harold Clurman, *On Directing* (New York: Simon & Schuster, 1972), pp. 80–1.
8. Kazan, *A Life* (1988), p. 38.
9. Exhibition on *America America*, Wesleyan Cinema Archives, 2004, citing materials from Kazan collection, WUCA.
10. Kazan on his performance in *City for Conquest*, B8, Kazan collection, WUCA.
11. Ray Ludlow, 'Pie in the Sky', *New Theatre*, May 1935, Kazan folders, Film Department, MOMA. See also Joel Stewart Zuker, *Ralph Steiner, Filmmaker and Still Photographer* (New York: Arno Press, 1978), pp. 187ff; William Alexander, *Film on the Left* (1981), pp. 62–4, 172–8; *Pie in the Sky* and *People of the Cumberland* viewed at Film Department, MOMA, New York. *Pie in the Sky* is

available as part of the set of DVDs, *Unseen Cinema: Early American Avant-Garde Film, 1894–1941* (released by Image Entertainment, 2005).

12. Brian Neve, *Film and Politics in America* (1992), pp. 86–90; Thomas Schatz, *Boom and Bust* (1997), pp. 289ff; David Thomson, *The Whole Equation* (2005), pp. 309–10; Martin Scorsese, 'Elia Kazan', *Entertainment Weekly*, 743–4, 26 December 2003.

13. See for example W.R. Wilkerson, 'Trade Views,' *Hollywood Reporter*, 25 July 1950, p. 1.

14. See Paul Buhle, *Radical Hollywood, Behind America's Favorite Movies* (New York: The New Press, 2002), Paul Buhle and Dave Wagner, *The Hollywood Blacklistees in Film and Television* (2003); Frank Krutnik, Steve Neale, Brian Neve, Peter Stanfield, eds., *'Un-American Hollywood': Politics and Film in the Blacklist Era* (2007). See also *Red Hollywood* (written and directed by Thom Andersen and Noël Burch, 1995), the excellent documentary survey of the film work of the Hollywood Left.

15. Lillian Hellman, *Scoundrel Time* (1976), p. 39; Williams to his grandfather, 3 June 1952, in Albert J. Devlin, ed., *The Selected Letters of Tennessee Williams* (2004), pp. 429–30; Bertrand Tavernier, Interview, Sydney Film Festival, 10 July 1999, http://www.wsws.org/articles/1999/jul (accessed, 10 August 2004). Adlai Stevenson speech, Albuquerque, New Mexico, clipping, *New York Times*, 15 September 1952, B25, F1, Kazan collection, WUCA.

16. Michel Ciment, 'Pour en finir avec les mises au point', *Positif, Revue Mensuelle de Cinéma*, 192 (April 1977), p. 23; Thom Andersen, 'Afterword', in Frank Krutnik, Steve Neale, Brian Neve and Peter Stanfield, eds., *'Un-American Hollywood'* (2007), p. 555; David Thomson, *The Whole Equation* (2005), p. 274.

17. Roger Tailleur, *Elia Kazan* (1971); Michel Ciment, ed., *Kazan on Kazan* (1973); Thomas H. Pauly, *An American Odyssey* (1983); Michel Ciment, ed., *Elia Kazan, An American Odyssey* (1988); Elia Kazan, *A Life* (1988); Jim Kitses, 'Elia Kazan: A Structural Analysis', *Cinema*, 7, 3 (Winter 1972–3), pp. 25–36; Robin Wood, 'The Kazan Problem', in *Movie*, 19 (Winter 1971–2); Lloyd Michaels, 'Critical Survey', in Michaels, *Elia Kazan* (1985), p. 27; Richard Schickel, *Elia Kazan, A Biography* (2005).

18. Kazan to Christopher Cook, 'Third Ear', BBC Radio 3, 3 June 1988.

19. James Naremore, *Acting in the Cinema* (1988), p. 210.

1. Kazan at Twentieth Century-Fox

1. On Zanuck see George F. Custen, *Twentieth Century's Fox* (1997), including pp. 99–102 on his role in production of *The Jazz Singer*. On Kazan's advice to Zanuck on 'One World' see John B. Wiseman, 'Darryl F. Zanuck and the Failure of "One World", 1943–1945', *Historical Journal of Film, Radio and Television*, 7, 3 (1987), p. 283.

2. Joseph McBride, *Searching for John Ford* (2003), p. 247.

3. Kazan to Arthur Miller, 2 May 1947, Arthur Miller correspondence, Kazan collection, WUCA.

4. Kazan questionnaire in Tay Garnett material, Folder 179, Lewis Milestone collection, AMPAS.

5. Bosley Crowther, *New York Times*, 9 March 1945; Manny Farber, 'The Brooklyn Dodger', *The New Republic*, cutting, Kazan folders, MOMA; James Agee, *The Nation*, 17 February 1945, in Agee, *Agee on Film* (Boston: Beacon Press, 1958), pp. 141–3.

6. 'Beginner's Notes' (1944), edited by Nick Ray, B13, F10, Kazan collection, WUCA.

7. 'Beginner's Notes' (1944), B13, F10, Kazan collection, WUCA; Joseph McBride, *Searching for John Ford* (2003), p. 490.

8. Elia Kazan, *A Life* (1988), p. 304; *Sea of Grass* file, PCA/MPAA collection, AMPAS.

9. Patrick McGilligan and Paul Buhle, *Tender Comrades* (1997), p. 578.

10. Kazan annotation on *Sea of Grass* script, B17, F1, Kazan collection, WUCA; *Hollywood Reporter*, 12 February 1947, in *Sea of Grass* file, PCA/MPAA, AMPAS.

11. William Lafferty, 'A Reappraisal of the Semi-Documentary in Hollywood, 1945–1948', *Velvet Light Trap*, 20 (1983), pp. 22–6; *Hollywood Reporter*, 24 January 1947.

12. Kazan testimony, 10 April 1952, in Eric Bentley, ed., *Thirty Years of Treason* (1971), p. 493.

13. David Garfield, *A Player's Place* (1980), pp. 52, 56–8.

14. See J.P. Telotte, *Voices in the Dark: The Narrative Patterns of Film Noir* (Urbana: University of Illinois Press, 1989), pp. 139–45.

15. *Boomerang* script, 10 September 1946, B17, F2, Kazan collection, WUCA; Martin Gottfried, *Arthur Miller, his Life and Work* (2003), p. 104.

16. Raymond Borde and Etienne Chaumeton, *A Panorama of American Film Noir, 1941–1953* (2002), p. 6; James Agee, *Agee on Film* (Boston: Beacon Press, 1958), p. 244.

17. *Daily Worker*, 19 March 1948, p. 12; *Daily Worker*, 18 March 1948, p. 17. See also Will Straw, 'Documentary Realism and the Postwar Left', in Frank Krutnik et. al., *'Un-American Hollywood'* (2007), pp. 130–41.

18. Kazan annotations, script, *Gentleman's Agreement*, B18, F4, Kazan collection, WUCA.

19. Larry Ceplair and Steven Englund, *The Inquisition in Hollywood* (1983), p. 289.

20. Donald Weber, 'The Limits of Empathy: Hollywood's Imaging of the Jews circa 1947', in Jack Kugelmass, ed., *Key Texts in American Jewish Culture* (2003), pp. 91–104; Zanuck to Kazan, 18 June 1947, in Rudy Behlmer, ed., *Memo from Darryl F. Zanuck* (1993), pp. 133–4; Kazan to Miller, 20 June 1947, Arthur Miller correspondence, Kazan collection, WUCA.

21. Kazan annotations, script, *Gentleman's Agreement* B18, F4, Kazan collection, WUCA.

22. *Time*, 17 November 1947, p. 105; Elliot E. Cohen, 'Mr Zanuck's "Gentleman's Agreement", Reflections on Hollywood's Second Film About Anti-Semitism', *Commentary* (January 1948), p. 53.

23. David Caute, *The Great Fear* (1978), p. 492; *Variety*, 29 October 1947, p. 14; Gerald Horne, *The Final Victim of the Blacklist* (2006), p. 193.

24. Caute, *The Great Fear* (1978), p. 499; *Hollywood Reporter*, 2 December 1947, cited in Joseph Foster, 'Entertainment Only', *New Masses*, 66 (1948), pp. 21–2.

25. Box 6, re: *Pinky*, Philip Dunne collection, USC; *Pinky* file, PCA/MPAA, AMPAS.

26. Joseph McBride, *Searching for John Ford* (2003), p. 489; *Time*, 10 October 1949; *Morning Telegraph*, 30 September 1949; *Variety*, 5 October 1949; Ralph Ellison, *The Reporter*, 6 December 1949; *New York Times*, 30 September 1949.

27. Alan Gevinson, ed., *American Film Institute Catalog: Within Our Gates, Ethnicity in American Feature Films, 1911–1960* (Berkeley: University of California Press, 1997), p. 778; Michael Rogin, *Blackface, White Noise, Jewish Immigrants in the Hollywood Melting Pot* (Berkeley: University of California Press, 1996), pp. 222–8; see also Thomas Cripps, *Making Movies Black* (1993), pp. 232–40.

28. Kazan note, 18 September 1944, *Viva Zapata* materials, Kazan collection, WUCA.

29. Ad for *Bicycle Thief*, Kazan collection, B21, F2, WUCA; Thomas Schatz, *Boom and Bust* (1997), p. 295; *Cue*, 8 February 1947, pp. 9–10.

30. Kazan notebook for *A Streetcar Named Desire*, August 1947, in Toby Cole and Helen Krich Chinoy, eds., *Directing the Play* (1953), p. 296; Raymond Borde and Etienne Chaumeton, *A Panorama of American Film Noir* (2002), p. 92.

31. Kazan script, *Panic in the Streets*, B21, F5, Kazan collection, WUCA; Walter Bernstein, *Inside Out* (1996), p. 17.

32. M.J. Heale, *American Anticommunism* (1990), pp. 134–44; Michael Wreszin, 'Arthur Schlesinger Jr., Scholar-activist In Cold War America: 1946–1956', *Salmagundi* (Spring–Summer 1984), pp. 268–9.

33. Arthur M. Schlesinger Jr., *The Vital Center, The Politics of Freedom* (New York: Da Capo Press, 1988, first published in 1949), p. 255.

34. Kazan annotation, script, 'Port of Entry', 25 November 1949, B21, F5, Kazan collection, WUCA; Peter Biskind, *Seeing is Believing* (1983), pp. 20–33.

35. Kazan annotation, script, 'Port of Entry', B21, F5, 25 November 1949, Kazan collection, WUCA; email to the author from Lenka Peterson O'Connor, 4 August 2007.

36. See the commentary by James Ursini and Alain Silver, to the *Panic in the Streets* DVD, Fox Film Noir series (2004).

37. David Lee Simmons, 'Panic Attack', *Gambit Weekly*, 4 April 2005, accessed, 20 June 2005, at http://www.bestofneworleans.com/dispatch/2005–04–05/cover_story.html; *Time*, 4 August 1950; L.G.A. (Lindsay Anderson), 'As They Go', *Sequence*, 12 (August 1950), pp. 14–15; Gavin Lambert, *Sight & Sound*, 19, 6 (August 1950), pp. 241–2.

38. Elia Kazan, *A Life* (1988), p. 294.

2. New Directions: *A Streetcar Named Desire* (1951) and *Viva Zapata!* (1952)

1. Williams to Kazan, 24 February 1950, Tennessee Williams correspondence, Kazan collection, WUCA.
2. Albert J. Devlin, ed., *The Selected Letters of Tennessee Williams* (2006), p. 260.
3. *A Streetcar Named Desire* production file, PCA/MPAA collection, AMPAS; Kazan to Jack Warner (JW), undated, WB/USC; Rudy Behlmer, ed., *Memo from Darryl F. Zanuck* (1993), pp. 168, 203.
4. Zanuck to Delmer Daves, 16 June 1950, in Behlmer, ed., *Memo from Darryl F. Zanuck* (1993), pp. 187–8.
5. 'Notebook for *A Streetcar Named Desire*', in Toby Cole and Helen Krich Chinoy, eds., *Directing the Play* (1953), pp. 296–320.
6. Brenda Murphy, *Tennessee Williams and Elia Kazan* (1992), p. 63; see also David Richard Jones, *Great Directors at Work* (1986), pp. 138–99.
7. Note on Kazan's draft script, *A Streetcar Named Desire*, June 1950, B24, Elia Kazan collection, WUCA.
8. Kazan notes, bound with June 1950 draft script, Kazan collection, WUCA; Kim Hunter, interviewed in a documentary released on the DVD of *A Streetcar Named Desire*, Warner Bros., 2006.
9. Kazan to JW, undated, WB/USC; Feldman memo, 3 March 1950, WB/USC; Breen, 'Memo from Breen office to Warner Bros. studio', 28 April 1950, WB/ USC.
10. Sam Staggs, *When Blanche Met Brando* (2005), pp. 191–2.
11. Sanya Shoilevska Henderson, *Alex North, Film Composer* (2003), pp. 97–9, 113.
12. Kazan to JW, undated, WB/USC; Tennessee Williams (TW) to Kazan, 19 July 1950, Williams Correspondence, Kazan collection, WUCA; Feldman to JW, 11 July 1950, WB/USC.
13. Kazan to Breen, 14 September 1950, PCA/MPAA, AMPAS; Kazan to JW, undated, WB/USC; 'Notes for the Files', 3 October 1950, PCA/MPAA, AMPAS.
14. Kazan to JW, 19 October 1950, WB/USC.
15. JW to Joseph Breen, 29 October 1950, PCA/MPAA, AMPAS.
16. Breen to TW, 2 November 1950, Steve Trilling to TW, 2 November 1950, WB/USC; TW wire to Kazan, 2 November 1950, PCA/MPAA, AMPAS; Kazan to JW, 7 December 1950, WB/USC.
17. Kazan to JW, 22 November 1950, Kazan to JW, 7 December 1950, WB/USC.
18. Charles Feldman to JW, 27 February 1951, WB/USC.
19. *Hollywood Reporter*, 14 June 1951, p. 4; Kazan to JW, undated, WB/USC.
20. Jack Vizzard to Breen, 9 July 1951, Vizzard to Breen, 12, 17, 22 July 1951, PCA/MPAA, AMPAS.
21. Kazan to Steve Trilling, 27 July 1951, WB/USC; Devlin, ed., *The Selected Letters of Tennessee Williams* (2006), 389; Kazan to Martin Quigley, 16 August 1951, B23, Kazan collection, WUCA; Kazan, 'Pressure Problem', *New York Times*, 21 October 1951, II, p. 5.

22. Hollis Alpert, 'SRL Goes to the Movies', *Saturday Review*, 34, 1 September 1951, pp. 28–31; Bosley Crowther, *New York Times*, 20 September 1951; McCarten, *New Yorker*, 29 September 1951; Karel Reisz, *Sight and Sound*, 21, 4 (April-June 1952), pp. 170–1; Farber in *The Nation*, 20 October 1951, and in Manny Farber, *Negative Space, Manny Farber on the Movies* (London: Studio Vista, 1971), pp. 71–6; Sam Kashner and Jennifer MacNair, *The Bad and the Beautiful, A Chronicle of Hollywood in the Fifties* (London: Little, Brown, 2002), p. 292; John Howard Lawson, *Film in the Battle of Ideas* (1953), pp. 43–4.

23. Laurence Jarvik, '"I Don't want Realism, I want Magic", Elia Kazan and *A Streetcar Named Desire*', unpublished paper, undated; *Hollywood Reporter*, 16 October 1950, p. 7.

24. Herb A. Lightman, 'Uninhibited Camera', *American Cinematographer*, 32, 10 (October 1951), pp. 400, 424–5, 428.

25. Karl Malden in Richard Schickel, *Elia Kazan, A Biography* (2005), p. 216.

26. Jack Vizzard to Breen, 22 July 1951, PCA/MPAA, AMPAS.

27. *Mary McCarthy's Theatre Chronicles, 1937–1962* (1999), pp. xvii, 135–9.

28. Marlon Brando, *Songs My Mother Taught Me* (1994), p. 152.

29. Kazan on Roberto Rossellini, opposite page 132 of draft script, *A Streetcar Named Desire*, June 1950, Kazan collection, WUCA.

30. 'Mexican horse epic', Kazan to JW, undated, WB/USC; Kazan, in June 1950 draft script, *A Streetcar Named Desire*, Kazan collection, WUCA.

31. Paul J. Vanderwood, 'An American Cold Warrior: *Viva Zapata!*', in John E. O'Connor and Martin A. Jackson, eds., *American History/American Film* (1979), pp. 185–7; telegram, Zanuck to Kazan, 1 June 1948, B25, Kazan collection, WUCA.

32. Jackson J. Benson, *John Steinbeck, Writer: A Biography* (1990), pp. 625–6; On Buck's role see Jonathan M. Schoenwald, 'Rewriting revolution: the origins, production and reception of *Viva Zapata!*', *Film History*, 8 (1996), pp. 109–30.

33. Steinbeck, 'A narrative, in dramatic form, of the life of Emiliano Zapata', in John Steinbeck (edited by Robert E. Morsberger), *Zapata* (London: Penguin, 2001), pp. 47–9, 132.

34. Kazan, 'Zapata' treatment, 17 October 1949, Twentieth Century-Fox collection, USC; Kazan to Zanuck, undated, typed notes, B25, Kazan collection, WUCA.

35. Corrido extract, in Revised Screenplay, 'Zapata', 27 April 1950, Kazan collection, WUCA.

36. Robert E. Morsberger, 'Steinbeck's Zapata, Revel versus Revolutionary', in John Steinbeck, *Zapata* (2001), 204; Elia Kazan, *A Life* (1988), p. 395.

37. Michel Ciment, ed., *Kazan on Kazan* (1973), p. 88; reference to 'commie revolutionary', written in Kazan's script, 6 February 1951, B27, Kazan collection, WUCA.

38. Zanuck to Steinbeck and Kazan, 3 May 1950, in Behlmer, ed., *Memo from Darryl F. Zanuck* (1993), p. 172.

39. Kazan letter, *Saturday Review*, 5 April 1952, pp. 22–3; Kazan, *A Life* (1988), pp. 397–8; Elena Feder, 'A Reckoning: Interview with Gabriel Figueroa', *Film Quarterly*, 49, 3 (Spring 1996), pp. 8–9; Steinbeck to Buck, 19 June 1950, in

Jonathan M. Schoenwald, 'Rewriting revolution', *Film History*, 8 (1996), p. 118; Kazan to 'Max', 14 February 1952, B29, Kazan collection, WUCA.

40. Kazan, *A Life* (1988), p. 419; Zanuck, Memo to Steinbeck and Kazan, 26 December 1950, Twentieth Century-Fox collection, USC.

41. Kazan, *A Life* (1988), p. 418; Schoenwald, 'Rewriting revolution', *Film History*, Volume 8 (1996), p. 119; Richard Slotkin, *Gunfighter Nation* (1992), p. 421.

42. Zanuck to Kazan, 18 April 1951, Kazan collection, WUCA; *Guardian*, 24 December 2007.

43. Kazan to North, two letters, undated, and North to Kazan, two letters, undated, Alex North collection, AMPAS; North to Kazan, three letters, one 28 March 1951, two undated, *Viva Zapata!* materials, Kazan collection, WUCA.

44. Zanuck to Kazan, 2 October 1951, Kazan to Zanuck, 29 January 1952, and Kazan to 'Max', 14 February 1952, Kazan collection, WUCA.

45. Catholic War Veterans, letter to Zanuck, 21 January 1952, *Viva Zapata!* materials, Kazan collection, WUCA; *Counterattack*, 6, 7, 15 February 1952, and *Firing Line*, 1, 5, 15 March 1952, in Harvey Matusow Papers, Special Collections, University of Sussex; Kazan testimony, 10 April 1952, in Eric Bentley, ed., *Thirty Years of Treason* (2002), p. 494.

46. Dan Georgakas, 'Still Good after all these Years', *Cineaste*, 7, 2 (Spring 1976), pp. 16–17; Peter Biskind, 'Ripping Off Zapata: Revolution Hollywood Style', *Cineaste*, 7, 2, pp. 11–15.

47. Kazan's note is on front cover of 11 May 1951 shooting script, *Viva Zapata!*, Kazan collection, WUCA.

48. Notes bound with 6 February 1951 script, '*Viva Zapata!*', B26, F2, in Kazan collection, WUCA.

49. Herb A. Lightman, 'The Filming of "*Viva Zapata!*"', *American Cinematographer*, 33, 4 (April 1952), pp. 54–5.

50. Mao's quotation dates from 1938.

51. Jeremy G. Butler, '*Viva Zapata!*: HUAC and the Mexican Revolution', in Donald R. Noble, ed., *The Steinbeck Question: New Essays in Criticism* (New York: Whitston Publishing Company, 1993), especially pp. 245–8.

52. Marked 'IMPORTANT' and written in red opposite p. 6 on Kazan's copy of the 6 February 1951 script, B27, Kazan collection, WUCA.

53. Mariano Azuela, *The Underdogs*, (New York: New American Library, 1963) (first written in 1915).

54. See Leo Braudy, *The World in a Frame* (1977), p. 243.

55. 6 February 1951 screenplay, *Viva Zapata!*, Kazan collection, WUCA.

56. *Hollywood Reporter*, 6 February 1952, *Viva Zapata!* File, PCA/MPAA, AMPAS; Hollis Alpert, 9 February 1952, pp. 25–6, Laura Z. Hobson, 1 March 1952, pp. 6–7, Kazan, 5 April 1952 and 24 May 1952, in reply to letter from Carleton Beals of same date (all in *Saturday Review*); Crowther, 8 February 1952; Lawson, *Film in the Battle of Ideas* (1953), pp. 42, 49; 'Hollywood's Viva Zapata Falsifies Mexican Revolution', *Daily Worker*, 16 March 1952, B25, Kazan collection, WUCA.

57. John Womack Jr., *Zapata and the Mexican Revolution* (Harmondsworth: Penguin, 1972), p. 565; Womack quoted in Robert E. Morsberger, 'Steinbeck's Screenplays and Productions', in Steinbeck, *Zapata* (2001), p. 352; Arthur Pettit, '*Viva Zapata!*: A Tribute to Steinbeck, Kazan and Brando', *Film & History* (May 1977), pp. 25–45; Raymond Fletcher, 'The Real Zapata', *Tribune*, 2 May 1952 (BFI); Dan Georgakas, 'Still Good after all these Years', *Cineaste*, 7, 2 (Spring 1976), pp. 16–17.

3. Elia Kazan and the House Committee on Un-American Activities

1. Brian Neve, 'HUAC, the Blacklist, and the Decline of Social Cinema', in Peter Lev, *The Fifties: Transforming the Screen* (2003), pp. 65–8. On the Hollywood blacklist see Larry Ceplair and Steven Englund, *The Inquisition in Hollywood* (1983); John Cogley, *Report on Blacklisting, I – Movies* (1956); David Caute, *The Great Fear* (1978); Howard Suber, 'The Anti-Communist Blacklist in the Hollywood Motion Picture Industry', PhD. Thesis, UCLA, 1968; Victor S. Navasky, *Naming Names* (1980); Patrick McGilligan and Paul Buhle, eds., *Tender Comrades* (1997); Paul Buhle and Dave Wagner, *Hide in Plain Sight* (2003), *Radical Hollywood, The Untold Story Behind America's Favorite Movies* (2003); Dan Georgakas, 'The Hollywood Reds Fifty Years Later', *American Communist History*, 2, 1 (June 2003), pp. 63–76.
2. Richard Pells, *The Liberal Mind in a Conservative Age* (1998), p. 272; Ellen Schrecker, *Many Are the Crimes* (1998), pp. 190, 203.
3. John Cogley, *Report on Blacklisting* (1956), pp. 92–4.
4. Walter Goodman, *The Committee* (1968), p. 312. The Matthews article appeared in *The American Legion Magazine*, December 1951, pp. 13–14, 49–56.
5. Kazan, typescript of letter to Zanuck, 7 December 1950, B29, Kazan collection, WUCA; Arthur Miller, *Timebends* (1987), p. 308; Kazan, *A Life* (1988), p. 412.
6. Kazan, *A Life* (1988), pp. 432, 445.
7. The Schulberg and Dmytryk testimonies are in Bentley, *Thirty Years of Treason* (1971), pp. 376–400, and pp. 434–57; Richard Collins, 12 April 1951, *Communist Infiltration of Hollywood Motion Picture Industry – Part 1, Hearings before the Committee on Un-American Activities* (Washington, 1951), p. 254; Schulberg in Victor Navasky, *Naming Names* (1980), p. 246. For Kazan's first testimony, see Executive Session, Hearings before the Committee on Un-American Activities, 82nd Congress, First Session, 14 January 1952 (RG 233 Records of the House of Representatives, National Archives); also in Brian Neve, 'Elia Kazan's First Testimony to the House Committee on Un-American Activities, Executive Session, 14 January 1952', *Historical Journal of Film, Radio and Television*, 25, 2 (June 2005), pp. 251–72.
8. Kazan, *A Life* (1988), p. 446.
9. Wendy Smith, *Real Life Drama* (1990), pp. 158, 252; elsewhere Kazan puts his exit from the party earlier, in 1935, Kazan, *A Life*, p. 131; Kazan, interview with

author, 15 September 1980; Kazan to Crawford and Strasberg, undated, *Paradise Lost* folder, B3–F7, Kazan collection, WUCA; on *Dimitroff*, a play dramatising the recent trial of two German Communists, see Thomas H. Pauly, *An American Odyssey* (1983), pp. 29–31.

10. V.J. Jerome was chairman of the Communist Party's National Cultural Commission. Budd Schulberg calls him a 'didactic party overseer', known at the time as the 'American cultural commissar'; Schulberg, 'Any Which Way He Could', *American Film*, 13, 9 (1988), p. 56. Jerome was the author of *The Negro in Hollywood Films* (New York, Masses & Mainstream, 1950). He was convicted under the Smith Act, of 'conspiracy to teach and advocate the overthrow by force and violence' of the US government, and served a three-year prison term, 1954–7; *Biographical Note*, Yale University Library; Wendy Smith, *Real Life Drama* (1990), p. 253.

11. Larry Ceplair and Steven Englund, *The Inquisition in Hollywood* (1983), p. 143; information on Kazan and the Nazi-Soviet Pact from Robert Hethmon, drawing on a letter to him from Robert Ardrey of 7 October 1966.

12. Jack Warner to Elia Kazan, 20 February 1952, WB/USC.

13. See Robert Sklar, *City Boys, Cagney, Bogart, Garfield* (Princeton, N.J.: Princeton University Press, 1992), pp. 220–4.

14. On John Howard Lawson see Gerald Horne, *The Final Victim of the Blacklist* (2006) and Gary Crowdus, *The Political Companion to American Film* (1994), pp. 243–4; Lawson was a key figure in organising the Screen Writers Guild, and wrote a number of respected texts on drama and film, including *Film in the Battle of Ideas* (1953). Nancy Lynn Schwartz, *The Hollywood Writers' Wars* (New York: Alfred A. Knopf, 1982), p. 88.

15. Kazan, *A Life* (1980), pp. 456–7. On the role of Lawson and the Communist Party in the demise of *New Theatre and Film* (previously *New Theatre*) see Herbert Kline, 'Afterword', in Kline, ed., *New Theatre and Film, 1934–1937, An Anthology* (San Diego: Harcourt Brace Jovanovich, 1985), pp. 363–7. Molly Thacher Kazan was assistant editor of the magazine.

16. Martin Gottfried, *Arthur Miller, His Life and Work* (2003), p. 193.

17. *Counterattack*, 15 February 1952, Harvey Matusow Papers, 1950–5, Special Collections, University of Sussex Library.

18. *Hollywood Reporter*, 19 March 1952, p. 2; Val Holley, *Mike Connolly and the Manly Art of Hollywood Gossip* (2003), pp. 104–5.

19. W.R. Wilkerson, in *Hollywood Reporter*, 2 December 1947, cited in Joseph Foster, 'Entertainment Only', *New Masses*, 66 (1948), pp. 21–2; Kazan, *A Life* (1988), pp. 451, 455.

20. George F. Custen, *Twentieth Century's Fox* (1997), pp. 312–16; *New York Times*, 25 November 1951, cutting, Kazan file, AMPAS; 'Spyros P. Skouras: Mr CinemaScope', *Films and Filming*, 1, 5 (February 1955), p. 3.

21. Holley, *Mike Connolly and the Manly Art of Hollywood Gossip* (2003), p. 6; Barbara Leaming, *Marilyn Monroe* (1988), pp. 44–5. Jeff Young discusses the effects of the *Hollywood Reporter* story on the Awards ceremony in an interview in *Arthur Miller, Elia Kazan and the Blacklist: None Without Sin*, Thirteeen/WNET broad-

cast, 1 September 2003; *Variety*, 26 April 1952, p. 17; Kazan, *A Life* (1988), pp. 455–6.

22. Navasky, *Naming Names* (1980), p. 201; Bosworth, 'Kazan's Choice', *Vanity Fair*, 469 (September 1999), p. 180; Steinbeck to Annie Laurie Williams, 17 June 1952, in Elaine Steinbeck and Robert Wallsten, *Steinbeck: A Life in Letters* (1975), p. 450; Kazan, *A Life* (1988), pp. 460, 465, 569; Gottfried, *Arthur* Miller (2003), p. 194. For other accounts of the meetings with Miller and Hellman see Arthur Miller, *Timebends, A Life* (1987), pp. 330–5, and Lillian Hellman, *Scoundrel Time* (1976), pp. 63–4. Molly Kazan, *The Egghead, A Comedy*, undated typescript in the Theatre collection, Library for the Performing Arts, NYPL/Lincoln Center, New York.

23. Sidney Hook, *HERESY, yes* – *CONSPIRACY, no!* (American Committee for Cultural Freedom, undated, 29pp), p. 14; Elia Kazan to Sidney Hook, undated, Box 54, Folder 1, Sidney Hook Collection, Hoover Institution Archives; Elia Kazan to Bertram D. Wolfe, 24 September 1952, and Bertram D. Wolfe to Elia Kazan, 22 February 1972, in Bertram Wolfe collection, Hoover Institution Archives, Box 9, Folder 4; phone interview, author with Herbert I. London, 11 January 2004; Ronald Radosh, Allis Radosh, *Red Star over Hollywood* (2005), p. 187.

24. Elia Kazan, Executive Hearing, 10 April 1952, in Eric Bentley, *Thirty Years of Treason* (1971), pp. 482–95; this includes Kazan's paid advertisement, which first appeared in the *New York Times*, 12 April 1952; on Tony Kraber see Kazan, *A Life*, pp. 684–5. See the testimony of Clifford Odets in Bentley, ed., *Thirty Years of Treason* (1971), pp. 498–533. In January Kazan had mentioned that there were nine members in the unit; in April he named eight, arguing that he did not, on reflection, remember attending any meeting with Michael Gordon. As well as three Party officials, V.J. Jerome, Andrew Overgaard and Ted Wellman (a.k.a. Sid Benson), Kazan's affidavit also 'named' four members of the League of Workers Theatres, which he called 'unquestionably a Communist-controlled unit', Bentley, *Thirty Years of Treason* (1971), pp. 487–8. While Kazan always maintained that he had been truthful, some have suggested that Kazan 'named names' selectively; see Pat McGilligan, 'Scoundrel Tome', *Film Comment*, June 1988, pp. 14–15. On the advertisement Kazan did say in 1988: 'I signed the ad. It was my fault. I've often wished I hadn't done that. It seemed like I was asking other people to join me. I had no right to ask them, did I?', *New York Post*, 5 May 1988, p. 37.

25. Molly Kazan, *The Egghead, A Comedy*, undated typescript (No. 3088) in the Theatre collection, Library for the Performing Arts, NYPL/Lincoln Center, New York.

26. Elia Kazan, interview with the author, New York, 15 September 1980. McGilligan on Jules Dassin, in Patrick McGilligan and Paul Buhle, eds., *Tender Comrades* (1997), p. 213; *The Nation*, 26 April 1952, p. 395; Arthur Schlesinger Jr., 'History of the Week', *New York Post*, 4 May 1952, p. 3M; Pauly, *An American Odyssey* (1983), p. 160. Schlesinger Jr., whose *The Vital Center, The Politics of Freedom* (New York), had been published in 1949, continued to support Kazan; see his piece

on Kazan's 1999 Award, *New York Times*, 28 February 1999. William Fitelson to Kazan, 13 May 1981, Kazan collection, WUCA. Kazan describes his family lawyer Fitelson politically as a left anti-Stalinist and a 'Trotskyist', *A Life* (1988), pp. 457–8; the lawyer has also been seen as advising Kazan to publish the *New York Times* advertisement urging others to cooperate with the Committee, Bernard Eisenschitz, *Nicholas Ray* (1993), p. 501.

27. Dassin interview, 'Cine Parade', Criterion Collection 2005 DVD of *Night and the City* (1950); Larry Adler, 'Hollywood on Trial', *New Statesman*, 9 November 1973, p. 684; Sanya Shoilevska Henderson, *Alex North, Film Composer* (2003), pp. 49–50; statement dated 8 October 1952 on the title page of Robert E. Sherwood, Annotated Final script, 31 July 1952, B29, Kazan collection, WUCA.

28. Victor Navasky, *Naming Names* (1980), pp. 319–24; credits in Howard Suber, 'The Anti-Communist Blacklist in the Hollywood Motion Picture Industry', 1968, pp. 187, 238–9, and Internet Movie Database.

29. On Navasky see Thom Andersen, 'Red Hollywood', in Suzanne Ferguson and Barbara Groseclose, eds., *Literature and the Visual Arts in Contemporary Society* (1985), pp. 158–65; Paul Jarrico quoted in Michael S. Ybarra, 'Blacklist Whitewash', *The New Republic*, 5–12 January 1998, p. 23.

30. Jules Dassin, *Hollywood Reporter*, 15 March 1999; Alan Wolfe, 'Revising a False History', *Los Angeles Times*, 21 March 1999, pp. M1, M6. See also Larry Ceplair, 'Preface to the Illinois Paperback', in Larry Ceplair and Steven Englund, *The Inquisition in Hollywood* (2003), pp. xi–xix.

31. Zanuck to Kazan, marked 'Confidential', 17 April 1952, B30, Kazan collection, WUCA.

32. On the goals of the American Committee for Cultural Freedom see the Preface to James Rorty and Moshe Dector, *McCarthy and the Communists* (Boston: The Beacon Press, 1954), pp. vii–viii; International Rescue Committee (IRC) and other research material for *Man on a Tightrope*, including Wolfe's paper, 'Culture and the Total State', Address delivered at conference, 'In Defence of Free Culture', under the auspices of the ACCF, 29 March 1952, B29, Kazan collection, WUCA; Richard H. Pells, *The Liberal Mind in a Conservative Age* (1985), p. 129; *New York Times*, 15 May 1952.

33. Kazan notebook on *Man on a Tightrope*, B29, Kazan collection, WUCA; Kazan to Steinbeck, 18 May, 1953, *East of Eden* notebook, B33, Kazan collection, WUCA; Zanuck to Kazan, 21 October 1952, B30, Kazan collection, WUCA.

34. Zanuck to Kazan, 29 July 1952, bound with script, Twentieth Century-Fox collection, USC; Robert Sherwood, 'Notes on "Man on a Tightrope"', sent to Darryl F. Zanuck, Elia Kazan and Robert Jacks, 4 August 1952, Sherwood correspondence, Kazan collection, WUCA.

35. Skouras to Kazan, 7 May 1953, B30, Kazan collection, WUCA.

36. Ciment, ed., *Kazan on Kazan* (1973), p. 83; Young, ed., *Kazan* (1999), p. 119; Kazan, *A Life* (1988), pp. 463, 466; Pauly, *An American Odyssey* (1983), pp. 163, 169.

4. Filming *On the Waterfront* (1954)

1. Kazan, *A Life* (1988), p. 486; Jack Newfield and Mark Jacobson, 'An Interview with Budd Schulberg', *Tikkun*, 15, 3 (May–June 2000), p. 11; Miller, *Timebends* (1987), p. 273; Gottfried, *Arthur Miller* (2003), p. 194.
2. Budd Schulberg testimony, 23 May 1951, in Eric Bentley, ed., *Thirty Years of Treason* (1971), pp. 434–57; Navasky, *Naming Names* (1980), p. 246.
3. Martin Gottfried, *Arthur Miller* (2003), pp. 116, 128, 168.
4. Arthur Miller, 1st Draft, *The Hook*, undated, B23, Kazan collection, WUCA.
5. Kazan, Typed Comments on First Version, *The Hook*, B23, Kazan collection, WUCA.
6. Arthur Miller, *The Hook*, 26 January 1951, 'Estimating Draft', B23 F3, Kazan collection, WUCA.
7. Budd Schulberg, interview with author, 13 October 2004.
8. Malcolm Johnson, *Crime on the Waterfront* (New York: McGraw-Hill, 1950), quoted in Brenda Murphy, *Congressional Theatre* (1999), p. 282.
9. Albert Wertheim, 'A View from the Bridge', in Christopher Bigsby, ed., *The Cambridge Companion to Arthur Miller* (1997), p. 105; Leo Braudy, *On the Waterfront* (2005), p. 17.
10. Stephen Schwartz, 'Arthur Miller's Proletariat: The True Stories of *On the Waterfront*, Pietro Panto, and Vincenzo Longhi', *Film History*, Volume 16 (2004), p. 380.
11. Miller, *Imagine*, BBC1, 24 November 2004.
12. 'Original Screenplay', undated, MOMA.
13. Schulberg, in 'A Contender', *Arena*, BBC2, 19 May 2001; Schulberg, 'Joe Docks: Forgotten Man of the Waterfront', *New York Times*, 28 December 1952.
14. Elaine Steinbeck, Robert Wallsten, eds., *Steinbeck: A Life in Letters* (1979), p. 450; contracts, Warner Bros. materials, Princeton University Library
15. *Variety*, 22 April 1953, pp. 5, 18.
16. Darryl Zanuck, undated, Western Union message to Joe Moskowitz, asking him to convey message to Kazan and Schulberg, B31–F8, Kazan collection, WUCA; Zanuck to Schulberg and Kazan, 12 February 1953, in Behlmer, ed., *Memo from Darryl F. Zanuck* (1993), pp. 225–8. On the State Department (and the CIA) and Hollywood in 1953, David N. Eldridge, '"Dear Owen": The CIA, Luigi Luraschi and Hollywood, 1953', *Historical Journal of Film, Radio and Television*, 20, 2 (2000), p. 149.
17. Zanuck to Kazan, 15 July 1954, in Behlmer, *Memo from Darryl F. Zanuck* (1993), pp. 229–30.
18. Schulberg, 'Afterword', in Budd Schulberg, *On the Waterfront, A Screenplay* (1980), p. 147. Arthur Miller, *Timebends* (1987), p. 401; Spyros Skouras to George Skouras, 8 July 1960, Spyros Skouras Collection, Box 32, Special Collections, Stanford University; Zanuck to Kazan, 27 January 1955, in Behlmer, *Memo from Darryl F. Zanuck* (1993), p. 253.

19. Natasha Fraser-Cavassoni, *Sam Spiegel, The Biography of a Hollywood Legend* (2003), pp. 21–58; on Spiegel, Kazan, interview with the author, 15 September 1980; Joanna E. Rapf, 'Introduction', in Joanna E. Rapf, ed., *On the Waterfront* (2003), p. 11.

20. Undated script, 148 pp., titled '*The Golden Warriors (On the Waterfront)*', available from Hollywood Scripts, London.

21. Production notebook, *Golden Warriors*, June 1953, Kazan collection, WUCA.

22. Production notebook, *Golden Warriors*, June 1953, Kazan collection, WUCA.

23. Christopher Cook, 'Third Ear', BBC Radio 3, 3 June 1988; Kazan, *A Life* (1988), p. 500; Budd Schulberg, interview with the author, 13 October 2004.

24. Kazan, *A Life* (1988), p. 529; Schulberg, 'The King Who Would be Man', *Vanity Fair* (March 2005), p. 244; Kazan production notebook, *Golden Warriors*, Kazan collection, WUCA.

25. Patricia Bosworth, *Marlon Brando* (2001), p. 102.

26. Lee Rogow, 'Brando on the Waterfront', *Saturday Review*, 37, 24 July 1954, pp. 25–6; Volker Schlöndorff, *The Daily Telegraph*, 16 November 2002; Patricia Bosworth, *Guardian*, 16 July 2001; John Coleman, *New Statesman*, 12 January 1962 (fiche, BFI); Roger Tailleur, *Elia Kazan* (1971), p. 80.

27. Todd Rainsberger, *James Wong Howe, Cinematographer* (San Diego, A.S. Barnes & Co., 1981), p. 116.

28. Sam B. Girgus, *Hollywood Renaissance* (1998), pp. 163, 172.

29. Director's script, Kazan collection, WUCA; Jeffrey Chown, 'Visual Coding and Social Class in *On the Waterfront*', in Joanna E. Rapf, ed., *On the Waterfront* (2003), pp. 106–23.

30. Jon Burlingame, 'Leonard Bernstein and *On the Waterfront*', in Joanna E. Rapf, ed., *On the Waterfront* (2003), pp. 126, 133–5.

31. Frances K. Pohl, *Ben Shahn* (1989), p. 5.

32. Kazan, letter to MOMA, Film Department, 5 September 1980, in Kazan folders, MOMA; Kenneth Hey, 'Ambivalence as a Theme in *On the Waterfront* (1954): An Interdisciplinary Approach to Film Study', *American Quarterly* (Winter 1979), p. 683; Edouard L. de Laurot and Jonas Mekas, 'An Interview with Boris Kaufman', in Rapf, ed., *On the Waterfront*, pp. 161–3.

33. *Time*, 9 August 1954; *Irish Times*, 2 July 1955, in PCA file for *On the Waterfront*, PCA/MPAA collection, AMPAS.

34. Thomas H. Pauly, *An American Odyssey* (1983), p. 213; Lindsay Anderson, 'The Last Sequence of *On the Waterfront*', *Sight & Sound*, 24, 3 (1955), pp. 127–30.

35. John M. Smith, 'Three Liberal Films', *Movie*, 19 (1971–2), p. 20; Thomas H. Pauly, *An American Odyssey* (1983), p. 213; Schulberg interview with the author, 13 October 2004; Kazan, in Jeff Young, ed., *Kazan* (1999), p. 122.

36. Budd Schulberg, interview with the author, 13 October 2004, and interview with Kevin Mitchell, *The Observer*, 22 July 2007, Sport section, pp. 6–7; Peter Biskind, 'The Politics of Power in "*On the Waterfront*"', *Film Quarterly* (Fall 1975), pp. 25–38; Michael Denning, *The Laboring of American Culture in the Twentieth Century* (1996), p. 257.

37. Lloyd Michaels, *Elia Kazan: A Guide to References and Resources* (1985), p. 33; Nicholas Ray, Susan Ray, eds., *I was Interrupted: Nicholas Ray on Making Movies* (Berkeley: University of California Press, 1995), p. 30.

5. Producer–Director: *East of Eden* (1955) and *Baby Doll* (1956)

1. Douglas Gomery, *The Hollywood Studio System* (London: BFI and Macmillan, 1986), p. 122; Janet Wasko, *Movies and Money, Financing the American Film Industry* (Norwood, N.J.: Ablex Publishing, 1982), p. 118; Thomas Schatz, *The Genius of the System* (New York: Pantheon Books, 1988), p. 439.
2. Contract information in Warner Bros. materials, Princeton University Library; Nick Roddick, *A New Deal in Entertainment* (London: BFI, 1983), pp. 16, 24.
3. Annie Laurie Williams to Elia Kazan, 19 August 1952, Annie Laurie Manuscript Collection, Columbia University, New York; Kazan to John Steinbeck, 10 December 1952, Annie Laurie Manuscript Collection, Columbia University, New York; David Wyatt, 'Introduction', in John Steinbeck, *East of Eden* (London: Penguin, 2000), p. vii.
4. Contract information in Warner Bros. materials, Princeton University Library and WB/USC; Kazan to Steinbeck, 10 December 1952, Annie Laurie Manuscript Collection, Columbia University, New York.
5. Peter Lev, *The Fifties* (2003), p. 108.
6. Kazan to Warner, 21 July 1954, WB/USC; notebook on *East of Eden*, 'Eden', 19 April 1953 entry, Kazan collection, WUCA; Kazan to John Steinbeck, 21 April 1953, Annie Laurie Manuscript Collection, Columbia University, New York. Letter, Kazan to John Steinbeck, 18 May 1953, pasted in 'Eden' notebook, Kazan collection, WUCA.
7. Kazan to John Steinbeck, 18 May 1953, 'Eden' notebook, Kazan collection, WUCA; Paul Osborn to Leland Hayward, 21 June 1954, Paul Osborn Papers, Wisconsin.
8. Warner to Kazan, 10 March 1954, in Leith Adams and Keith Burns, *James Dean* (1990), p. 17; Kazan to Sidney Skolsky, 20 December 1954, Folder 21, Sidney Skolsky collection, AMPAS; Paul Osborn to Kazan, undated, Paul Osborn Papers, Wisconsin.
9. Kazan to Paul Osborn, 19 April 1954, Paul Osborn Papers, Wisconsin.
10. Arthur Gavin, 'The Photography of "East of Eden"', *American Photographer* (March 1955), p. 149; Kazan to Steve Trilling, 9 December 1954, Jack L. Warner collection, USC.
11. Christopher Palmer, *The Composer in Hollywood* (London: Marion Boyars, 1990), pp. 302–8; Publicity notes, *East of Eden* files, WB/USC; Kazan to Steve Trilling, 3 July 1954, Jack L. Warner Collection, USC; on the love story between Adam and Cal, see Kazan, *East of Eden* notebook, 3 April 1953 entry, B33, Kazan collection, WUCA.

12. Breen to Jason Joy, 22 April 1952, Breen to Jack Warner, 2 December 1953, PCA/MPAA Files, AMPAS; Kazan to Steinbeck, 10 December 1952, Annie Laurie Manuscript Collection, Columbia University, New York.

13. Letter, Kazan to Steve Trilling, undated, clipped with memo of 16 February 1954, PCA/MPAA, AMPAS; Vizzard, Memo for the Files, 16 February 1954, PCA/MPAA, AMPAS; Breen to Warner, 29 June 1954, PCA/MPAA, AMPAS; Kazan to Warner, 9 October 1953, Warner file, *East of Eden*, WB/USC.

14. Kazan, *A Life* (1988), p. 535.

15. Michel Ciment, ed., *Kazan on Kazan* (1973), p. 121.

16. David Bordwell, Janet Staiger and Kristin Thomson, *The Classical Hollywood Cinema* (1985), p. 361.

17. Andrew Sarris, *Film Culture*, 1, 3 (May–June 1955), p. 24; Leo Braudy, *The World in a Frame* (1977), p. 241; Michael Butler, 'Shock Waves', in Joanna E. Rapf, ed., 'In Focus: Children of the Blacklist, an Extended Family', *Cinema Journal*, 44, 4 (Summer 2005), p. 85.

18. *Time*, 21 March 1955, p. 98; Jonathan Miller, *New Statesman*, 11 August 1961, fiche on *Baby Doll*, BFI; Jeff Young, *Kazan* (1999), p. 196; John Howard Lawson, *Theory and Technique of Playwriting and Screenwriting* (1949), pp. 174–86.

19. Kazan to Jack Warner, 8 April 1955, WB/USC; J.S. Hummel to Warner, 17 May 1955, WB/USC; on Dean, Kazan to Jack Warner, 4 October 1955, WB/USC.

20. Devlin, ed., *The Selected Letters of Tennessee Williams* (2006), p. 410; Breen to Warner, 1 August 1952, PCA/MPAA, AMPAS; Kazan to Warner, 2 August 1952, WB/USC; contract information, WB/Princeton.

21. Tennessee Williams, *Baby Doll* (1957).

22. Albert J. Devlin, *Selected Letters* (2006), pp. 589, 597.

23. 24 October 1955, PCA/MPAA, AMPAS; Kazan to Jack Warner, 7 November 1955, WB/USC; Kazan to Finlay/Warner, 15 November 1955, WB/USC; Jack Warner to Kazan, 10 November 1955, WB/USC.

24. Production Notes on *Baby Doll*, *Baby Doll* folder, MOMA.

25. Jack Vizzard, *See No Evil* (1970), pp. 206–8.

26. Vincent Brook, 'Courting Controversy: The Making and Selling of *Baby Doll* and the Demise of the Production Code', *Quarterly Review of Film & Video*, 18, 4 (2001), p. 354; Arthur Knight, 'The Williams–Kazan Axis', *Saturday Review*, 39, 29 December 1956, pp. 22–4.

27. Kazan to Finlay/Warner, 15 November 1955, WB/USC; Press Release, National Legion of Decency, WB/USC; *Motion Picture Herald*, 8 December 1956.

28. Frank Walsh, *Sin and Censorship* (1996), p. 275; *Time*, 24 December 1956, p. 61; Brook, 'Courting Controversy', *Quarterly Review of Film & Video*, 18, 4 (2001), p. 357.

29. Kazan to George Stevens, 14 October 1955, Stevens collection, AMPAS; Leo Braudy, *The World in a Frame* (1977), p. 241; Carroll Baker, *Baby Doll, An Autobiography* (1983), p. 151; Eli Wallach, *The Good, the Bad and Me* (2005), p. 172; Michel Ciment, 'Entretien avec Elia Kazan', FR3 TV interview on French DVD of *Baby Doll*; Karl Malden, with Carla Malden, *When Do I Start?* (1997), pp.

249–50; translation of article, 'Cardinal Spellman's Condemnation of "Baby Doll"', *Le Monde*, 27 December 1956, Kazan clippings file, AMPAS.

30. Kazan notebook on *Baby Doll*, B34, F4, Kazan collection, WUCA; Bertrand Tavernier, 'The Fanny Trilogy: An Appreciation', with Kino DVD edition of *The Fanny Trilogy* (2004); Kazan to Williams, undated letter in Ciment, ed., *Elia Kazan* (1988), p. 109, Williams to Kazan, 28 July 1955, in Devlin, ed., *The Selected Letters of Tennessee Williams* (2006), p. 577. On vacation in 1949, Kazan had visited Marseilles, mentioning Pagnol enthusiastically in a postcard he sent to Cheryl Crawford, Billy Rose Theatre Collection, NYPL/Lincoln Center.

31. Kazan, 'I did the best …', poster, *Baby Doll* materials, Kazan collection, WUCA; *Baby Doll* Production Notes, MOMA.

32. Ciment, ed., *Elia Kazan* (1988), p. 84; Michael Stragow, *Phoenix Post*, 23 July 1985, MOMA.

33. Philip C. Kolin, 'Civil Rights and the Black Presence in *Baby Doll*', *Literature Film Quarterly*, 24, 1 (1996), p. 3; V.O. Key, *Southern Politics in State and Nation* (New York: Vintage, 1949), p. 229.

34. Boris Kaufman, 'Filming "Baby Doll"', *American Cinematographer*, 38, 2 (February 1957), pp. 92–3; Kazan, letter, 5 September 1980, to MOMA Film Department, MOMA.

35. Anna Hill Johnstone, *Baby Doll* Production Notes, MOMA; comments on the *Baby Doll* music at http://www.musicfromthemovies.com/review.asp?ID= 4010 (accessed, 2 August 2006); Kazan to Steve Trilling, 16 November 1955, WB/USC.

36. Bosley Crowther, *New York Times*, 19 December 1956; Knight, 'The Williams–Kazan Axis', *Saturday Review*, 39, 29 December 1956, pp. 22–4; Max Lerner, *New York Post*, 23 December 1956; Williams, *Memoirs* (1976), pp. 169–70; Brenda Murphy, *Tennessee Williams and Elia Kazan* (1992), p. 132.

37. Synopsis, Warner Bros., *Baby Doll* folder, MOMA.

38. François Truffaut, *The Films in My Life* (Harmondsworth: Penguin, 1982), pp. 110–13.

6. Journeys in the American South

1. Molly Kazan quoted in Kazan 'TVA Production Diary' on *Wild River*, 13 January 1958 entry, Kazan collection, WUCA.

2. Ardrey to Kazan, 27 November 1955, Robert Ardrey correspondence, Kazan collection, WUCA.

3. Budd Schulberg, 'Your Arkansas Traveller', in Schulberg, *Some Faces in the Crowd* (1954), pp. 7–49.

4. Elia Kazan, 'Introduction', in Budd Schulberg, *A Face in the Crowd* (1957), p. xvi; Peter C. Rollins, 'Will Rogers and the Relevance of Nostalgia', in John O'Connor and Martin A. Jackson, ed., *American History, American Television: Interpreting the Video Past* (New York: Frederick Ungar, 1983), p. 78; Vance Packard, *The Hidden*

Persuaders (Harmonsworth: Penguin, 1960), p. 103; Kazan, notebook for *A Face in the Crowd*, 6 July 1956 entry, B36, F5, Kazan collection, WUCA.

5. Kathleen Hall Jamieson, *Packaging the Presidency, A History and Criticism of Presidential Campaign Advertising* (New York: Oxford University Press, 1996), p. 44; Budd Schulberg, interview with the author, 13 October 2004.

6. Kazan to Robert Ardrey, 6 March 1957, Ardrey correspondence, Kazan collection, WUCA; on Gold Medal Studios, *A Face in the Crowd* materials, WB/USC; Kazan to Schulberg, 7 November 1955, Schulberg correspondence, Kazan collection, WUCA.

7. Kazan to Budd Schulberg, 22 April 1956, entry of 20 April 1956 on Molly Kazan's script criticisms, and Paul Osborn to Kazan, 31 May 1956, all in *Face in the Crowd* notebook, B36, F5, Kazan collection, WUCA; Typescript on meetings of 31 May 1956, *A Face in the Crowd* materials, B36, Kazan collection, WUCA.

8. Geoffrey Shurlock, 10 July 1956, and Kazan to Shurlock, 22 May 1957, *A Face in the Crowd* file, PCA/MPAA, AMPAS.

9. Kazan, notebook, 25 August 1956, B36, Kazan collection, WUCA; Kazan, *A Life* (1988), p. 568.

10. Kazan notebook, 25 May 1956 and 25 March 1956 entries, B36, Kazan collection, WUCA.

11. Kazan, *A Life* (1988), p. 569.

12. Kazan on 'Know-nothingism', and James Dean fan clubs, *A Face in the Crowd* notebook, B36, Kazan collection, WUCA. Kazan notes Dean being corrupted by his new success and power.

13. *Peoples World* review in Kazan, *A Life* (1988), p. 567; on Brownie McGhee see *Jazz Journal* (June 1958), pp. 1–5, at www.blues.co.nz/dig-this/documents/S (accessed, 15 August 2006); on Tom Glazer see Michael Denning, *The Cultural Front* (1996), p. 469.

14. David Riesman, *The Lonely Crowd* (Garden City, NY: Doubleday, 1953).

15. C. Wright Mills, *The Power Elite* (New York: Oxford University Press, 1956).

16. Kazan to Schulberg, 3 June 1957, Kazan collection, WUCA; Kazan's notes, 4 January 1958, in Ciment, ed., *Elia Kazan* (1988), pp. 112, 114.

17. *Time* review, undated clipping, MOMA; Bosley Crowther, *New York Times*, 29 May 1957; Arthur Knight, *Saturday Review*, 25 May 1957; Andrew Sarris, *Film Culture*, 3 (October 1957), pp. 13–14; François Truffaut, *The Films in My Life* (1982), p. 115.

18. William Bradford Huie, *Mud on the Stars* (London: Hutchinson, 1944); Kazan to Osborn, 17 December 1954, Paul Osborn Papers, Wisconsin.

19. William Bradford Huie to 'Gadge' Kazan, 1 October 1955, B43, F6, Kazan collection, WUCA.

20. Kazan to Robert Ardley, 6 March 1957, Robert Ardrey correspondence, Kazan collection, WUCA; 'Ben Maddow: The Invisible Man', in Pat McGilligan, *Backstory* 2 (1991), pp. 157–92; Kazan notes, 5 August 1957, B41, Kazan collection, WUCA.

21. Kazan's reference to federal interference, 5 August 1957 note, B41, Kazan collection, WUCA.

22. Ciment, ed., *Kazan on Kazan* (1973), p. 24; Kazan, *A Life* (1988), pp. 105, 263; Brian Black, 'Authority in the Valley: TVA in *Wild River* and the Popular Media, 1930–1940', *Journal of American Culture*, 18, 2 (1995), p. 2; Charles Silver, 'Elia Kazan's *Wild River*', *Studies in Modern Art*, 1 (1991), pp. 165–81.

23. Elia Kazan draft screenplay, 'The Coming of Spring', 7 April 1958, MSS collection, Wisconsin; Kazan diary entry on Maddow draft, 17 January 1958, Kazan collection, WUCA.

24. 'Actually I was Dave once', typescript, pasted in Kazan notebook, February 1958, Kazan collection, WUCA.

25. Ciment, ed., *Kazan on Kazan* (1973), p. 130, Kazan, 'The Coming of Spring' ('3rd E.K. version'), 7 April 1958, p. 90, MSS collection, Wisconsin.

26. Notes on script by Molly Kazan, 23 January 1958, Kazan notebook, Kazan collection, WUCA; reference to Skourus, Kazan notebook of 3 March 1958, Kazan collection, WUCA; Buddy Adler, 26 April 1958 letter to Kazan, Twentieth Century-Fox collection, USC.

27. Geoffrey Shurlock to Frank McCarthy, Twentieth Century-Fox, 14 September 1959, and other letters to 7 March 1960 re: *Wild River*, PCA/MPAA collection, AMPAS.

28. Kazan to Marlon Brando, 24 August 1959 and telegram in reply, 26 August 1959, in *Wild River* materials, B44, F2, Kazan collection, WUCA; Patricia Bosworth, *Montgomery Clift* (1978), p. 135.

29. Kazan to Osborn, undated, Paul Osborn Papers,Wisconsin,

30. Kazan to Osborn, undated, Paul Osborn Papers,Wisconsin.

31. Kazan annotation, opposite p. 39, 5 October 1959 script, B42–F3, Kazan collection, WUCA.

32. Kazan to Osborn, undated, Paul Osborn Papers, Wisconsin. (References 29–30 and 32 relate to three separate letters.)

33. Marquerite Duras, conversation with Elia Kazan, 'L'homme tremblant', *Cahiers du Cinéma*, No. 318, December 1980, pp. 5–13; Donald Chase, '*Wild River*', *Film Comment*, 32, 6 (November–December 1996), pp. 10–15.

34. Kazan, *A Life* (1988), p. 601; Robin Wood, 'The Kazan Problem', *Movie*, 19, 1971–2, p. 31; see Stéphane Delorme, 'Par-dessus bord', *Cahiers du Cinéma* (November 2004), pp. 27–8; Jean-Pierre Coursoden, 'Deau tragedies américaines', in *Positif, Revue Mensuelle de Cinéma*, No. 518 (April 2004), pp. 94–7.

7. *Splendour in the Grass* (1961) and *America America* (1963)

1. Ciment, *Kazan on Kazan* (1973), p. 139; Kazan to Inge, 7 June 1963, William Inge correspondence, Kazan collection, WUCA.

2. William Inge, 'New Scenarist's Views', *New York Times*, 8 October 1961 (MOMA); Kazan to Inge, 7 June 1963, Kazan collection, WUCA.

3. Kazan note, 5 May 1958, notebook on *Splendour in the Grass*, Kazan collection, B45, WUCA.

4. Kazan annotation, Inge screenplay of 7 March 1960, B46, Kazan collection, WUCA.
5. Kazan, *A Life* (1988), p. 584; Ardrey to Kazan, 21 January 1961, Robert Ardrey correspondence, Kazan collection, WUCA; Suzanne Finstad, *Warren Beatty* (2005), p. 231; Jeff Young, ed., *Kazan* (1999), p. 267.
6. Kazan, 11 March 1960, to Head, International Photographers of the Motion Picture Industries Local, New York, B48, Kazan collection, WUCA.
7. Production-Distribution agreement, 20 January 1960, *Splendour in the Grass* folders, WB/USC.
8. Ciment, *Kazan on Kazan* (1973), p. 142; Vincent LoBrutto, *By Design* (1992), p. 54; Peter Ettedqui, *Production Design and Art Direction Stagecraft* (Crans-Pres-Celigny: RotoVision, 1999), p. 40.
9. Kazan, 11 March 1960, to Motion Picture Industries Local, New York, B48, Kazan collection, WUCA.
10. Geoffrey Shurlock to Kazan, 6 April 1960, Shurlock to Kazan, 13 February 1961, and Memo for the Files, 21 February 1961, all in *Splendour in the Grass* file, PCA/MPAA collection, AMPAS.
11. Kazan to Ben Kalmenson, 4 January 1961, Kazan to Jack Warner, 27 February 1961 (unsent); Kazan to Jack Warner, 27 February 1961, all in B47, Kazan collection, WUCA.
12. Kazan to Jack Warner and Ben Kalmenson, 25 May 1961, Kazan collection, WUCA.
13. Kazan to Inge, 7 June 1963, William Inge correspondence, Kazan collection, WUCA.
14. Kazan to Clifford Odets, 28 June 1961, Odets correspondence, folder for 1961, Kazan collection, WUCA; Memo for the Files, Re: *Splendour in the Grass*, 26 June 1961, with enclosures of Inge re-writes, PCA/MPAA, AMPAS; *Splendour in the Grass* files, WB/USC; Kazan to Wolfe Cohen, Warner Bros., New York, 8 November 1961, Warner Bros. materials, Princeton University Library.
15. Ettedqui, *Production Design and Art Direction Stagecraft* (1999), p. 40; Kazan note, 2 April 1958, notebook, *Splendour in the Grass*, B45, Kazan collection, WUCA.
16. Kazan annotation to 7 March 1960 screenplay, B46, Kazan collection, WUCA.
17. Kazan annotation to 7 March 1960 screenplay, B46, Kazan collection, WUCA.
18. Kazan annotation to 7 March 1960 screenplay, B46, Kazan collection, WUCA; Paul Jacobs and Saul Landau, *The New Radicals* (Harmondsworth: Penguin, 1966), p. 159.
19. Kazan interview with Robin Bean, *Films and Filming* (March 1962), p. 26.
20. Michael Walker, '*Splendour in the Grass*', *Movie*, 19 (Winter 1971–2), pp. 32–4.
21. Arthur Knight, *Saturday Review*, 16 September 1961, p. 36.
22. Kazan annotation to 7 March 1960 screenplay, B46, Kazan collection, WUCA.
23. Paul V. Beckley, *New York Herald Tribune*, 11 October 1961; *Newsweek*, 16 October 1961, pp. 112–13; Knight, *Saturday Review*, 16 September 1961; Dwight Macdonald, *Esquire*, December 1961, reprinted in Dwight Macdonald, *On Movies* (New York, De Capo Press, 1981), pp. 140–2; *Time*, 13 October 1961, p. 95.

24. Jacques Rivette, *Cahiers du Cinéma*, 132 (June 1962), reproduced in Roger Tailleur, *Elia Kazan* (1971), pp. 176–8; Robin Wood, 'The Kazan Problem', *Movie*, 19 (1971–2), pp. 29–31; Penelope Houston, *Monthly Film Bulletin* (NFT programme note, June 1962); Bertrand Tavernier, Interview, Sydney Film Festival, 10 July 1999, http://www.wsws.org/articles/1999/jul (accessed, 10 August 2004).

25. Kazan, *Films and Filming*, March 1962, p. 26.

26. Kazan's opening narration, *America America*.

27. Kazan, *A Life* (1988), p. 559.

28. Frederic Morton interview, 'Gadg!', Esquire, 47 (February 1957), in William Baer, ed., *Elia Kazan Interviews* (2000), p. 36.

29. Pauly, *An American Odyssey* (1983), p. 239.

30. Notebook on 'Stavros' and 'Other Characters', Kazan collection, WUCA.

31. 'Stavros' Notebook', 22 March 1962 entry, Kazan collection, WUCA.

32. Marginal note on blank pages opposite script pages, *America America* draft screenplay, 26 February 1962, Kazan collection, WUCA.

33. 'Stavros' Notebook', 31 May 1962 entry, Kazan collection, WUCA.

34. 'Stavros' Notebook', Kazan collection, WUCA.

35. 'Stavros' Notebook', Kazan collection, WUCA.

36. Marginal note on *America America* draft screenplay, 26 February 1962, Kazan collection, WUCA.

37. Michael Butler, emails to author, 11, 18, 20 October 2005.

38. 'Painting exhibition by two-time Oscar winner Vassilis Fotopoulos', http://cultureguide.gr/events (accessed 9 May 2004).

39. Steve Paley, remarks to author, Los Angeles, 11 July 2005.

40. Note by Manos Hadjidakis, 8 November 1963, *America America* materials, Warner Bros. materials, Princeton University Library.

41. Elia Kazan, *The Arrangement* (London: William Collins, 1967), p. 416.

42. Kazan, guest on *Desert Island Discs* (BBC Radio 4), circa 1979.

43. Kazan to Richard Lederer, undated, from Istanbul, Warner Bros. materials, Princeton University Library.

44. Michelangelo Antonioni to Elia Kazan, 1 June 1961, F45, F1, Kazan collection, WUCA.

45. Lyrics for song, Nikos Gatzos (Gatsos), final version, displayed in WUCA exhibit on *America America*, September 2004. The reference to 'two homesicknesses' is in typed material pasted at the front of the *America America* draft screenplay, 26 February 1962, Kazan collection, WUCA.

46. *America America* draft screenplay, 26 February 1962, Kazan collection, WUCA.

47. Charles Silver, Programme notes for October 1977 MOMA showing of *America America*, Kazan material, MOMA Film Department.

48. Andrew Sarris, undated review, *Village Voice*, Kazan file, MOMA.

49. Interview with Suzanne Schiffman, in Royal S. Brown, ed., *Focus on Godard* (Englewood Cliffs, NJ: Prentice-Hall, 1972), p. 48. Kazan remembers that it was the filming of *A Woman Is a Woman* (*Une Femme est une Femme*) (1961) that he

sat in on, see American Film Institute (AFI), 'Dialogue on Film: Elia Kazan', in Baer, *Elia Kazan Interviews* (2000), p. 202.

50. Stavros notebook, Kazan collection, WUCA.
51. Dede Allen, phone interview with author, 4 February 2006; Allen, in Jeanine Basinger et. al., *Working with Kazan* (1973), unpaginated.
52. Richard Lederer to Wolfe Cohen, 8 August 1963, Warner Bros. materials, Princeton University Library.
53. Kazan letter, 14 November 1962, Warner Bros. materials, Princeton University Library.
54. *Newsweek*, 23 December 1963, p. 52; Stanley Kauffman, *A World in Film: Criticism and Comment* (New York: Harper & Row, 1966), pp. 155–6; Joan Didion, *Vogue*, 1 February 1964 (cutting, Kazan file, MOMA).
55. Hollis Alpert, *Saturday Review*, 28 December 1964; telegram, King Vidor to Kazan, 24 December 1963, exhibition on *America America*, WUCA, 2004; Wexler quoted in Robert Koehler, 'One from the heart', *Variety*, 8 March 1999.
56. Kazan to Richard Lederer, 25 March 1964, Warners collection, Princeton University Library.

8. Into Myself: *The Arrangement* (1969) and After

1. William Baer, ed., *Elia Kazan Interviews* (2000), p. 90; Elia Kazan, *A Life* (1988), p. 680.
2. Kazan, *A Life* (1988), pp. 573, 650, 721–2.
3. Interview with Kazan, *Saturday Review*, 4 March 1967, p. 27.
4. Granville Hicks; R.V. Cassill, *Book Week*, 26 February 1967; Robert Ardrey to Kazan, 1 June 1967, Kazan collection, WUCA; James Baldwin, 'God's Country', *New York Review of Books*, 8, 23 March 1967, pp. 17–20.
5. Jeff Young, ed., *Kazan* (1999), pp. 296; Kazan, *A Life* (1988), p. 754.
6. Kirk Douglas, *The Ragman's Son* (1966), p. 405–6.
7. Elia Kazan screenplay, *The Arrangement*, 21 June 1968, p. 154, and changes of 1 October 1968, in Box 47, Folder 2, Kirk Douglas Collection, Wisconsin.
8. Jeff Young, ed., *Kazan* (1999), p. 294.
9. Kazan, 'My Work with Actors', in Ciment, ed., *Elia Kazan* (1988), p. 221.
10. Michel Cieutat, 'L'Arrangement, Un roman, un film, une vie', *Positif, Revue Mensuelle de Cinéma*, 518 (April 2004), pp. 102–4; Michel Ciment, *Kazan par Kazan* (1973, French edition), p. 263.
11. Kazan, 'Political Passion Play: Act II', *New York*, 1, 23 September 1968, pp. 26–7; on *A Face in the Crowd*, Claudine Tavernier, interview with Kazan, 'Kazan vieux comme le monde', *Cinema 70*, 143 (February 1970), p. 53; Richard Roud, *A Passion for Film, Henri Langlois and the Cinematheque Française* (Baltimore: Johns Hopkins Press, 1999), p. 154.
12. Andrew Sarris, *The American Cinema* (1968), pp. 158–9; Andrew Sarris, *Village Voice*, 27 November 1969; Lloyd Michaels, *Elia Kazan* (1985), p. 110.

13. Pauline Kael, *New Yorker*, 22 November 1969; Vincent Canby, *New York Times*, November 19, 1969.

14. Jean-Louis Cosmolli, *Cahiers du Cinéma*, 222 (July 1970), in Roger Tailleur, *Elia Kazan* (1971), pp. 168–70; Robert Benayoun, 'L'Enfance est un Mensonge', *Positif, Revue Mensuelle de Cinéma*, 117 (June 1970), in Roger Tailleur, *Elia Kazan* (1971), pp. 136–43; Gilles Jacob, *Nouvelles Littéraires*, 28 March 1970, in Tailleur, *Elia Kazan* (1971), pp. 180–1.

15. Budd Schulberg, interview with the author, 13 October 2004; Barbara Loden, quoted in Berenice Reynaud, 'For *Wanda*', *Senses of cinema*, http://www. sensesofcinema.com/contents/02/22/wanda.html accessed, 7 July 2007.

16. Daniel Lang, 'Casualties of War', *New Yorker*, 18 October 1969, pp. 61–146; Young, *Kazan* (1999), p. 304.

17. Production Notes, *The Visitors*, United Artists Corporation, *The Visitors* folder, MOMA.

18. Ric Gentry, 'Interview: James Woods', *Post Script, Essays in Film and the Humanities*, 18, 3 (Summer 1999), pp. 20–1.

19. William H. Chafe, *The Unfinished Journey: America Since World War II* (New York: Oxford University Press, 1995), p. 406.

20. Kazan, note on *The Visitors*, Kazan collection, WUCA.

21. Kazan, 'Home Free', Notes, 25 December 1970, Kazan collection, WUCA; Elia Kazan, *The Assassins* (1972).

22. Kazan, Notes, *The Visitors*, 25 December 1970, Kazan collection, WUCA.

23. Earl G. Ingersoll, 'Bringing the (Gender) war Home: Vietnam and Elia Kazan's *The Visitors*', *Post Script, Essays in Film and the Humanities*, 17, 3 (Summer 1998), pp. 55–68.

24. Jeff Young, Kazan (1999), p. 306; James Boatwright, 'Another Pot Shot at Liberals', *New Republic*, 11 March 1972, p. 19; William Kennedy, Review of *The Assassins*, *Saturday Review*, 1 April 1972, pp. 75–6.

25. Ciment, ed., *Kazan on Kazan* (1973), p. 163.

26. Rex Reed, *Chicago Tribune*, 6 February 1972, MOMA.

27. Earl G. Ingersoll, 'Bringing the (Gender) War Home', *Post Script* (1998), p. 65; Jonathan Rosenbaum, in Richard Roud, ed., *Cinema, A Critical Dictionary, The Major film-makers, Vol. 1* (London: Secker & Warburg, 1980), p. 541.

28. Vincent Canby, *New York Times*, 3 February 1972; Charles Michener, *Newsweek*, 7 February 1972; Andrew Sarris, *Village Voice*, 30 March 1972; Hollis Alpert, *Saturday Review*, 19 February 1972 (Kazan folders, MOMA).

29. *L'Auore*, 7 May 1972, MOMA.

30. David Caute, *Joseph Losey: A Revenge on Life* (London: Faber and Faber, 1994), p. 405.

9. *The Last Tycoon* (1976): A Coda

1. Steven H. Gale, *Sharp Cut, Harold Pinter's Screenplays and the Artistic Process* (Lexington: University Press of Kentucky, 2003), p. 226; Spiegel, in Natasha Fraser-Cavassini, *Sam Spiegel* (2003), p. 315.

2. Hollis Alpert, 'Fitzgerald, Hollywood and *The Last Tycoon*', *American Film*, 1, 5 (March 1976), pp. 9, 11; Kazan, 'Notes on Monroe Stahr in "The Last Tycoon"', 19 February 1975, in Michel Ciment, ed., *Elia Kazan: An American Odyssey* (1988), pp. 145–7.

3. Ingrid Boulting, telephone interview with the author, 26 October 2005; Christopher C. Hudgins, '*The Last Tycoon*: Elia Kazan's and Harold Pinter's Unsentimental Hollywood Romance', in Kimball King, ed., *Hollywood on Stage, Playwrights Evaluate the Culture Industry* (New York: Garland, 1997), p. 182.

4. Kazan, 'Notes on Monroe Stahr in "*The Last Tycoon*"', 20 December 1974, in Ciment, ed., *Elia Kazan* (1998), pp. 145–7; for the published screenplay see Harold Pinter, *The French Lieutenant's Woman and other Screenplays* (London: Methuen, 1982); Fitzgerald, 29 September 1939, on his plans for the novel, in F. Scott Fitzgerald, *The Last Tycoon*, edited by Edmund Wilson (Harmondsworth: Penguin, 1965), p. 168.

5. Joanna E. Rapf, '*The Last Tycoon* or "A Nickel for the Movies"', *Literature Film Quarterly* (1988), pp. 80–1.

6. See Peter Lev, *The Euro-American Cinema* (Austin: University of Texas Press, 1993), pp. 30–7.

7. Kazan annotations, Harold Pinter screenplay, 11 August 1975, Kazan collection, WUCA.

8. Ingrid Boulting, email to author, 9 November 2005.

9. Ingrid Boulting, telephone interview with the author, 26 October 2005.

10. Kazan to Lester Cowan, 7 July 1944, Lester Cowan collection, AMPAS.

11. Kazan annotations to Pinter screenplay of 19 February 1975, Kazan collection, WUCA.

12. Kazan annotations to Pinter screenplay of 19 February 1975, Kazan collection, WUCA.

13. See Yannick Lemarié, 'Kazan ou le regard captif', *Positif, Revue Mensuelle de Cinéma*, 518 (April 2004), pp. 87–9.

14. Kazan, *A Life* (1988), p. 775.

15. Andrew Sarris, *Village Voice*, 15 November 1976.

16. Pauline Kael, *New Yorker*, 29 November 1976; Richard Corliss, *New Times*, 26 November 1976.

17. I. Lloyd Michaels, 'Auteurism, Creativity, and Entropy in *The Last Tycoon*', *Literature/Film Quarterly*, 10, 2 (1982), pp. 110–18.

18. Kazan to George Stevens, 3 May 1968, George Stevens collection, AMPAS.

19. Jean-Pierre Cousoden, 'Elia Kazan', in Coursidon with Pierre Sauvage, *American Directors, Volume II* (1983), p. 172; the Kazan films listed in the 'Annual top Moneymaking Films' from 1947 onwards were *The Sea of Grass* (1947, 19th),

Gentleman's Agreement (1948, 8th), *Pinky* (1949, 2nd), *A Streetcar Named Desire* (1951, 5th), *On the Waterfront* (1954, 15th), *East of Eden* (1955, 13th) and *Splendour in the Grass* (1961, 10th), in Cobbett Steinberg, *Reel Facts, The Movie Book of Records* (New York: Vintage Books, 1978), pp. 339–54; DGA website, 'A Tribute to Elia Kazan', http://www.dga/news/v29_2/evnt_kazan (accessed, 10 November 2005); Eugene L. Miller Jr., and Edwin T. Arnold, eds., *Robert Aldrich Interviews* (Jackson, University Press of Mississippi, 2004), p. xii; Alan Rosenthal, 'Emile de Antonio: An Interview', *Film Quarterly*, 32, 1 (1978), p. 14; Elia Kazan, 'The View from a Turkish Prison', *New York Times Magazine*, 4 February 1979, pp. 33–5, 48–50; Abraham Polonsky, interview with the author, 20 August 1988.

20. Richard Schickel, *Elia Kazan, A Biography* (2005), pp. 428–32, 441–7; for a synopsis of *Beyond the Aegean*, see Jacques Gerber, ed., *Anatole Dauman* (1992), pp. 180–3; on the collapse of the project see also Victor Navasky, 'Afterword to the Third Edition', in Navasky, *Naming Names* (New York: Hill and Wang, 2003), pp. 437–8; Budd Schulberg, interview with the author, 13 October 2004; Dan Ranvaud, 'Sorcerer and the Sword', *Guardian*, 2 August 1984; Robert Evans, *The Kid Stays in the Picture* (London: HarperCollins, 1995), p. 218; Elia Kazan, 'The Hyphenated Americans', in John Boorman and Walter Donohue, eds., *Projections* 4½ (1995), p. 93. One of Kazan's last visits to the cinema in New York was to see *Topsy-Turvy* (2000), a film by another director, Mike Leigh, whose cinema works in particular through performance and close observation of behaviour (information from Leonard Quart).

21. Robin Wood, 'The Kazan Problem', *Movie*, 19 (Winter 1971–2), p. 31.

22. Peter Cowie, *Revolution, The Explosion of World Cinema in the 60s* (London: Faber and Faber, 2004), p. 2.

23. Kazan, *America America* notebook, Kazan collection, WUCA.

24. Patricia Neal, 'What Kazan Did for Me', *Films and Filming*, 4, 1 (October 1957), p. 9; Kazan to Tay Garnett, 13 August 1974, Folder 179, Lewis Milestone collection, AMPAS.

25. Kazan to Tay Garnett, 13 August 1974, Folder 179, Lewis Milestone collection, AMPAS.

26. Brando and Wallach quoted in Jeanine Basinger et. al., eds., *Working with Kazan* (1973); Remick in Jay Leyda, ed., *Film Makers Speak, Voices of Film Experience* (New York: Da Capo Paperback, 1977), p. 383.

27. Kazan, 'What a Film Director Needs to Know', in Elia Kazan, *A Kazan Reader* (1977), p. 270; Colin McArthur, *Underworld USA* (1972), p. 120.

28. Kazan on Marlon Brando, 'The Tick-Tock of Time', Actors Studio Dinner, 5 November 1980, in Michel Ciment, ed., *Elia Kazan* (1988), p. 214.

29. Steven Cohan, *Masked Men, Masculinity and the Movies in the Fifties* (1997), p. 249; Dunnock, in Jeanine Basinger et. al., eds., *Working with Kazan* (1973).

30. Berenice Reynaud, 'For *Wanda*', *Senses of cinema*, http://www.sensesofcinema. com/contents/02/22/wanda.html accessed, 7 July 2007.

31. 'A Brief History of the Actors Studio', Folder 528, Martin Ritt collection, AMPAS; Kazan paper to Board of Actors Studio, 16 June 1987, Folder 528, Martin Ritt collection, AMPAS.
32. David Thomson, *America in the Dark, Hollywood and the Gift of Unreality* (London: Hutchinson, 1978), p. 198.
33. Kazan, 1958 Diary, re: *Wild River*, 19 February 1958, Kazan collection, WUCA.
34. David Bordwell, 'The Art Cinema as a Mode of Film Practice', in Catherine Fowler, ed., *The European Cinema Reader* (London: Routledge, 2002), p. 96; for Kazan on films 'that say life is meaningless', see James F. Fixx, 'Who cares what the Boss Thinks', *Saturday Review*, 28 December 1963, p. 14; for his comment on Godard, American Film Institute, 'Dialogue on Film: Elia Kazan' (1976), in William Baer, *Elia Kazan Interviews* (2000), p. 204.

Filmography

Note: Years given are release dates. Credits and casts are transcribed from the films, supplemented by filmographies in Michel Ciment, ed., *Kazan on Kazan*, 1973 (by Ciment and Olivier Eyquem), Lloyd Michaels (*Elia Kazan*, 1985), Leo Braudy (*On the Waterfront*, 2005), Jeanine Basinger et. al. (*Working with Kazan*, 1973), and the Internet Movie Database (http://www.imdb.com/name/nm0001415 (accessed 6 April 2008)). In the thirties Kazan was involved in short films: as an actor in *Café Universal* (Ralph Steiner, 1934), *Pie in the Sky* (Ralph Steiner, Nykino, 1934), and as assistant director of *People of the Cumberland* (Ralph Steiner, Frontier Films, 1937). He also appeared in *City for Conquest* (Anatole Litvak, Warner Bros., 1940) and *Blues in the Night* (Anatole Litvak, Warner Bros., 1941). There were also film inserts in Kazan's stage production of *It's Up to You* (1941, for the US Department of Agriculture).

A Tree Grows in Brooklyn (1945)

128 minutes, Twentieth Century-Fox; DIR: Elia Kazan; PROD: Louis D. Lighton; SCRIPT: Tess Slesinger and Frank Davis, adapted from the novel by Betty Smith; PH: Leon Shamroy; ART DIR: Lyle Wheeler; SET DECORATION: Thomas Little, Frank E. Hughes; ED: Dorothy Spencer; MUSIC: Alfred Newman; SOUND: Bonnie Cashin; ASS. DIRS: Saul Wurtzel, Nicholas Ray.

CAST: Dorothy McGuire (Katie Nolan), Joan Blondell (Aunt Sissy), James Dunn (Johnny Nolan), Lloyd Nolan (Officer McShane), James Gleason (McGarrity), Ted Donaldson (Neeley Nolan), Peggy Ann Garner (Francie), Miss McDonough (Ruth Nelson), Grandma Rommely (Ferike Boros), John Alexander (Steve Edwards), J. Farrell MacDonald (Garney), B.S. Pully (Christmas tree salesman), Charles Halton (Mr Barker), Art Smith (ice cream seller), Lillian Bronson (Librarian), Nicholas Ray (Bakery Clerk).

The Sea of Grass (1947)

131 minutes, Metro Goldwyn Mayer; DIR: Elia Kazan; PROD: Pandro S. Berman; SCRIPT: Marguerite Roberts and Vincent Lawrence, based on a novel by Conrad Richter; PH: Harry Stradling; ART DIR: Cedric Gibbons, Paul Groesse; SET DECORATION: Edwin B. Willis, Mildred Griffiths; ED: Robert J. Kern; MUSIC: Herbert Stothart; SOUND: Douglas Shearer; COSTUMES: Walter Plunkett; ASS. DIR: Sid Sidman.

CAST: Spencer Tracy (Jim Brewton), Katherine Hepburn (Luie Cameron), Robert Walker (Brock Brewton), Melvyn Douglas (Brice Chamberlain), Phyllis Thaxter (Sarah Bess), Edgar Buchanan (Jeff), Harry Carey (Dr Reid), Ruth Nelson (Selena Hall), William 'Bill' Phillips (Banty), Robert Armstrong (Floyd McCurtin), James Bell (Sam Hall), Robert Barrat (Judge Seth White), Charles Trowbridge (George Cameron).

Boomerang! (1947)

88 minutes, Twentieth Century-Fox; DIR: Elia Kazan; PROD: Louis de Rochemont, for Darryl F. Zanuck; SCRIPT: Richard Murphy, based on an article by Anthony Abbot (Fulton Oursler) published in *The Reader's Digest*, December 1945; PH: Norbert Brodine; ART DIR: Richard Day, Chester Gore; SET DECORATION: Thomas Little; ED: Hermon Jones; MUSIC: David Buttolph; SOUND: W.D. Flick, Roger Heman.

CAST: Dana Andrews (Henry Harvey), Jane Wyatt (Mrs Harvey), Lee J. Cobb (Chief Robinson), Cara Williams (waitress/witness), Arthur Kennedy (John Waldron), Sam Levene (Woods), Taylor Holmes (T. M. Wade), Robert Keith (McCreery), Ed Begley (Paul Harris), Leona Roberts (Mrs Crossman), Philip Coolidge (Crossman), Lester Lonergan (Cary), Lewis Leverett (Harvey's assistant), Richard Garrick (Mr Rogers), Karl Malden (Lieutenant White), Joe Kazan (Mr Lukash), Barry Kelley (Desk Sgt. Dugan), Herbert Ratner (questioner), Guy Thomajan (Cartucci), E.J. Ballantine (McDonald), Wyrley Birch (Father Lambert), Arthur Miller (line-up suspect).

Gentleman's Agreement (1948)

118 minutes, Twentieth Century-Fox; DIR: Elia Kazan; PROD: Darryl F. Zanuck; SCRIPT: Moss Hart, from the novel by Laura Z. Hobson; PH: Arthur Miller; ART DIR: Lyle Wheeler, Mark-Lee Kirk; SET DECORATION: Thomas Little, Paul S. Fox; ED: Harmon Jones; MUSIC: Alfred Newman; SOUND: Alfred Bruzlin, Roger Heman; COSTUMES: Charles Le Maire, Kay Nelson; ASS. DIR: Saul Wurtzel.

CAST: Gregory Peck (Phil Green), Dorothy McGuire (Kathy), John Garfield (Dave Goldman), Celeste Holm (Anne), Anne Revere (Mrs Green), June Havoc (Miss Wales), Albert Dekker (John Minify), Jane Wyatt (Jane), Dean Stockwell (Tommy Green), Nicholas Joy (Dr. Craigie), Sam Jaffe (Professor Lieberman), Harold Vermilyea (Jordan), Ransom M. Sherman (Bill Payson), Roy Roberts (Calkins), Kathleeen Lockhart (Mrs Minify), Robert Warwick (Irving Weisman), Morgan Farley (Resort Clerk), Roy Roberts (Mr Calkins), Herbert Ratner, Lewis Leverett (Father).

Pinky (1949)

102 minutes, Twentieth Century-Fox; DIR: Elia Kazan; PROD: Darryl F. Zanuck; SCRIPT: Philip Dunne and Dudley Nichols, based on the novel *Quality*, by Cid Ricketts Sumner; PH: Joe MacDonald; ART DIR: Lyle Wheeler, J. Russell Spencer; SET DECORATION: Thomas Little, Walter M. Scott; ED: Harmon Jones; MUSIC: Alfred Newman; COSTUMES: Charles Le Maire; SOUND: Eugene Grossman, Roger Heman; ASS. DIR: Wingate Smith.

CAST: Jeanne Crain (Pinky Johnson), Ethel Barrymore (Miss Em), Ethel Waters (Aunt Dicey), William Lundigan (Dr Thomas Adams), Basil Ruysdael (Judge Walker), Kenny Washington (Dr Canady), Nina Mae McKinney (Rozelia), Griff Barnett (Dr Joe), Frederick O'Neal (Jake Walters), Evelyn Varden (Melba Wooley), Raymond Greenleaf (Judge Shoreham), Dan Riss (Stanley).

Panic in the Streets (1950)

96 minutes, Twentieth Century-Fox; DIR: Elia Kazan; PROD: Sol C. Siegel; SCRIPT: Richard Murphy, adaptation by Daniel Fuchs from a story by Edna and Edward Anhalt; PH: Joe MacDonald; ART DIR: Lyle Wheeler, Maurice Ransford; SET DECORATION: Thomas Little, Fred J. Rode; ED: Harmon Jones; MUSIC: Alfred Newman; COSTUMES: Charles Le Maire; SOUND: W.D. Flick, Roger Heman.

CAST: Richard Widmark (Dr Clinton Reed), Paul Douglas (Police Captain Warren), Barbara Bel Geddes (Nancy Reed), Walter Jack Palance (Blackie), Zero Mostel (Raymond Fitch), Dan Riss (Neff), Tommy Cook (Vince), Alexis Minotis (John Mefaris), Guy Thomajan (Poldi), Edward Kennedy (Jordan), H.T. Tsiang (Cook), Lewis Charles (Kochak), Emile Meyer (Captain).

A Streetcar Named Desire (1951)

122/125 minutes, Group Productions, for Warner Bros; DIR: Elia Kazan; PROD: Charles K. Feldman; SCRIPT: Tennessee Williams, adaptation by Oscar Saul, based on the original play, 'A Streetcar Named Desire', as presented on the stage by Irene Mayer; PH: Harry Stradling; ART DIR: Richard Day; SET DECORATION: George James Hopkins; ED: David Weisbart; MUSIC: Alex North; SOUND: C.A. Riggs; COSTUMES: Lucinda Ballard.

CAST: Vivien Leigh (Blanche DuBois), Marlon Brando (Stanley Kowalski), Kim Hunter (Stella Kowalski), Karl Malden (Mitch), Rudy Bond (Steve), Nick Dennis (Pablo), Peg Hillias (Eunice), Wright King (A collector), Richard Garrick (Doctor), Ann Dere (Matron), Edna Thomas (Mexican woman), Mickey Kuhn (Sailor).

Viva Zapata! (1952)

113 minutes, Twentieth Century-Fox; DIR: Elia Kazan; PROD: Darryl F. Zanuck; SCRIPT: John Steinbeck; PH: Joe MacDonald; ART DIR: Lyle Wheeler, Leland Fuller; SET DECORATION: Thomas Little, Claude Carpenter; ED: Barbara McLean; MUSIC: Alex North; COSTUMES: Charles Le Maire, Travilla; SOUND: W.D. Flick, Roger Heman.

CAST: Marlon Brando (Emiliano Zapata), Jean Peters (Josefa), Anthony Quinn (Eufemio), Joseph Wiseman (Fernando), Arnold Moss (Don Nacio), Alan Reed (Pancho Villa), Margo (Soldadera), Harold Gordon (Madero), Lou Gilbert (Pablo), Mildred Dunnoock (Señora Espejo), Frank Silvera (Huerta), Nina Varela (Aunt), Florenz Ames (Señor Espejo), Bernie Gozier (Zapatista), Frank De Kova (Colonel Guajardo), Joseph Granby (General Fuentes), Pedro Regas (Innocente), Richard Garrick (Old General), Fay Roope (Diaz), Harry Kingston (Don Garcia), Will Kuluva (Lazaro).

Man on a Tightrope (1953)

105 minutes, Twentieth Century-Fox; DIR: Elia Kazan; PROD: Robert L. Jacks; SCRIPT: Robert E. Sherwood, based on a story by Neil Paterson; PH: Georg Krause; ART DIR: Hans H. Kuhnert, Theo Zwirsky; ED: Dorothy Spencer; MUSIC: Franz Waxman; COSTUMES: Ursula Maes; SOUND: Martin Mueller, Karl Becker, Roger Heman.

CAST: Fredric March (Karel Cernik), Terry Moore (Tereza Cernik), Gloria Grahame (Zama Cernik), Cameron Mitchell (Joe Vosdek), Adolphe Menjou (Commissioner of Police Fesker), Robert Beatty (Barovik), Alex d'Arcy (Rudolph), Richard Boone (Krofta),

Pat Henning (Konradin), Paul Hartman (Jaromir), John Dehner (The Chief), Dorothea Wieck (Duchess), William Castello (Czech captain), Margaret Slezak (Mrs Jaromir), Gert Froebe (Plainclothes Policeman), Hansi (Kalka, the midget), and the Brumbach Circus as the Cernik Circus.

On the Waterfront (1954)

108 minutes, Horizon Pictures, for Columbia Pictures; DIR: Elia Kazan; PROD: Sam Spiegel; SCRIPT: Budd Schulberg, based on an original story by Budd Schulberg, suggested by articles by Malcolm Johnson; ASS. DIR: Charles H. Maguire; PH: Boris Kaufman; ART DIR: Richard Day; ED: Gene Milford; MUSIC: Leonard Bernstein; COSTUMES: Anna Hill Johnstone; SOUND: James Shields.

CAST: Marlon Brando (Terry Malloy), Karl Malden (Father Barry), Lee J. Cobb (Johnny Friendly), Rod Steiger (Charley Malloy), Eva Marie Saint (Edie Doyle), Pat Henning ('Kayo' Dugan), Leif Erickson (Inspector Glover, Crime Commission), James Westerfield ('Big Mac'), Tony Galento ('Truck'), Tami Mauriello (Trillo), John Hamilton ('Pop' Doyle), John Heldabrand (Mutt), Rudy Bond (Moose), Don Blackman (Luke), Arthur Keegan (Jimmy Collins), Abe Simon (Barney), Pat Hingle (Bartender), Fred Gwynne ('Slim'), Barry Macollum (Johnny Friendly's Banker), Martin Balsam (Gillette, Crime Commission investigator), Anne Hegira (Mrs Collins), Tommy Handley (Tommy Collins), Mike O'Dowd ('Specs'), Michael V. Gazzo (waiter, Johnny's bar), Robert Downing (Father Vincent), Nehemiah Persoff (cab driver), Dan Bergin (Sidney, the butler), John Finnegan (Joey Doyle), Lee Oma (Johnny Friendly's bartender), Richard Marnell, Sr. (Mr Upstairs).

East of Eden (1955)

115 minutes, Warner Bros.; DIR: Elia Kazan; PROD: Elia Kazan; SCRIPT: Paul Osborn, from the novel by John Steinbeck; PH: Ted McCord; ART DIR: James Basevi, Malcolm Bert; SET DECORATION: George James Hopkins; ED: Owen Marks; MUSIC: Leonard Rosenman; COLOUR CONSULTANT: John Hambleton; COSTUMES: Anna Hill Johnstone; SOUND: Stanley Jones; ASS. DIRS: Don Page, Horace Hough.

CAST: Julie Harris (Abra), James Dean (Cal Trask), Raymond Massey (Adam Trask), Burl Ives (Sam, the Sheriff), Richard Davalos (Aron Trask), Jo Van Fleet (Kate), Albert Dekker (Will Hamilton), Lois Smith (Ann), Harold Gordon (Mr Albrecht), Nick Dennis (Rantani), Timothy Carey (Joe), Lonny Chapman (Roy), Barbara Baxley (Nurse), Mario Siletti (Piscora).

Baby Doll (1956)

114 minutes, Newtown Productions, for Warner Bros.; DIR: Elia Kazan; PROD: Elia Kazan; SCRIPT: Tennessee Williams, based on two one act plays; ASS. DIR: Charles H. Maguire; PH: Boris Kaufman; ART DIR: Richard Sylbert (associate art director: Paul Sylbert); ED: Gene Milford; MUSIC: Kenyon Hopkins; COSTUMES: Anna Hill Johnstone; SOUND: Edward J. Johnstone.

CAST: Karl Malden (Archie Lee), Carroll Baker (Baby Doll Meighan), Eli Wallach (Silva Vacarro), Mildred Dunnock (Aunt Rose), Lonny Chapman (Rock), Eades Hogue (Town Marshal), Noah Williamson (Deputy); Madeleine Sherwood (Nurse, Doctor's office), Rip Torn (Dentist), Jimmy Williams (Mayor), Will Sheriff (Sheriff), John Stuart Dudley (Doctor), and 'some people of Benoit, Mississippi'.

A Face in the Crowd (1957)

126 minutes, Newtown Productions, for Warner Bros.; DIR: Elia Kazan; PROD: Elia Kazan; SCRIPT: Budd Schulberg, based on his short story, 'Your Arkansas Traveller'; PH: Harry Stradling, Gayne Rescher; ART DIRS: Richard Sylbert, Paul Sylbert; ED: Gene Miford; MUSIC: Tom Glazer (lyrics: Tom Glazer and Budd Schulberg); COS-TUMES: Anna Hill Johnstone; SOUND: Don Olson, Ernest Zatorsky; ASS. DIR: Charles H. Maguire.

CAST: Andy Griffith (Lonesome Rhodes), Patricia Neal (Marcia Jeffreys), Anthony Franciosa (Joey De Palma), Walter Matthau (Mel Miller), Lee Remick (Betty Lou Fleckum), Percy Waram (General Hainesworth), Paul McGrath (Macey), Rod Brasfield (Beanie), Marshal Neilan (Senator Fuller), Alexander Kirkland (Jim Collier), Charles Irving (Mr Luffler), Howard Smith (J.B. Jeffries), Kay Medford (first Mrs Rhodes), Big Jeff Bess (Sheriff Hesmer), Henry Sharp (Abe Steiner), P. Jay Sidney (Llewellyn), Eva Vaughan (Mrs Cooley), Rip Torn ('new' Lonesome Rhodes), Burl Ives, Walter Winchell, Mike Wallace, John Cameron Swayze, Earl Wilson, Bennett Cerf (themselves).

Wild River (1960)

109 minutes, Twentieth Century-Fox; DIR: Elia Kazan; PROD: Elia Kazan; SCRIPT: Paul Osborn, based on the novels Mud on the Stars, by William Bradford Huie, and Dunbar's Cove, by Borden Deal; ASS. DIR: Charles Maguire; PH: Ellsworth Fredericks; ART DIR: Lyle R. Wheeler, Herman A. Blumenthal; SET DECORATION: Walter M. Scott, Joseph Kish; ED: Williams Reynolds; MUSIC: Kenyon Hopkins; COSTUMES: Anna Hill Johnstone; MAKE-UP: Ben Nye; COLOUR CONSULTANT: Leonard Doss; SOUND: Eugene Grossman, Richard Vorisek.

CAST: Montgomery Clift (Chuck Glover), Lee Remick (Carol Garth), Jo Van Fleet (Ella Garth), Albert Salmi (Frank Bailey), J.C. Flippen (Hamilton Garth), James Westerfield (Cal Garth), Barbara Loden (Betty Jackson), Frank Overton (Walter Clark), Malcolm Atterbury (Sy Moore); Robert Earl Jones (Ben), Bruce Dern (Jack Roper), Big Jeff Bess (Joe John), James Streakley (Mayor), Hardwick Stewart (Marshal Hogue), Judy Harris (Barbara-Ann), Jim Menard (Jim Junior), Patricia Perry (Mattie), John Dudley (Todd), Alfred E. Smith (Thompson), Pat Hingle (narrator).

Splendour in the Grass (1961)

124 minutes, Newtown Productions/NBI, for Warner Bros.; DIR: Elia Kazan; PROD: Elia Kazan; SCRIPT: William Inge; PH: Boris Kaufman; PRODUCTION DESIGN: Richard Sylbert; SET DECORATOR: Gene Callahan; ED: Gene Milford; MUSIC: David Amram; COSTUMES: Anna Hill Johnstone; ASS. DIRS: Don Kranze, Ulu Grosbard; SOUND: Edward Johnstone.

CAST: Natalie Wood (Deanie Loomis), Warren Beatty (Bud Stamper), Pat Hingle (Ace Stamper), Barbara Loden (Ginny Stamper), Zohra Lampert (Angelina), Fred Stewart (Del Loomis), Joanna Ross (Mrs Stamper), John McGovern (Doc Smiley), Jan Norris (Juanita Howard), Martine Bartlett (Miss Metcalf), Gary Lockwood (Toots), Sandy Dennis (Kay), Crystal Field (Hazel), Marla Adams (June), Lynn Loring (Carolyn), Phyllis Diller (Texas Guinan), Sean Garrison (Glenn), William Inge (Reverend Whiteman), Jake La Motta (Waiter), Adelaide Klein (Italian Mother), Phoebe Mackay (Maid), Lou Antonio (Roustabout), Charles Robinson (Johnny Masterson).

America America (1963)

168 minutes, Athena Enterprises, for Warner Bros.; DIR: Elia Kazan; PROD: Elia Kazan; ASS. PROD: Charles H. Maguire; SCRIPT: Elia Kazan, based on his novel America America; PH: Haskell Wexler; PRODUCTION DESIGN: Gene Gallahan; ART DIR: Vassilis Photopoulos (uncredited); ED: Dede Allen; MUSIC: Manos Hadjidakis (Lyrics: Nikos Gatsos); COSTUME DESIGN: Anna Hill Johnstone; SOUND: L. Robbins, Richard Vorisek.

CAST: Stathis Giallelis (Stavros Topouzoglou), Frank Wolff (Vartan Damadian), Harry Davis (Isaac Topouzoglou), Elena Karam (Vasso Topouzoglou), Estelle Hemsley (Grandmother Topouzoglou), Gregory Rozakis (Hohannes Gardashian), Lou Antonio (Abdul), Salem Ludwig (Odysseus Topouzoglou), John Marley (Garabet), Joanna Frank (Vartuhi), Paul Mann (Aleko Sinnikoglou), Linda Marsh (Thomna Sinnikoglou), Robert H. Harris (Aratoon Kebabian), Katharine Balfour (Sophia Kebabian).

The Arrangement (1969)

125 minutes, Athena Enterprises for Warner Bros.–Seven Arts; DIR: Elia Kazan; PROD: Elia Kazan; SCRIPT: Elia Kazan, based on his novel; PH: Robert Surtees; PRODUCTION DESIGN: Gene Callahan; ART DIR: Malcolm C. Bert; SET DECORATION: Audrey Blasdel; ED: Stefan Arnsten; MUSIC: David Amram; COSTUMES: Theodora Van Runkle; ASS. DIR: Burtt Harris; SOUND: Richard Vorisek.

CAST: Kirk Douglas (Eddie Anderson/Evangelos), Faye Dunaway (Gwen), Deborah Kerr (Florence Anderson), Richard Boone (Sam Anderson), Hume Cronyn (Arthur), Michael Higgins (Michael), Carol Rossen (Gloria), William Hansen (Dr Weeks), Harold Gould (Dr Liebman), Michael Murphy (Father Draddy), John Randolph Jones (Charles), Anne Hegira (Thomna), Charles Drake (Finnegan), E.J. Andre (Uncle Joe), Philip Bourneuf (Judge Morris), Dianne Hull (Ellen), Barry Sullivan (Chet Collier), Ann Doran (Nurse Costello), Chet Stratton (Charlie), Paul Newlan (Banker).

The Visitors (1971)

90 minutes, Chris Kazan–Nick Proferes Productions, distributed by United Artists; DIR: Elia Kazan; PROD: Chris Kazan, Nick Proferes; SCRIPT: Chris Kazan; PH: Nicholas T. Proferes; ED: Nick Proferes; MUSIC: Bach's Suite No. 1, played by William Matthews (guitar); SOUND: Dale Whitman.

CAST: Patrick McVey (Harry Wayne), Patricia Joyce (Martha Wayne), James Woods (Bill Schmidt), Steve Railsback (Sgt. Mike Nickerson), Tony Rodriguez (Chico Martinez).

The Last Tycoon (1976)

125 minutes, Paramount; DIR: Elia Kazan; PROD: Sam Spiegel; SCRIPT: Harold Pinter, from F. Scott Fitzgerald's novel; PH: Victor Kemper; PROD. DESIGN: Gene Callahan; ART DIR: Jack Collins; SET DECORATION: Bill Smith, Jerry Wunderlich; ED: Richard Marks; MUSIC: Maurice Jarre; COSTUMES: Anna Hill Johnstone, Anthea Sylbert.

CAST: Robert DeNiro (Monroe Stahr), Tony Curtis (Rodriguez), Robert Mitchum (Pat Brady), Joanne Moreau (Didi), Jack Nicholson (Brimmer), Donald Pleasence (Boxley), Ray Milland (Fleishacker), Dana Andrews (Red Ridingwood), Ingrid Boulting (Kathleen Moore), Theresa Russell (Cecelia Brady), Peter Strauss (Wylie), Tige Andrews (Popolos), Morgan Farley (Marcus), John Carradine (Guide), Jeff Corey (Doctor), Diane Shalet (Stahr's secretary), Seymour Cassell (seal trainer), Angelica Huston

(Edna), Bonnie Bartlett (Brady's secretary), Sharon Masters (Brady's secretary), Eric Christmas (Norman), Leslie Curtis (Mrs Rodriguez), Lloyd Kino (butler), Brendan Burns (assistant editor), Carrie Miller (lady in restaurant), Peggy Feury (hairdresser), Betsy Jones-Moreland (writer), Patricia Singer (girl on beach).

Select Bibliography

Archive Material

British Film Institute Library, London (BFI).

Center for Legislative Archives, National Archives and Records Administration, 700 Pennsylvania Avenue, Washington, DC.

Elia Kazan collection, Wesleyan University Cinema Archives, Middletown, Connecticut (WUCA).

Hoover Institution Archives, Stanford University, Stanford, California.

Library for Rare Books and Manuscripts, 801 Butler Library, Columbia University, New York (Columbia University).

MPAA Production Code Administration Records and other collections at Margaret Herrick Library, Center for Motion Picture Study, Academy of Motion Picture Arts and Sciences, Los Angeles, California (PCA/MPAA, AMPAS).

Special Collections, University of Sussex.

Study Center of Department of Film, Museum of Modern Art, New York (MOMA).

Theatre Collection, Library of the Performing Arts, New York Public Library, Lincoln Center, New York.

Twentieth Century-Fox and other collections at Doheny Library, University of Southern California, Los Angeles, California (USC).

Twentieth Century-Fox collection at University College of Los Angeles, California (UCLA).

USC Warner Bros. Archives, School of Cinema-Television, University of Southern California, Los Angeles, California (WB/USC).

Warner Bros. materials, Princeton University Library.

Wisconsin Center for Film and Theater Research, Film and Manscripts Archive, The State Historical Society of Wisconsin, Madison, Wisconsin (Wisconsin).

Published Sources
Books

Leith Adams and Keith Burns, *James Dean: Behind the Scenes* (New York: Citadel Press, 1990).

William Alexander, *Film on the Left: American Documentary Film from 1931 to 1942* (Princeton, NJ: Princeton University Press, 1981).

Robert C. Allen and Douglas Gomery, *Film History, Theory and Practice* (New York: McGraw-Hill, 1985).

William Baer, ed., *Elia Kazan Interviews* (Jackson: University of Mississippi, 2000).

Carroll Baker, *Baby Doll: An Autobiography* (New York: Arbor House, 1983).

Jeanine Basinger, John Frazer and Joseph W. Reed Jr., eds., *Working with Kazan* (Middletown CT, Wesleyan University, 1973).

Rudy Behlmer, ed., *Memo from Darryl F. Zanuck, The Golden Years of Twentieth Century-Fox* (New York: Grove Press, 1993).

Jackson J. Benson, *John Steinbeck, Writer: A Biography* (New York: Penguin, 1990).

Eric Bentley, ed., *Thirty Years of Treason: Excerpts from Hearings Before the House Committee on Un-American Activities, 1938–1968* (New York: The Viking Press, 1971).

Walter Bernstein, *Inside Out, A Memoir of the Blacklist* (New York: Alfred A. Knopf, 1996).

Christopher Bigsby, ed., *The Cambridge Companion to Arthur Miller* (Cambridge: Cambridge University Press, 1997).

Raymond Borde and Etienne Chaumeton, *A Panorama of American Film Noir, 1941–1953* (San Francisco: City Lights Books, 2002).

David Bordwell, Janet Staiger and Kristin Thomson, *The Classical Hollywood Cinema: Film Style and Mode of Production to 1960* (London: Routledge & Kegan Paul, 1985).

Patricia Bosworth, *Montgomery Clift* (New York: Bantam Books, 1978).

Patricia Bosworth, *Marlon Brando* (London: Weidenfeld & Nicolson, 2001).

Marlon Brando with Robert Lindsey, *Songs My Mother Taught Me* (London: Century, 1994).

Leo Braudy, *The World in a Frame: What We See in Films* (New York: Anchor Books, 1977).

Leo Braudy, *On the Waterfront* (London: British Film Institute, 2005).

Stella Bruzzi, *Bringing Up Daddy: Fatherhood and Masculinity in Post-war Hollywood* (London: BFI, 2005).

Paul Buhle and Dave Wagner, *The Hollywood Blacklistees in Film and Television* (New York: Palgrave Macmillan, 2003).

Paul Buhle and Dave Wagner, *Radical Hollywood, The Untold Story Behind America's Favorite Movies* (New York: New Press, 2003).

David Caute, *The Great Fear, The Anti-Communist Purge Under Truman and Eisenhower* (London: Secker & Warburg, 1978).

David Caute, *Joseph Losey, A Revenge on Life* (London: Faber and Faber, 1994).

David Caute, *The Dancer Defects, The Struggle for Cultural Supremacy during the Cold War* (Oxford: Oxford University Press, 2003).

Larry Ceplair and Steven Englund, *The Inquisition in Hollywood: Politics in the Film Community, 1930–1960* (Berkeley: University of California Press, 1983, and paperback edition, Urbana: University of Illinois Press, 2003).

William H. Chafe, *The Unfinished Journey: America Since World War II* (New York: Oxford University Press, 1995).

Michel Ciment, *Kazan par Kazan: Entretiens avec Michel Ciment* (Paris: Stock, 1973).

Michel Ciment, ed., *Kazan on Kazan* (London: Secker & Warburg/BFI, 1973).

Michel Ciment, ed., *Elia Kazan: An American Odyssey* (London: Bloomsbury, 1988).

Harold Clurman, *The Fervent Years: The Group Theatre and the Thirties* (New York: Alfred A. Knopf, 1975).

John Cogley, *Report on Blacklisting, I – Movies* (New York, The Fund for the Republic, 1956).

Toby Cole and Helen Krich Chinoy, eds., *Directing the Play: A Source Book of Stagecraft* (New York: Bobbs-Merrill Co., 1953).

Florence Colombani, *Elia Kazan, Une Amérique du Chaos* (Paris: Philippe Rey, 2004).

Jean-Pierre Coursidon with Pierre Sauvage, *American Directors, Volume II* (New York: McGraw-Hill, 1983).

Thomas Cripps, *Making Movies Black: The Hollywood Message Movie from World War II to the Civil Rights Era* (Oxford: Oxford University Press, 1993).

Gary Crowdus, *The Political Companion to American Film* (Chicago: Lakeview Press, 1994).

Efrén Cuevas, *Elia Kazan* (Madrid: Cátedra, 2000).

George F. Custen, *Twentieth Century's Fox: Darryl F. Zanuck and the Culture of Hollywood* (New York: Basic Books, 1997).

Michael Denning, *The Laboring of American Culture in the Twentieth Century* (London: Verso, 1996).

Albert J. Devlin, ed., *The Selected Letters of Tennessee Williams, Vol. II 1945–1957* (London: Oberon Books, 2006).

Thomas Doherty, *Cold War, Cool Medium: Television, McCarthyism, and American Culture* (New York: Columbia University Press, 2003).

Kirk Douglas, *The Ragman's Son* (London: Simon & Schuster, 1988).

Bernard Eisenschitz, *Nicholas Ray: An American Journey* (London: Faber and Faber, 1993).

Manny Farber, *Negative Space: Manny Farber on the Movies* (London: Studio Vista, 1971).

Suzanne Finstad, *Warren Beatty, A Private Man* (London: Aurum, 2005).

F. Scott Fitzgerald, *The Last Tycoon*, Edmund Wilson, ed. (New York: Charles Scribner's Sons, 1941).

Natasha Fraser-Cavassoni, *Sam Spiegel: The Biography of a Hollywood Legend* (London: Little, Brown, 2003).

Steven H. Gale, *Sharp Cut: Harold Pinter's Screenplays and the Artistic Process* (Lexington: University Press of Kentucky, 2003).

David Garfield, *A Player's Place: the Story of the Actors Studio* (New York: Macmillan, 1980).

Kenneth L. Geist, *People Will Talk: The Life and Times of Joseph L. Mankiewicz* (New York: Charles Scribner's Sons, 1978).

Jacques Gerber, ed., *Anatole Dauman: Pictures of a Producer* (London: BFI, 1992).

Sam B. Girgus, *Hollywood Renaissance: The Cinema of Democracy in the Era of Ford, Capra, and Kazan* (Cambridge: Cambridge University Press, 1998).

Douglas Gomery, *The Hollywood Studio System* (London: BFI and Macmillan, 1986).

Walter Goodman, *The Committee* (London, Secker & Warburg, 1968).

Martin Gottfried, *Arthur Miller, his Life and Work* (New York: Da Capo Press, 2003).

David Halberstam, *The Fifties* (New York: Fawcett Columbine, 1993).

M.J. Heale, *American AntiCommunism: Combating the Enemy Within, 1830–1970* (Baltimore: The Johns Hopkins University Press, 1990).

Lillian Hellman, *Scoundrel Time* (Boston: Little, Brown, 1976).

Sanya Shoilevska Henderson, *Alex North, Film Composer* (Jefferson, NC, McFarland & Co., 2003).

Val Holley, *James Dean: The Biography* (New York: St. Martin's Griffin, 1995).

Val Holley, *Mike Connolly and the Manly Art of Hollywood Gossip* (Jefferson, NC, 2003).

Sidney Hook, *HERESY, yes – CONSPIRACY, no!* (American Committee for Cultural Freedom, undated).

Sidney Hook, *Heresy, Yes – Conspiracy, No* (New York: John Day, 1953).

Gerald Horne, *The Final Victim of the Blacklist: John Howard Lawson, Dean of the Hollywood Ten* (Berkeley: University of California Press, 2006).

William Bradford Huie, *Mud on the Stars* (London: Hutchinson, 1944).

V.J. Jerome, *The Negro in Hollywood Films* (New York: Masses and Mainstream, 1950).

Malcolm Johnson, *Crime on the Waterfront* (New York: McGraw-Hill, 1950).

David Richard Jones, *Great Directors at Work: Stanislavsky, Brecht, Kazan, Brook* (Berkeley: University of California Press, 1986).

Sam Kashner and Jennifer MacNair, *The Bad and the Beautiful: A Chronicle of Hollywood in the Fifties* (London: Little, Brown, 2002).

Elia Kazan, *America America* (New York: Stein and Day, 1962).

Elia Kazan, *The Arrangement* (New York: Stein and Day, 1967).

Elia Kazan, *The Assassins* (New York: Stein and Day, 1972).

Elia Kazan, *The Understudy* (New York: Stein and Day, 1974).

Elia Kazan, *A Kazan Reader* (New York: Stein and Day, 1977).

Elia Kazan, *Acts of Love* (New York: Alfred A. Knopf, 1978).

Elia Kazan, *The Anatolian* (New York: Alfred A. Knopf, 1982).

Elia Kazan, *A Life* (London: Andre Deutsch, 1988).

Elia Kazan, *Beyond the Aegean* (New York: Alfred A. Knopf, 1994).

Frank Krutnik, Steve Neale, Brian Neve, Peter Stanfield, eds., *'Un-American Hollywood': Politics and Film in the Blacklist Era* (New Brunswick, NJ: Rutgers University Press, 2007).

Jack Kugelmass, ed., *Key Texts in American Jewish Culture* (New Brunswick, NJ: Rutgers University Press, 2003).

John Howard Lawson, *Theory and Technique of Playwriting and Screenwriting* (New York: G.P. Putnam's Sons, 1949).

John Howard Lawson, *Film in the Battle of Ideas* (New York, Masses and Mainstream, 1953).

Barbara Leaming, *Marilyn Monroe* (London: Orion, 1988).

Leonard J. Leff and Jerold L. Simmons, *Dame in the Kimono: Hollywood, Censorship and the Production Code* (Lexington, Kentucky: University of Kentucky Press, 2nd ed., 2001).

Peter Lev, *The Euro-American Cinema* (Austin, Texas: University of Texas Press, 1993).

Peter Lev, *The Fifties: Transforming the Screen, 1950–1959* (New York: Charles Scribner's Sons, 2003).

W.T. Lhamon, *Deliberate Speed: The Origins of a Cultural Style in the American 1950s* (Washington: Smithsonian Institution Press, 1990).

Vincent LoBrutto, *By Design: Interviews with Film Production Designers* (Westport CT: Praeger Publishers, 1992).

Alan Lovell and Peter Krämer, eds., *Screen Acting* (London: Routledge, 1999).

Dwight Macdonald, *On Movies* (New York, De Capo Press, 1981).

Charles J. Maland, *Chaplin and American Culture: The Evolution of a Star Image* (Princeton: Princeton University Press, 1989).

Karl Malden with Carla Malden, *When Do I Start? A Memoir* (New York: Simon and Schuster, 1997).

Lary May, *The Big Tomorrow: Hollywood and the Politics of the American Way* (Chicago: The University of Chicago Press, 2000).

Colin McArthur, *Underworld USA* (London: Secker & Warburg/BFI, 1972).

Joseph McBride, *Searching for John Ford: A Life* (London: Faber and Faber, 2003).

Mary McCarthy, *Mary McCarthy's Theatre Chronicles, 1937–1962* (San Jose: Author's Guild, BackinPrint, 1999).

Patrick McGilligan and Paul Buhle, *Tender Comrades: A Backstory of the Hollywood Blacklist* (New York: St. Martin's Press, 1997).

Pat McGilligan, *Backstory 2, Interviews with Screenwriters of the 1940s and 1950s* (Berkeley: University of California Press, 1991).

Lloyd Michaels, *Elia Kaza:, A Guide to References and Resources* (Boston, Mass.: G.K. Hall, 1985).

Arthur Miller, *Timebends, A Life* (London: Methuen, 1987).

Brenda Murphy, *Tennessee Williams and Elia Kazan, A Collaboration in the Theatre* (Cambridge: Cambridge University Press, 1992).

Brenda Murphy, *Congressional Theatre: Dramatising McCarthyism on stage, film, and Television* (Cambridge: Cambridge University Press, 1999).

James Naremore, *Acting in the Cinema* (Berkeley: University of California Press, 1988).

Victor S. Navasky, *Naming Names* (New York: Viking, 1980).

Brian Neve, *Film and Politics in America: A Social Tradition* (London: Routledge, 1992).

Donald R. Noble, ed., *The Steinbeck Question: New Essays in Criticism* (New York: Whitston Publishing Company, 1993).

John E. O'Connor and Martin A. Jackson, eds., *American History/American Film: Interpreting the Hollywood Image* (New York: Frederick Ungar, 1979).

Christopher Palmer, *The Composer in Hollywood* (London: Marion Boyars, 1990).

Thomas H. Pauly, *An American Odyssey: Elia Kazan and American Culture* (Philadelphia: Temple University Press, 1983).

Richard H. Pells, *The Liberal Mind in a Conservative Age* (New York: Harper & Row, 1985).

Harold Pinter, *The French Lieutenant's Woman and other Screenplays* (London: Methuen, 1982).

Frances K. Pohl, *Ben Shahn: New Deal Artist in a Cold War Climate, 1947–1954* (Austin, Texas: University of Texas Press, 1989).

Dana Polan, *Power and Paranoia: History, Narrative, and the American Cinema, 1940–1950* (New York: Columbia University Press, 1986).

Ronald Radosh and Allis Radosh, *Red Star over Hollywood: The Film Colony's Long Romance with the Left* (San Francisco: Encounter Books, 2005).

Joanna E. Rapf, ed., *On the Waterfront* (Cambridge: Cambridge University Press, 2003).

Susan Ray, *I was Interrupted: Nicholas Ray on Making Movies* (Berkeley: University of California Press, 1995).

Nick Roddick, *A New Deal in Entertainment* (London: BFI, 1983).

Andrew Sarris, *The American Cinema: Directors and Directions, 1929–1968* (New York: E.P. Dutton, 1968).

Thomas Schatz, *The Genius of the System* (New York: Pantheon Books, 1988).

Thomas Schatz, *Boom and Bust: The American Cinema in the 1940s* (New York: Charles Scribner's Sons, 1997).

Richard Schickel, *Elia Kazan: A Biography* (New York: Harper Collins, 2005).

Arthur M. Schlesinger, Jr., *The Vital Center: The Politics of Freedom* (New York: Da Capo Press, 1988, first published in 1949).

Ellen Schrecker, *Many Are the Crimes: McCarthyism in America* (Boston: Little, Brown, 1998).

Budd Schulberg, *Some Faces in the Crowd* (London: The Bodley Head, 1954).

Budd Schulberg, *A Face in the Crowd: A Play for the Screen* (New York: Random House, 1957).

Budd Schulberg, *On the Waterfront, A Screenplay* (Carbondale: Southern Illinois University Press, 1980).

Nancy Lynn Schwartz, *The Hollywood Writers' Wars* (New York, Alfred A. Knopf, 1982).

Robert Sklar, *City Boys: Cagney, Bogart, Garfield* (Princeton, NJ: Princeton University Press, 1992).

Richard Slotkin, *Gunfighter Nation, The Myth of the Frontier in Twentieth Century America* (New York: Athenaeum, 1992).

Donald Spoto, *The Kindness of Strangers: the Life of Tennessee Williams* (London: The Bodley Head, 1985).

Wendy Smith, *Real Life Drama: The Group Theatre and America, 1933–1940* (New York, Alfred A. Knopf, 1990).

Sam Staggs, *When Blanche Met Brando, The Scandalous Story of 'A Streetcar Named Desire'* (New York: St. Martins Press, 2005).

Elaine Steinbeck, Robert Wallsten, eds., *Steinbeck: A Life in Letters* (London: Pan Books, 1979).

John Steinbeck, *Zapata* (Robert E. Morsberger, ed.) (London: Penguin, 2001).

Howard Suber, 'The Anti-Communist Blacklist in the Hollywood Motion Picture Industry', PhD. Thesis, UCLA, 1968.

Roger Tailleur, *Elia Kazan* (Paris: Éditions Seghers, 1971).

J.P. Telotte, *Voices in the Dark: The Narrative Patterns of Film Noir* (Urbana: University of Illinois Press, 1989).

David Thomson, *A Biographical Dictionary of Film* (New York: William Murrow, 1976).

David Thomson, *The Whole Equation: A History of Hollywood* (New York: Alfred A. Knopf, 2004).

Margaret Bradham Thornton, *Tennessee Williams Notebooks* (New Haven: Yale University Press, 2006).

François Truffaut, *The Films in My Life* (Harmondsworth: Penguin, 1982).

Jack Vizzard, *See No Evil: Life Inside a Hollywood Censor* (New York: Simon and Schuster, 1970).

Eli Wallach, *The Good, the Bad and Me: In My Anecdotage* (Orlando: Harcourt Inc., 2005).

Frank Walsh, *Sin and Censorship, the Catholic Church and the Motion Picture Industry* (New Haven: Yale University Press, 1996).

Janet Wasko, *Movies and Money: Financing the American Film Industry* (Norwood, NJ: Ablex Publishing, 1982).

Stephen J. Whitfield, *The Culture of the Cold War* (Baltimore: The Johns Hopkins Press, 1991).

Tennessee Williams, *Baby Doll, The Script for the Film* (Harmondsworth: Penguin, 1957).

Tennessee Williams, *Memoirs* (London: W.H.Allen, 1976).

John Womack Jr., *Zapata and the Mexican Revolution* (Harmondsworth: Penguin, 1972).

Jeff Young, *Kazan: the Master Director Discusses his Films* (New York: Newmarket Press, 1999).

Joel Stewart Zuker, *Ralph Steiner, Filmmaker and Still Photographer* (New York: Arno Press, 1978).

Articles and Book Chapters

Larry Adler, 'Hollywood on Trial', *New Statesman*, 9 November 1973, p. 684.

Hollis Alpert, 'Fitzgerald, Hollywood and *The Last Tycoon*', *American Film*, 1, 5 (March 1976), pp. 8–13.

Thom Andersen, 'Afterword', in Frank Krutnik, Steve Neale, Brian Neve and Peter Stanfield, eds., *'Un-American Hollywood': Politics and Film in the Blacklist Era* (New Brunswick, NJ: Rutgers University Press, 2007), pp. 264–75.

Thom Andersen, 'Red Hollywood', in Suzanne Ferguson and Barbara Groseclose, eds., *Literature and the Visual Arts in Contemporary Society* (1985), pp. 141–96; also in Frank Krutnik et. al., eds., *'Un-American Hollywood': Politics and Film in the Blacklist Era* (New Brunswick, NJ: Rutgers University Press, 2007), pp. 225–63.

Lindsay Anderson, 'The Last Sequence of *On the Waterfront*', *Sight & Sound*, 24, 3 (1955), pp. 127–30.

James Baldwin, 'God's Country', *New York Review of Books*, 8, 23 March 1967, pp. 17–20.

Eric Bentley, *What is Theatre? A Query in Chronicle Form* (London: Dennis Dobson, 1957), pp. 55–63, 98–102.

Peter Biskind, 'The Politics of Power in "On the Waterfront"', *Film Quarterly* (Fall 1975), pp. 25–38.

Peter Biskind, 'Ripping off Zapata – Revolution Hollywood Style', *Cineaste*, 7, 2 (1976), pp. 11–15.

Brian Black, 'Authority in the Valley: TVA in *Wild River* and the Popular Media, 1930–1940', *Journal of American Culture*, 18, 2 (1995), pp. 1–14.

Patricia Bosworth, 'Kazan's Choice', *Vanity Fair*, 469 (September 1999), pp. 165–84.

Leo Braudy, '"No Body's Perfect": Method Acting and 50s Culture', *Michigan Quarterly Review*, 35 (1996), pp. 191–215.

Vincent Brook, 'Courting Controversy: The Making and Selling of *Baby Doll* and the Demise of the Production Code', *Quarterly Review of Film & Video*, 18, 4 (2001), pp. 347–60.

Jeremy G. Butler, '*Viva Zapata!*: HUAC and the Mexican Revolution', in Donald R. Noble, ed., *The Steinbeck Question: New Essays in Criticism* (Troy, New York: Whitston Publishing Company, 1993), pp. 239–50.

Michael Butler, 'Shock Waves', *Cinema Journal*, 44, 4 (2005), pp. 79–85.

Terence Butler, 'Polonsky and Kazan', *Sight & Sound*, 57, 4 (Autumn 1988), pp. 262–7.

Estelle Changas, 'Elia Kazan's America', *Film Comment*, 8, 2 (Summer 1972), pp. 8–19.

Donald Chase, '*Wild River*', *Film Comment*, 32, 6 (November–December 1996), pp. 10–15.

Michel Ciment, 'Pour en finir avec les mises au point', *Positif*, 192 (April 1977), p. 23.

Elliot E. Cohen, 'Mr Zanuck's "Gentleman's Agreement": Reflections on Hollywood's Second Film About Anti-Semitism', *Commentary* (January 1948), pp. 51–6.

Gary Collins, 'Kazan in the Fifties', *The Velvet Light Trap*, 11 (Winter 1974), pp. 41–5.

Marianne Conroy, 'Acting Out: Method Acting, the National Culture, and the Middlebrow Disposition in Cold War America', *Criticism*, 35, 2 (Spring 1993), pp. 239–63.

Jean-Pierre Coursoden, 'Deau tragedies américaines', *Positif*, No. 518 (April 2004), pp. 94–7.

Michel Delahaye, interview with Elia Kazan, *Cahiers du Cinéma in English*, 9 (1967), pp. 13–35.

Stéphane Delorme, 'Par-dessus bord', *Cahiers du Cinéma* (November 2004), pp. 27–8.

Marguerite Duras, conversation with Elia Kazan, 'L'homme tremblant', *Cahiers du Cinéma*, No. 318 (December 1980), p. 5–13.

Ralph Ellison, 'The Shadow and the Act', *The Reporter*, 1, 17, 6 December 1949, pp. 17–19.

Joseph Foster, 'Entertainment Only', *New Masses*, 66 (1948), pp. 21–2.

Arthur Gavin, 'The Photography of "East of Eden"', *American Photographer* (March 1955), pp. 149, 169–72.

Dan Georgakas, 'Still Good after all these Years', *Cineaste*, 7, 2 (1976), pp. 16–17.

Dan Georgakas, 'The Screen Playwright as Author: An Interview with Budd Schulberg', *Cineaste*, 11, 4 (1982), pp. 7–15, 39.

Dan Georgakas, 'Don't Call him "Gadget": A Reconsideration of Elia Kazan', *Cineaste*, 16, 4 (1988), pp. 4–7.

Dan Georgakas, 'The Hollywood Reds Fifty Years Later', *American Communist History*, 2, 1 (June 2003), pp. 63–76.

Robert Gottlieb, 'Force of Nature', *New York Review of Books*, LIII, 6, 6 April (2006), pp. 54–7.

John Earl Haynes, 'A Bibliography of Communism, Film, Radio and Television', *Film History*, 16 (2004), pp. 396–423.

Kenneth Hey, 'Ambivalence as a Theme in *On the Waterfront* (1954): An Interdisciplinary Approach to Film Study', in Peter C. Rollins, ed., *Hollywood as Historian: American Film in a Cultural Context* (Lexington, Ky: University Press of Kentucky, 1983), pp. 159–89.

Robert Hughes, 'On the Waterfront: A Defence', *Sight and Sound*, 24, 4 (Spring 1955), pp. 214–15.

Earl G. Ingersoll, 'Bringing the (Gender) war Home: Vietnam and Elia Kazan's *The Visitors*', *Post Script, Essays in Film and the Humanities*, 17, 3 (Summer 1998), pp. 55–68.

Laurence Jarvik, '"I Don't want Realism, I want Magic", Elia Kazan and A Streetcar Named Desire', unpublished paper, undated.

Boris Kaufman, 'Filming "Baby Doll"', *American Cinematographer*, 38, 2 (February 1957), pp. 92–3, 106.

Elia Kazan, 'Pressure Problem', *New York Times*, 21 October 1951, II, p. 5.

Elia Kazan, letter, 5 April 1952, *Saturday Review*, 5 April 1952, pp. 22–3.

Elia Kazan letter, 24 May 1952, *Saturday Review*, 24 May 1952, p. 28.

Elia Kazan, 'Pursuit of Usey-Less', *Williams Alumni Review*, LVII, 1 (November 1964), pp. 4–7 (MOMA).

Elia Kazan, 'A Natural Phenomenon', *Cahiers du Cinema in English*, 9 (1967), pp. 13–35.

Elia Kazan, 'Political Passion Play: Act II', *New York*, 1, 23 September 1968, pp. 16, 19–27.

Elia Kazan, 'On What Makes a Director', *Directors Guild of America*, 1973.

Elia Kazan, 'Dialogue on Film', *American Film*, 1, 5 (March 1976), pp. 33–48.

Elia Kazan, 'The hyphenated Americans', in John Boorman and Walter Donohue, eds., *Projections 4½* (London: Faber and Faber, 1995), pp. 92–3.

Jim Kitses, 'Elia Kazan: A Structural Analysis', *Cinema*, 7, 3 (Winter 1972–3), pp. 25–36.

Arthur Knight, 'The Williams-Kazan Axis', *Saturday Review*, 39, 29 December 1956, pp. 22–4.

Philip C. Kolin, 'Civil Rights and the Black Presence in Baby Doll', *Literature Film Quarterly*, 24, 1 (1996), pp. 2–11.

William Lafferty, 'A Reappraisal of the Semi-Documentary in Hollywood, 1945–1948', *Velvet Light Trap*, 20 (1983), pp. 22–6.

Daniel Lang, 'Casualties of War', *New Yorker*, 18 October 1969, pp. 61–146.

Yannick Lemarie, 'Kazan ou le regard captif', *Positif, Revue Mensuelle de Cinéma*, 518 (April 2004), pp. 87–9.

Herb A. Lightman, 'Uninhibited Camera', *American Cinematographer*, 32, 10 (October 1951), pp. 400, 424–5, 428.

Herb A. Lightman, 'The Filming of "Viva Zapata"', *American Cinematographer*, 33, 4 (April 1952), pp. 154–5, 183.

Charles J. Maland, 'On the Waterfront (1954): Film and the Dilemmas of American Liberalism in the McCarthy Era', *American Studies in Scandinavia*, 14 (1982), pp. 107–27.

·Courtney Maloney, 'The Faces of Lonesome's Crowd: Imagining the Mass Audience in *A Face in the Crowd*', *Journal of Narrative Theory*, 29, 3 (1999), 251–77.

Pat McGilligan, 'Scoundrel Tome', *Film Comment*, 24, 3 (June 1988), pp. 11–16.

I. Lloyd Michaels, 'Auteurism, Creativity, and Entropy in *The Last Tycoon*', *Literature/ Film Quarterly*, 10, 2 (1982), pp. 110–18.

Robert E. Morsberger, 'Steinbeck's Zapata, Rebel versus Revolutionary', in Robert E. Morsberger, ed., *Zapata* (London: Penguin, 2001).

Movie, special issue on Elia Kazan, 19 (Winter 1971–2).

Patricia Neal, 'What Kazan Did For Me', *Films and Filming*, 4, 1 (October 1957), p. 9.

Brian Neve, 'Elia Kazan's First Testimony to the House Committee on Un-American Activities, Executive Session, 14 January 1952', *Historical Journal of Film, Radio and Television*, 25, 2 (June 2005), pp. 251–72.

Jack Newfield and Mark Jacobson, 'An Interview with Budd Schulberg', *Tikkun*, Volume 15, No. 3 (May–June 2000), pp. 9–12.

Thomas H. Pauly, 'Black Images and White Culture During the Decade before the Civil Rights Movement', *American Studies*, 31, 2 (Fall 1990), pp. 101–19.

Arthur Pettit, 'Viva Zapata!: A Tribute to Steinbeck, Kazan and Brando', *Film & History* (May 1977), pp. 25–45.

Positif, Revue Mensuelle de Cinéma, articles on Elia Kazan, 241 (April 1981), pp. 2–21.

Positif, Revue Mensuelle de Cinéma, 'Dossier', Elia Kazan, 518 (April 2004), pp. 78–104.

Leonard Quart, 'A Second Look', (on A Face in the Crowd), *Cineaste*, 17, 2 (1989), pp. 30–1.

Joanna E. Rapf, '*The Last Tycoon* or "A Nickel for the Movies"', *Literature Film Quarterly*, 16 (1988), pp. 76–81.

Joanna E. Rapf, ed., 'In Focus: Children of the Blacklist, an Extended Family', in *Cinema Journal*, 44, 4 (Summer 2005), pp. 75–114.

Jonathan Rosenbaum, in Richard Roud, ed., *Cinema, A Critical Dictionary, The Major Film-makers, Vol 1* (London: Secker & Warburg, 1980), pp. 536–42.

Andrew Sarris, *Film Culture*, 1, 3 (May–June 1955), pp. 1, 3, 24.

Andrew Sarris, *Film Culture*, 3 (October 1957), 13–14.

Jonathan M. Schoenwald, 'Rewriting revolution: the origins, production and reception of Viva Zapata!', *Film History*, 8 (1996), pp. 109–30.

Budd Schulberg, 'Joe Docks: Forgotten Man of the Waterfront', *New York Times Magazine*, Section 6, 28 December 1952.

Budd Schulberg, 'Waterfront: From Docks to Film', *New York Times*, 11 July 1954, sec. 2, p. 5.

Budd Schulberg, letter, 'Life, Not Politics, Inspired "On the Waterfront"', *New York Times*, 14 September 1994.

Budd Schulberg, 'The King Who Would be Man', *Vanity Fair* (March 2005), pp. 206–8, 241–7.

Stephen Schwartz, 'Arthur Miller's Proletariat: The True Stories of On the Waterfront, Pietro Panto, and Vincenzo Longhi', *Film History*, 16 (2004), pp. 378–92.

Charles Silver, 'Elia Kazan's *Wild River*', *Studies in Modern Art*, 1 (1991), pp. 165–81.

John M. Smith, 'Three Liberal Films', *Movie*, 19 (1971–2), pp. 19–21.

Michael Stragow, 'Second Sight: Song of the South', *Phoenix Post*, 23 July 1985, pp. 3, 12–14.

Bertrand Tavernier, 'The Fanny Trilogy: An Appreciation', with Kino DVD edition of *The Fanny Trilogy* (2004).

Claudine Tavernier, 'Kazan vieux comme le monde', *Cinema* 70, 143 (February 1970), pp. 29–57.

Kenneth Turan, 'In the end, his most creative works matter most', *Los Angeles Times*, 30 September 2003, E1, 5.

Paul J. Vanderwood, 'An American Cold Warrior: Viva Zapata!' in John E. O'Connor and Martin A. Jackson, eds., *American History/American Film* (New York: Frederick Ungar, 1979), pp. 183–201.

Michael Walker, '*Splendour in the Grass*', *Movie*, 19 (Winter 1971–2), pp. 32–4.

Mike Wilmington, 'Elia Kazan: The Post-HUAC Years', *L.A. Weekly*, January 20–6, 1984, pp. 27–9, 31.

Alan Wolfe, 'Revising a False History', *Los Angeles Times*, 21 March 1999, pp. M1, M6.

Robin Wood, 'The Kazan Problem', in *Movie*, 19 (Winter 1971–2), pp. 29–31.

Michael Wreszin, 'Arthur Schlesinger, Jr., Scholar-Activist in Cold War America: 1946–1956', *Salmagundi* (Spring–Summer 1984), pp. 255–85.

Michael S. Ybarra, 'Blacklist Whitewash', *The New Republic*, January 5–12, 1998, pp. 20–3.

Carole Zuker, 'Love Hurts: Performance in Elia Kazan's *Splendour in the Grass*', *Cineaste*, Vol. 31, No. 4 (2006), pp. 18–23.

Audio–Visual Material

None without Sin: Arthur Miller, Elia Kazan and the Blacklist (written, produced and directed by Michael Epstein for PBS), broadcast, 3 September 2003.

Imagine, on Arthur Miller, broadcast, BBC1, 24 November 2004.

'A Contender', *Arena*, on Budd Schulberg, broadcast BBC2, 19 May 2001.

Jules Dassin interview, 'Cine Parade', 1972, Criterion Collection DVD of *Night and the City*, 2005.

Elia Kazan: A Director's Journey (Written and Directed by Richard Schickel, First Run Features, New York, 1995).

Elia Kazan Outsider (Annie Tresgot, Argos Films, France, 1982).

'Entretien avex Elia Kazan' (Kazan, interviewed by Michel Ciment), *Ciné Regards* (Jean Baronnet, FR3, 1980).

Index

NOTE: Page numbers in **bold** refer to illustrations